BOOKS BY KATHRYN HULME

ARAB INTERLUDE

DESERT NIGHT

WE LIVED AS CHILDREN

THE WILD PLACE
(*Atlantic Nonfiction Prize Award, 1953*)

THE NUN'S STORY

ANNIE'S CAPTAIN

UNDISCOVERED COUNTRY

Undiscovered Country

Undiscovered Country

A SPIRITUAL ADVENTURE

by

Kathryn C. Hulme

◆

An AtlanticMonthly Press Book

LITTLE, BROWN AND COMPANY · BOSTON · TORONTO

ATLANTIC–LITTLE, BROWN BOOKS
ARE PUBLISHED BY
LITTLE, BROWN AND COMPANY
IN ASSOCIATION WITH
THE ATLANTIC MONTHLY PRESS

Published simultaneously in Canada
by Little, Brown & Company (Canada) Limited

PRINTED IN THE UNITED STATES OF AMERICA

For Marie Louise Habets

Undiscovered Country

CHAPTER ONE

IN the Paris of the Thirties the great adventure of my life began, the only event in it which seems worth recording in personal narrative form — a form, incidentally, which I love to read but dread to write. The event which compels me into this book was my meeting with the celebrated mystic, teacher and philosopher, George Ivanovitch Gurdjieff, whom I encountered as if by chance and came to love as if by design.

The experience of my years as one of his disciples dominates the landscape of my life like a single mountain looming out of context. This extraordinary and enigmatic man was the definitive turning point in my haphazard career. He uncovered in me a hidden longing I never knew I had — the desire for an inner life of the spirit — and taught me how to work for it as one works for one's daily bread.

After his death in 1949, I became a convert to the Roman Catholic Church, whose voice of conscience was the only one that made sense to me, after his. Much later, some of the understanding gained from him was reflected in *The Nun's Story,* my biography of a religious life dedicated to an aim not of this world. Between the lines of that biography is the story of my own years of inner struggle with the "Gurdjieffian" work aim.

The strange chance steps which led me to Gurdjieff, the high adventure of my encounter with him and the new directions my life took afterwards make this the story of "finding myself," as the easy expression goes . . . as if finding oneself bore no relation to knowing oneself.

Know thyself — short simple-sounding words that hold the most difficult lesson in the world to learn. With Gurdjieff I began trying and I've been working at it ever since; but I have not yet met all the strangers who inhabit me. Many of the earlier selves vanished with the attrition of time, but I have pictures to help me remember them.

One, framed in a Victorian oval of ebony beaded in bronze, catches at my heart when I look at it. My beautiful young mother with her arms about my sister and me looks straight into the camera with steady smiling eyes, straight into her husbandless life which began just about the time the photograph was taken — sometime around 1904 in San Francisco. She was divorced from my father soon after she produced the son he so passionately desired; but by then it was too late. I used to think, in my days of innocence, that had I been a boy, my father would have been spared his terrible disappointment and not made of my mother a "grass widow" for life.

From my first memory of his commanding voice until his death, I never heard my given name from him. He called me Tom and had my hair cut off like a boy's — a manly send-off into my female life which did not, however, confuse me. I also wished passionately that I had been born a boy and, moreover, one who would grow up to look exactly like him — six feet tall, lean, fair-haired and devastatingly handsome. Though I never knew him as a domestic parent, I adored him and spent my childhood believing that he might be enticed back home after our saintly mother had seen us safely through the trials of the nursery years — the bed-wetting, the nail-biting and all the customary children's diseases in triplicate. ("Mump them all together," my mother used to say.)

I grew up in what is now called "a broken home" but with no trace of anger or criticism for the restless father who had made it that. There was no divorce in my mother's heart and, as consequence, none in ours. Whatever agonies of unrequited love she lived through, we never heard a word of reproach for our father. She said he had "special devils," which made him even more interesting to his children and the wait for his next visit was a real ordeal of suspense.

He came to inspect our growth and condition usually once a month, at alimony time, when he remembered. Our mother combed and dressed us for each visitation, and put a dab of rouge on her own pale cheeks, enhancing her game of *As if*. As if it was normal paternal activity that plucked us from the familiar frame of a simple rented house in a middle-class family neighborhood and swung us off (in a 1905 Oldsmobile entered by folding steps at the rear) into another world, my father's luxurious domain presided over by his current attraction. For her, we paraded every virtue, real or read about, to drive home to the interloper what a wealth of promising children he had swapped for her.

As if . . . Long after our father remarried and we knew we would never get him back, we went right on playing our mother's game. We lived as children together, our pretty young mother and her brood of three. I think I began being a writer then, imagining what a home with a father would *really* be like, peopling our quiet flat with his single presence (worth ten men any day) and picturing my beloved mother in the one situation in which I had never seen her — in the arms of a man.

San Francisco's earthquake and fire of 1906 ended all daydreaming with an explosive punctuation mark. Like the self-contained little Emily in Hughes's classic *A High Wind in Jamaica,* I could say ever afterwards to people who had always lived safely, "I have been in an earthquake."

It was a firsthand experiencing of natural catastrophe that showed, in one prolonged and terrifying temblor, the relativity of security anywhere on earth. Our house fell inward upon us in showers of plaster and bricks. Our safe neighborhood street turned into a writhing horror of live wires; the city of our parents' births and of ours tumbled into a dump heap in less than a minute, then fire from the broken gas mains reached into the rubble and completed the holocaust in towers of flame. The ashes of our pasts powdered our hair for days thereafter.

Like all San Franciscans who lived through it, I dated everything connected with early youth before the 'Quake or after the 'Quake. Before it, I had lived in the cocoon of a child's daydreaming which encompassed mother, sister and brother, and the part-time father. After it, I began to see life as it really was. Safety was a mirage. The sense of completeness was nothing that came from outside, nothing that anyone could set around you like comfortable furniture or a regularly appearing father; it had to come from within. I had my first bittersweet taste of living inwardly alone and I liked it.

The people in books were my world (I read the way other children ate, with unappeasable voracity) — the princes and princesses of fairy tales, the Rover Boys, the Henty and Alger heroes; then, as vocabulary increased, the characters of

Dickens, Twain, Stevenson and Victor Hugo, whose collected works, sold in sets on the installment plan, appeared like manna in our home promptly after each salesman's call and kept my book-loving mother in debt for years. I lived so many lives simultaneously that I had no time for growing pains.

At the age of fourteen when I entered high school, the first self that did not wear the borrowed raiment of book characters emerged and took charge of my life. I fell in love with my clay-modeling teacher, Miss D. She was an artist from the crown of her chestnut pompadour (which fell askew when she worked) to the tips of her long fingers that pulled shapes of beauty from wet clay. I adored her with the unconditional surrender of first love that asked nothing, expected nothing, desired nothing. I remained in this rapt state until my senior year and it seemed as natural as breathing.

Those were my formative years when the passionate hoyden was clay at the feet of an artist. Tastes were developed, not only for the plastic arts but for the many related ones musical and literary. Miss D. was of Norwegian extraction; her musical appreciation centered on Grieg, her literary taste was for Ibsen and Hamsun. Thus, in emulation of my goddess, I was listening to the *Peer Gynt Suite* on our home phonograph and reading *A Doll's House* and *Hunger* while my contemporaries were occupied with the songs of Carrie Jacobs Bond and Elinor Glyn's sultry stories.

More significantly for my future, I was learning to build an altar. That I put a teacher on my altar and kept her there for three years is not half so important as that she inspired the altar-building. One learns best what altars mean by building one. Through these first emotions, I discovered that love begets love and that if you can feel it truly for one person, you can feel it for many. An inexhaustible spring in me had been tapped and its bright spray fell over everyone and everything touching my life . . .

. . . over Maxwell Anderson, my English teacher, a shy handsome man with the build of a football hero, who taught Chaucer and Shakespeare like an author revealing his own works, blushing and perspiring as he read their poetry, magnetizing me into loving it as he did and revering the men who had written it . . .

. . . over Charlotte Cerf, my French teacher, who died a little each day before the map of France over which she moved colored pins representing the German Army's advances, implanting in my heart a love for that land she mourned for, telling me of its nobility, grace and enlightenment, making of me an ardent francophile even before I had mastered the French irregular verbs . . .

. . . over things inanimate — the plaster casts of classic Greek sculptures I copied in clay for Miss D. — and things animate, like the sight down a microscope tube in biology class of living blood flowing through the capillaries in the web of a frog's foot, the disklike red cells wheeling along on their edges, tumbling, jostling, crowding up at corners, then breaking loose on the next heartbeat to stream wildly again through the transparent corridors of the magnified network. To see this, I thought, was to believe in God.

I remember how we knitted through the first of the war years — khaki scarves, helmet liners and socks — from wool handed out by the Red Cross. It was a sign of world concern (on the part of female students) to carry to classes huge flowered cretonne bags with bone knitting needles protruding. I knitted enough knotty socks to cripple an army; then suddenly, in the summer of 1917, knitting was not enough. General Pershing landed in France with the first troops of the American Expeditionary Force and I decided to try to follow, as a war nurse.

I walked up the hill behind our school to the Affiliated Colleges and offered myself for nursing training, stressing the science courses I had been following and the manual dexterity acquired in the sculpture classes. A chief nurse, intimidatingly starched, heard me out, then shook her head. I was only seventeen, underage for their requirements, she said. She advised me to stay in school and graduate; later, if I felt the same zeal, I might apply again though she hoped and believed that the war would be over by then. I went away crushed by my failure to help "make the world safe for democracy," fearful that it might be the last chance I would ever have.

I graduated in June of 1918, valedictorian of my class. Our graduation song was "Long, Long Trail," our dresses austere white cotton, the sashes red, white and blue. Miss D. sat with my mother far back under the shadow of the cheering-section balcony, the two trusted beings who had given me my real start in life, for whom I had prepared in secret the address that would prove their expectations of "great things" from me had not been in vain. I talked, of all things, about the perils of aviation and of the terrible loneliness of night skies hundreds, possibly thousands, of feet above the earth, as if I were at that moment over the Marne battlefields. It was not a bad speech for one who had never been off the ground.

CHAPTER TWO

I HAD dreamed of the University of California, folded in among the Berkeley hills, as a sacred grove of learning where, beneath the eucalyptus and live oaks, one would stroll with lecturing professors in selected groups, absorbing wisdom like the followers of Socrates. My awakening was abrupt. I entered with a freshman class numbering two thousand and listened to lectures in auditoriums that seated one thousand; the professor was a remote figure whose voice (loud speakers were not yet invented) seldom carried beyond the first ten rows center.

Only in the science labs was the scholarly intimacy I had dreamed of to be found. There you not only saw and spoke with your professor but actually touched hands with him occasionally as he guided your biology scalpel in the dissection of a snail's intestinal tract, or in the setting up of elaborate apparatus for chemistry experiments. I drifted into the sciences to escape the horrors of mass education in the liberal arts halls, and inadvertently prepared my mind for some kind of understanding of today's world which science rules. At least I know the difference between nucleus and nuclear, tropism and isotope.

I leavened my heavy science program with many literature

courses — Slavic 30, the great Russian novelists Tolstoi, Dostoievski, Gogol, Chekhov and Turgenev; Sanskrit 21, the anonymous epics *Mahabharata* and *Ramayana* which for me were pure spiritual adventures, my first . . . But chemistry, inorganic and organic, was my main study, calculated sagely to support me later when I would start to write (since who could ever hope to live by writing?). The thing that never entered my calculations was that chemistry would launch me into the career of a factory girl and put me back on the path I had meant to be on all along — the zigzag way of a writer in search of material. I took my first job during a summer vacation, in a pharmaceutical factory which turned out to be a laboratory of humanity. Equally interesting was the new self the job brought forth — a wildly exultant being, independent, venturesome, reaching out for life in the raw with both hands.

It was 1920, the start of the postwar boom. Industry was accepting anyone who displayed the normal number of feet and fingers; wages for the inexperienced started at $22.50 a week — a windfall to me trying to scrape through college on fifty dollars a month. "How the other half lives" — a phrase heard often in the Economics lecture hall — lost all its deprived connotations by the end of my first day as factory hand.

The factory was in San Francisco's "South of the Slot" section behind the historic old Palace Hotel, on a narrow cobbled street filled with trucks and horse-drawn drays and at noon with scarlet tamale wagons trailing redolent clouds of chili steam. To comfort my anxious mother to whom "South of the Slot" was a euphemism for gateway to hell, I told her I was going to work in Commercial Chemistry, obviously helpful in my college major. The fiction lasted until I returned home the first night looking like a gilded circus queen.

For my debut into the pharmaceutical world, the forelady set me to brushing gold dust on gummed labels for Florida Water. She hinted that as soon as I showed I was "good with my hands" I would be promoted to bottling and corking. She dusted one label for me and walked off, warning me not to waste gold dust.

Dusting was a simple task in manual dexterity which involved all eighty-eight muscles of arms and hands (anterior and palmar, posterior and dorsal) including the shoulder deltoids. A stack of five hundred labels was before me, a dish of water and small sponge to the left and a box of gold dust with cotton swab to the right. Moisten the top label from the left, dust it gold from the right, flip it face up off the stack, ahead of you, to dry.

I trained my body like a dog for the first two hours. Then the glue-printed FLORIDA WATER flew up gold on a single dusting stroke, its twelve letters shining evenly, one label per second like the production of the girl beside me who had no college education to hold her back: no compulsion to read every word on every label (including the fine print describing the soothing pleasure of Florida Water after bathing) or to steal glances at reagents shelved along the walls and put the mind over the jumps deciphering chemical formulae — C_2H_5OH, ethyl alcohol; $(C_2H_5)_2O$, ethyl oxide or ether; NH_4OH, ammonia water, also known as spirits of hartshorn. When the lunch whistle blew, my table companion grinned, told me we ate on the roof and led the way. As we passed a barrel of aspirin, she scooped up a handful of tablets and swallowed them dry. I suppressed my surprise and acted as if such massive doses of aspirin were the normal thing in a drug factory. (I later found out that they were; the girls ate aspirin like candy every time they passed the aspirin barrel.)

On the roof I met the remainder of my aproned fellow workers — all girls of varying ages, types and temperaments knit into a homogeneous group by shoptalk. They accepted me as one of them after Dora, my tablemate, told them I had "run up a stack of labels" as fast as she. They asked no questions; my educated diction seemed to pass unperceived. They promised to show me the secrets of the lab as soon as the forelady put me onto bottling. Then I could walk around, go from place to place collecting bottles, corks, cartons and labels, and talk with them behind the stacks. They began immediately to make life easier for me by telling which orders to shun, which to put in for. Beef, Iron and Wine, for instance, was pleasanter to bottle than Cod Liver Oil. Filling jars with cold cream was good for the hands; tamping talcum into cartons ruined the hair. Cough drops and pills were nice to work with *if* you liked to count. It was like being initiated into a special sorority of rough-handed working girls with frank and open hearts. I knew I was In when one of them wet the corner of her apron and, with proprietary air, wiped a smear of gold dust from my cheek.

My real initiation came a few days later after I was promoted to bottling and had free run of the container floor below the main filling room where the forelady prowled. Here, amid thousands of racked bottles that glimmered like a crystal palace in the dim storeroom light, behind bins of sweet-smelling corks and battlements of stacked folded cartons, the girls met in whispering intimacies of talk (forbidden above) and, toward quitting time, to take nips from a gallon jug of "hooch" they had hidden there. It was a pink concoction of pure grain alcohol and the grenadine the company manufactured for soda fountains. Dora and two others of "the club" showed me where the bottle was buried, at the bottom of a huge bin of two-inch flat corks left over from a discontinued jarred product. Safe as a grave, they whispered. They tilted the jug toward my mouth and nodded invitingly. I felt the hair rise straight up on my head when I swallowed, but I took a second swig at their insistence to show gratitude for my acceptance into their secret speakeasy. I agreed with them (when I got my breath) that this stuff straight out of the U.S. Pharmacopoeia was the safest you could find in those Prohibition days. I remember reaching automatically into the aspirin barrel when I went back to my work upstairs.

I became attached to the drug factory and to its working girls whom Heaven really *did* protect, considering the quantities of stimulants, calmatives and purgatives they swallowed daily. I enjoyed punching-in at the time clock and watching my card's work record lengthen through the weeks. Manual labor, I discovered, had the magical power of releasing mind and emotions from involvements with the physical body. I soon learned to fill (from shut-off tubes dangling through the ceiling direct from the mixing vats above) a gross of twelve-ounce flats (or ovals) of Bay Rum, Peroxide, Milk of Magnesia, Cough Syrup, Glycerine and Rose Water Lotion, etc., pound in the one hundred and forty-four corks, slap on the labels and box the lot in one-dozen cartons without once thinking what the hands were doing. My mind wrote stories set in drug factories as I worked; my emotions winged off to New York where all writers born in the west had to go first. Go east, young woman, go east . . . With each pay envelope the dream came nearer, until I confided it to my mother who put her foot down firmly. I was not self-supporting, she said, I was still living at home where, moreover, I belonged until I was at least twenty. And what about my finishing college?

Since it was difficult to formulate without reflecting some disenchantment with my father, I spared her one of the compelling reasons underlying my decision not to continue. I could no longer face up to the monthly ordeal of visiting him to ask for my allowance, which he never thought to send by mail and probably would have forgotten altogether had I not turned up to collect. My pride suffered unbearably in the presence of his wife, especially when she kindly interceded in my behalf and reminded him that it was the first of the month again. I longed to have him sense what it cost me to have to hint and prod each time, but he never did and I always went away feeling as if I had accepted money from a stranger. I told my mother only the partial truth, speaking glibly about the "school of life" and how my summertime job had opened my eyes.

I bargained and cajoled. I would go to some nearby city, say Los Angeles, and prove I could support myself. She agreed to a six-month trial with no conditions, only the hope that I might find employment in a more "elevated atmosphere" than factories.

Like a first love, you can have a first job only once. You put into it your first fruits — an overabundance of eagerness and delight, a passion to please and fulfill. Ever after in the memory it has a special shine which repetition cannot dull or diminish. I repeated factory jobs again and again, became handy with many new tools, agile in many new situations, but I never recaptured the thrill of first earnings, coins of purest gold.

I worked in a Los Angeles shirtwaist factory for the next six months and demonstrated for my mother that I could support myself in any strange city without funds from home. In that half year that passed like a day, a champion-of-the-underdog self emerged. The "underdogs" were the beautiful Mexican hand embroiderers whom the tough American machine operators called greasers, warning me to stay away from such trash. I studied Spanish so I could talk with them and learn their stories. They were refugees — the first of the Displaced Persons I was destined to know en masse in later years, though that horrendous expression was not even dreamed of then, nor the Second World War which was to displace not only humans but God Himself from the hearts of men. My embroiderers were refugees from the Mexican revolutions. Their mine-owner fathers had been shot against walls by the followers of Villa or Carranza, the mines nationalized, the great family haciendas seized and these girls, gently reared in convents and knowing nothing more practical than the art of embroidering, had fled to Los Angeles with mothers and maiden aunts and established themselves, small enclaves of alien grace, in the middle of the yammering garment industry. They called me by my Spanish name, Catalina, and when my time was up and I left them, they presented me with a hand-embroidered blouse which they had stretched on their hoops (sleeves here, collar there, back panel and front panel with two others and so forth) and worked on piecemeal when the factory forelady was not around.

I felt as if I owned the United States as I rode across the continent for three nights and four days in a Pullman car in the spring of 1921. Every factory town we hooted through was like a familiar milepost with hieroglyphics written by tall stacks in smoke and sparks against the sky, which I read complacently. The message was *Bread and butter here.* I could have stopped off anywhere and supported myself simply but adequately. (Bed, table and chair, three meals daily, what else did a writer need?) The massive concentration of industry over the flats of New Jersey, just before the train plunged into the tunnel under the Hudson River, made a splendid climax. No matter how long it takes to learn to write, I thought, I shall never starve.

I rode into New York on a wave of self-assurance and found a room in a young women's hostel on the East River for $5.50 a week with breakfast included. On my second day I took a job in a nearby factory which, as a welcome change from drugs and shirtwaists, manufactured Pyrene Fire Extinguishers. I signed on as a solderer at double any wage I had ever earned and was given a numbered badge to wear at all times over the left breast pocket — a security measure hung over from 1918 when the company had manufactured something secret. I liked the badge. It gave me a number in the numberless metropolis.

I liked my job, wielding a gas-lit soldering iron, until the muscle-binding began. The pain was like a plant rooted in the shoulder muscles, growing down day after day from pectoral to trapezius, to deltoid and sacrospinal, until my whole right side was bound tight in a mesh of suffering. I saw women twice my age eating their lunches from the left hand as I did, to give the aching right a precious half hour of total repose. Many had been soldering for years; it was the best-paying factory work you could get in New York, they said. I thought, but was too weary to say aloud, It damned well *ought* to be.

I stayed on the job for two months, not that I had to (daily papers listed scores of white-collar positions I believed I could fill) but because now I was really seeing how the other half lives, locked in the monotony of a production line that dropped you off at day's end like a flogged body spent and senseless. My California factory work seemed child's play by comparison. I never made a note during those days. All I had strength for at the end of them, and that barely, was to hoist myself (by the left hand) up the spiral iron stairs of a Fifth Avenue bus to ride the open top deck down to Washington Square, letting the summer wind blow my hair while I gazed at the splendid towered city I had entered by the back door, with my soldering iron as key.

Often, as the bus rocked over the crosstown trolley lines of 23rd Street, I looked across the square at the New York World building and thought of Maxwell Anderson sitting up there under its gold dome, writing editorials for his newspaper and, on the side, poetry which occasionally appeared in F.P.A.'s *Herald-Tribune* column. I pretended romantically that certain poems were written for me. When he had quit the San Francisco high school and gone East to the wider horizon, I had told him, in a voice husky with adoration, that I planned to follow him to New York one fine day, to try my luck also in the big town. And he had given me his address, with the suggestion that I look him up; perhaps he might help me to find a job in the writing field. Pride for one thing kept me from calling on him. I wanted to conquer New York alone, unaided, like an immigrant starting at the bottom.

After producing enough fire extinguishers to put out the fires of Hell, I moved up the scale from factory to department store. A new-found friend in the employment agency I patronized, a Vassar graduate getting her first experiences in the working world, thought I should find work that did not sap all my energies, and sent me forth to B. Altman & Company where I remained for several months as a salesgirl in the Ladies' Neckwear Department.

Ladies' neckwear in those days featured Irish lace jabots, fichus of Valenciennes, Chantilly and Venetian Point and, for dowagers, the whaleboned silk net collars with frontal bib which concealed wattled throats when an opera evening called for décolleté. As nowadays, the neckwear counter was placed like a trap just inside the store's main entrance. Few women could walk past it without pausing. In the pause, you could watch the battle of temptation play itself out on the tempted face — firm determination *not* to buy, at grips with a lust for lace. It was better than a college course in female psychology.

From my stand at the forward end of the counter I could see through the revolving doors the old Waldorf-Astoria on the corner of 34th Street, a handsome façade of red sandstone exuding luxury from every portal. Willa Cather, whom I revered above all women writers, had set one of her most poignant early stories in that hotel — "Paul's Case," which always put a catch in my throat. Often in my lunch hour I prowled the Waldorf's plush and gold lobby, gathering impressions of crystal chandeliers, violin music and the perfumes of women and flowers, as Willa Cather must have done while imagining herself a beauty-starved boy escaped from a sordid background. It excited me to follow in her footsteps. Though I knew that a lifetime of trying would never enable me to write as she wrote (she had a God-given gift, not simply a "way with words") I believed it did me no harm to aspire. I would write only from my own self. For the time being, the salesgirl in Ladies' Neckwear was writing my stories, all set in department stores and all doomed (like the preceding factory girl's writings set in drug or shirtwaist factories) to come home with rejection slips.

New York in the early Twenties was a magnetic place. Sherwood Anderson had published *Winesburg, Ohio* and F. Scott Fitzgerald *This Side of Paradise;* Willa Cather followed her incomparable *My Antonia* with her masterpiece, *A Lost Lady*. The newly formed Theatre Guild gave a Shaw cycle with *Back to Methuselah* in three endless evenings, with an intermission for supper. Morris Guest imported the Moscow Art Theatre with *Chauve Souris; Charlot's Revue* arrived from London with Beatrice Lillie, Jack Buchanan and Gertrude Lawrence. Eugene O'Neill had two plays going — *The Hairy Ape* in a converted Greenwich Village stable and *Anna Christie* in a Times Square theatre.

I had moved with Tuny, my Vassar friend, into a large one-room cockroach-ridden "apartment" in a brownstone rooming house in the West Seventies. Two could always do better than one, especially two of a kind. There I cooked cheap nourishing concoctions of tomatoes, rice and kidney beans, to save every possible penny for theatre tickets. We bought our front row top-balcony-center seats weeks in advance and stuck them around the frame of our cracked mirror. It was one of those last periods of innocent delight.

I was a "Gerry Flapper" in the Metropolitan Opera's top gallery every time Geraldine Farrar sang *Madame Butterfly, La Bohème* or *Carmen,* stamping my feet and clapping in unison with the hordes of young girls she mesmerized. I attended the sooty old church of the Paulist Fathers under the Ninth Avenue El — a Catholic church where I didn't belong but ventured into to hear the Paulist Choristers sing Mass on Sundays, a glorious Gregorian Chant. The only voice I missed in those first New York years was that of A. R. Orage, former editor of a London literary review, who arrived in December of '23 and gave talks about a man named Gurdjieff and the school called Institute for the Harmonious Development of Man he had established in France. Having missed Orage, I missed also the first coming of Gurdjieff to New York in January '24, which Orage had arranged, and the subsequent demonstrations of exercises and sacred dances performed in the Neighborhood Playhouse by the dancing disciples who had accompanied the mystic from France.

I seldom moon over the might-have-beens. I have never asked myself what might have happened had I met Gurdjieff then, but I do believe that had such an encounter occurred, he would have dismissed me with a kindly wave of the hand as, a decade later, I was to see him send away the eager but immature.

I still had a long way to go through the undiscovered country inside myself, before coming to the realization that life as I was leading it was essentially aimless. On the surface it looked very busy with purpose, especially after I moved with my friend to a century-old barn on her surgeon father's estate in Stamford, Connecticut, and raised chickens to earn money for a trip to Europe. Every weekend for a year, we beheaded, drew and plucked some thirty fryers and roasters and sold them to the matrons of Greenwich. Then we sailed on a slow freighter and spent a half year tramping through cathedrals, art galleries, châteaux and palaces with a *Guide Bleu* always open in the hand. We were both having our final fling as bachelor girls.

On our return we parted company — Tuny going to California eventually to marry the man she had set her heart on, while I waited in New York for the arrival from California of the man I had settled on in college days, an old beau, a "best friend" with whom I was positive I could make a successful marriage. While waiting, I held on to my job for the sake of our future budget.

There is a part of me difficult to get at because it all but died during the year of trying to make my marriage a success. We lived in a Greenwich Village apartment which had a small iron balcony overlooking Ninth Street — my weeping place, my place of endless self-probing. I hated the thought of divorce as only a child of divorce could hate it, but when I was sure there could be no alternative, I went home to California where a divorce could be had for more respectable reasons than New York's sole ground — adultery. The final blow was having my mother as witness in Judge Graham's court; there was no one else I could ask. She had always stood by me loyally, and now did so once again although saddened to see me starting down the long road of those who would never marry again, which she had known so well.

She scolded me only once after the sorry windup of my experiment with matrimony, when she heard me taking the whole blame for its failure on my own shoulders. "I want you to stop talking nonsense," she said. "It takes *two* to make a marriage and *two* to break it. The divorce courts make it look one-sided as a matter of expediency. But I know otherwise . . . ["More mother than wife" was how she had explained her failure when we were old enough to understand] . . . So will *you*, when you get your thinking cap back on!"

That was the kind of mother I had . . .

By letter before leaving New York, I had applied for work with a charity organization in San Francisco, describing myself as an athletic young woman with an unhappy life behind her and a great wish to be useful in her future, and had been accepted as Recreation Director of the Associated Charities, to whose orphan charges I now gave my time and affection.

Every other Sunday I tramped up the hogback trail to the summit of Mt. Tamalpais with a band of thirty boys, whom I had to frisk for bluejay slingshots before starting up. Alternate Sundays, I accompanied my charges to the municipal ballpark where I rested my aching arches but ruined my vocal chords. Weekdays I ran the Recreation House on Pacific Avenue, organizing cooking classes and Camp Fire groups for the daughters of broken homes and manual-training classes in the basement for the boys. But I was discovering to my dismay that I was not cut out to be a social worker; I identified too readily with every fatherless child. I suspected that despite my high-sounding promises of continuity on the job, I was using myself up too fast. I looked with envy at my sister happily married and making a family, my brother at sea content with his lot and at my mother doing a work she loved, managing a suite of doctors' offices. I seemed to be the only unsettled one in the family.

Toward the end of that year of recreating the underprivileged, I listened to two camera artist friends describe their current "find" — the city's most fashionable milliner — and looked at pictures they had taken of her, not one of which, they said, really had "caught" her. I knew her name. It was the trademark label in the hats of most of San Francisco's chic matrons, which she created on their heads like a Parisian modiste. She was French, my friends thought; she lived alone with a colored maid on the top floor of an office building which she had converted to an apartment furnished in Louis XV rococo. *She* was someone who would take my mind off those charity children, they said, and urged me to meet her.

I resisted for a time. I was suspicious of milliners and hats bored me. They tempted me with the suggestion that their "little milliner" had a story in her which I, speaking French, might be able to write up. Eventually, I went with them to meet the famous Madame X who was to change the course of my life while changing hers. I did not see as fate my first encounter with the woman my friends called Wendy. I saw only the hand she extended upon introduction. The Fragonard face and the body's emaciated elegance had an ethereal quality, but it was a working hand I held in mine, an artist's in the truest sense. It was like a thin bundle of steel rods.

The milliner took charge of my personal appearance almost at once, scolding at the way I wore my hair, covering up what she called "the best part of a woman's face." She swept it straight up off my cheeks and pinned it back above the ears, calling on my friends to see what a difference it made. Then she propelled me to a mirrored Venetian screen to have a look at myself while she stood behind me, laughing at my confusion. Her reflection in a mirror — a pale oval countenance dominated by splendid deep-set dark eyes professionally preoccupied with what her hands were doing . . . thus I saw Wendy for the next several months.

Wendy had made her fortune with her hands. In the cliché of the day she was a "self-made woman" whose lovely exterior was untouched by her struggles but whose interior, you sensed, was composed of coiled springs and small shiny wheels of business competence geared with the precision of a Swiss watch. Her career spanned the decades from turn-of-the-century to the mid-Twenties (when I met her), from the Edwardian double-decker "flower garden" hats built on buckram frames, to the simple felt cloches of the jazz age, tall-crowned and scoopy-brimmed with all their chic depending not on ornaments but on the drape. She had been married and had dropped off en route the "good little man" who had not been able to keep up with her.

I watched her hands at work in the designer's mirror of her vast empty workroom to which she often returned in the night when all was quiet and her thirty girls gone home. She would ask if she might "use my head" for a while, then forget time altogether as she created hat after hat around my difficult long-nosed face — cutting, stretching and draping the felts while she talked through the looking glass, through a mouthful of pins, of her early days.

It was a Horatio Alger success — the country girl from the

Cumberland Mountains who had run away from the family farm in her early teens and apprenticed herself to a millinery wholesaler in Baltimore. She had had to put up her hair with the big black Alsatian bow then fashionable, to make herself look old enough to work. Never allowed to touch a hat at first, but only the scaffoldings of wired buckram and willow frames which others would turn into aviaries and flower gardens, she stole with her eyes (as she expressed it) all the secrets of the master milliners at the head of the long worktables, watching how they applied plumes or Parma violets to cover a crown, how they tied the satin bows that gave the definitive touch of elegance to the brim. At the end of each day, after sweeping up the workroom, she stole the snippets of ribbons from the dustpan and took them home to her boardinghouse to practice on.

From wide-eyed apprentice, to blocker, to trimmer, to fitter and at last to master designer, she had moved West as she progressed up the ladder of the millinery hierarchy. San Francisco was her goal; it was written in her horoscope that there in the city of culture and chic she would have the success she believed she could win. Want ads in trade journals mapped her route. She followed the millinery seasons, timing her arrival in each strange new town to coincide with its hat harvest — spring bonnets at Easter, sunshade straws in summer, autumn's satin toques, winter's lustrous beavers. She had arrived on the Coast some fifteen years before I met her — an unknown who had chosen a French name to put over the door of her first small shop, and had become known by that name before the end of her first season in business. San Francisco put two and two together and gave it to her because she looked the part, as did her hats that had Paris written all over them. Yet she had never been abroad, and understood not a word of French . . . this was the embarrassment she lived through daily when her French-Jewish dowagers, the social and cultural arbiters of the city, chatted at her through the looking glass, in French.

The Madame X role that had been thrust upon her by adoring customers had become part of her after some fifteen years of living it. She would pause in the midst of a girlhood memory and stare searchingly at herself in the mirror. No imagination could put a farm in the background of that sophisticated figure with swept-back coiffure feathered at the temples with chic streaks of silver. Only France could have produced it. She was a woman without a country, I thought.

I had known her perhaps a year when she came to her crossroads. One night, in the midst of stretching a brim about the pot of felt she had set on my head, she announced that she had decided to see France, if I would take her. "You speak the language, you drive the car, you manage the monies . . . and I pay!" she said gaily. Then, as if I needed some special inducement, she added: "Maybe you can write some travel articles as we go."

It was an arrangement that suited me to a T. I had no feeling then, nor at any time during the years I was to travel with Wendy, that I was living like a parasite on the bounty of a rich woman — as the lifted eyebrows of some of my friends seemed to suggest. I knew exactly what I would be putting into the partnership — all the knowledge gained from my previous trip abroad, all the passion to communicate my love for art, books, ballet and music, all my skill as driver-mechanic, road expert, travel planner — in short, the total accretion of my Jack-of-all-trades life. We had a clear understanding about the finances: for my services she was to pay in travel expenses the equivalent of about a hundred dollars a week. My mother, characteristically, was delighted by the turn of events that freed me from my grueling charity work. "And you'll get a book out of it to boot," she said.

I was actually to get two books as a result of my first journey with Wendy, but in the excitement of its initial stages I had the feeling that I was giving up writing for the duration. I could not imagine how there would be time to do more than count continuously en route the luggage she assembled for the proposed travel year.

Besides two handsewn cowhide steamer trunks, innumerable suitcases, shoe bags and beauty kits, she bought a Louis Vuitton hat trunk imported from Paris for voyaging ladies who would never be seen in the same hat for two days running. The trunk held fifty hats, with space in the corners for a cork head mold and some trimmings, in case changes would be needed later. Wendy created her own hats, then mine, in the last weeks before she sold her shop, trade name and the goodwill of a grateful clientele that had made her rich in less than two decades.

I had a final conference with her lawyer and financial adviser, the one great friend she had had since her earliest days in San Francisco. He told me to watch out for Italian counts and Spanish fortune hunters ("Don't forget she's in Dun & Bradstreet!"), never to permit her to drive a car and to get some weight on her if I could. "Let her have her fun . . . my God, she has earned it!"

We left San Francisco in early May of 1928. From the awninged platform of the Overland Limited, waving farewell to family and friends, I remembered as from some

previous life my first departure for Europe on a freighter out
of New York with my Vassar friend. We had had exactly one
suitcase and six hundred dollars each, which was to see us
through a half year of travel, including North Africa, and
did. Now I was setting forth with a waterproof money belt
strapped about my waist in which reposed Wendy's appalling
$25,000 letter of credit and a thick stack of dollar bills for
use in towns that might have no banks. My briefcase, like
my waistline, bulged with other valuables — insurance on
Wendy's fur coats and jewelry, passports loaded with visas,
steamship tickets for outside top-deck staterooms . . .

I had some difficulty recognizing the self that had taken
over, without a quiver of dismay, the responsibility of showing Europe to one who had dreamed about it luxuriously for
most of her hard-working life. All that I knew with certainty
was that I had become, in a very practical sense, my sister's
keeper.

CHAPTER THREE

WHAT nostalgia to recall the delights of travel before jets were invented! You did not then swoop down out of the stratosphere; you came to the Old World majestically on a fifty-thousand-ton steamship a quarter of a mile long. The coast of Europe presented itself gently to the senses — visually, as a band of green low on the horizon; then orally as you came close enough to hear dockside voices singing out over the water; and finally, as you walked down the gangplank, you smelled the stacked cargos — cheeses and wines, fruits and legumes, with the scent of the land itself behind the odors of its exports. It was apple-blossom time in Normandy when we debarked in Le Havre.

I had plotted for Wendy a journey covering twenty degrees of earth's latitudes, from our Le Havre landing on the 50th parallel to the Sahara on the 30th. I had promised among other things to show her the Arab lands of North Africa, then like glamorous extensions of France on the sunnier side of the Mediterranean. One of her travel aims was to discover how the Arabs wrapped their turbans.

We made Cayre's Hotel on the Left Bank (which I knew from my previous visit) our Paris headquarters, then set out in search of a convertible car, a rarity in France in the

Twenties, considered by most Frenchmen to be an American barbarism. To motor with the wind and sun in your face, *mon Dieu!* Salesmen in the Champs Elysées auto salons stared at us, especially at Wendy who looked as if the first breeze could carry her off. We finally found the only convertible on the market, produced by Renault (possibly as an experiment to test the public taste) — a black four-passenger sedan with canvas top. Its hood, huge enough to accommodate an airplane motor, actually covered a shoebox-sized engine of four cylinders, six (European) horsepower, a dwarf hiding under the hood of an embassy vehicle. But it turned out to be the most reliable and efficient car I had ever driven.

Our "six horses" gave thirty kilometers to the liter of gasoline and saw us through some ten thousand miles crisscrossing France, Italy and Sicily and finally traversing North Africa from Tunis in the east to Casablanca in the west, with detours south to the Sahara wherever there were roads and oases en route in which to put up. We paid about eleven hundred dollars for the car and sold it a year later in Paris for eight hundred, with its tires worn down to the fabric and a cough in one of its pitiful small cylinders.

We traveled either like queens or gypsies. Wendy adored the quick changes from deluxe resorts to provincial pensions, which provided also personality changes for us both; in the *grands hotels de luxe* she was treated like a countess traveling incognito with her female driver-companion; in the little pensions we were taken as sisters, the elegant elder being very obviously the rare bird of the family.

As I watched Wendy spellbound before the great art of Europe's museums or clapping hands with delight for the fairs and folk festivals toward which we always steered, the Madame X of San Francisco days who had never learned how to play was a girl again. With car top folded back, we bowled over the ancient river-following highways of France and Italy, watching out for Roman aqueducts, amphitheatres, Renaissance palaces and pillared ruins.

We read as we traveled. We were in that prewar age of the Tauchnitz Editions — those 4½- by 6½-inch paperback reprints of famous British and American authors published in Leipzig before World War II and, under continental copyright protection, forbidden to be taken into the British Empire or the United States. We found Tauchnitz paperbacks in every bookshop and in the multilingual libraries of every hotel and pension which had collected and kept the dog-eared castoffs of its previous English-speaking patrons. Mark Twain, Stevenson, Bret Harte and Gertrude Atherton predominated in the reading rooms of hotels favored by Americans; Galsworthy, Arnold Bennett, Ruskin and Shaw were the popular writers for the British. But on all hotel bookshelves in liberal supply were the novels, travel memoirs and art appreciations relating to the locale.

In an old Loire Valley inn in Chinon, Shaw's *St. Joan* made the château-fortress come alive with the Maid's presence. In a plushy Monte Carlo palace E. Phillips Oppenheim's *Prodigals of Monte Carlo* lent spice to that spicy setting, and so did Henry James's *A Little Tour of France*. Ruskin's *The Stones of Venice* and *Mornings in Florence* guided us in those cities of the Renaissance. In Naples, Bulwer Lytton's *Last Days of Pompeii* made wonderful reading after visiting the ruins, especially when you had Vesuvius visible from the hotel balcony, smoking so ominously that ascents to the crater were momentarily forbidden.

I typed as we traveled, reams of diary-letters in multiple copies for friends, families and Wendy's lawyer. Each monument I described in a white heat of personal discovery as if no one before us had ever seen Venice's San Marco, the mosaics of Ravenna, the Greek temples of Sicily adrift in seas of almond blossoms. Words flowed from me in torrents and, after arrival in North Africa, they turned purple.

We were lost to the world for four months in Saharan oases and the Sultanate cities of Morocco. Wendy's lawyer sent out a tracer for us through the Passport Division in Washington. A consular agent located us in Marrakesh where we were spending every day in the huge market square, Djemna El Fna, watching snake charmers, merchants of love potions, acrobats, storytellers and patriarchal preachers of Mohammed's words weave spells over the Arab crowds to the thrumming of drums and the high-pitched music of reed flutes.

We had planned to cross over into Spain after Morocco, but a rebellion against Primo de Rivera's military dictatorship broke out in that spring of 1929. Officers who led the revolt were facing de Rivera's firing squads and a ruthless manhunt for the remaining insurgents was under way in Barcelona, Valencia and Seville. From the abyss of my political ignorance I assured Wendy that the trouble would blow over before Easter's lucrative Holy Week which, said I, no dictator in his right financial mind would put in jeopardy. Meanwhile we could wait it out on the French Riviera.

We were to "wait it out" during subsequent trips right up to the beginning of World War II — through de Rivera's forced resignation, the reestablishment of the monarchy and subsequent deposing of King Alfonso XIII; through the blood-soaked civil war that tore Spain apart and produced (besides rehearsal for a second world war) Generalissimo Franco, the International Brigade and the climax of Guernica whose apocalyptic horrors only the art of Picasso would communicate to the world.

I was never able to read writing on the wall.

Back in Paris a letter awaited me, saying that a short story I had sent to *transition* before leaving for North Africa would be accepted for publication if I would make a few changes. Wendy shared my excitement and led me to Maxim's to celebrate. She had a proprietary interest in that short story. I had conceived it in San Francisco where, from a window of her flat, we used to look down through the fog on Union Square at the young male prostitutes plying their trade. Opposite the square, in the pillared doorways of Post Street's fashionable shops, the female prostitutes plied theirs. One night I had said to her: "Suppose one of those whores discovered she was the mother of one of those boys!" and "Competition" was born.

I made the suggested changes and saw my piece in print just before we sailed for home. It appeared in the 1929 Spring-Summer number, in the United States section which led off with Gertrude Stein's "Four Saints in Three Acts," followed by stories signed Erskine Caldwell, Kay Boyle, Whit Burnett, Hamilton Basso . . . all but Miss Stein unknown to me then. I felt as if my name had been shot up in lights against the Paris sky. The self that sometimes worried me about gallivanting around the planet with a rich woman, acquiring expensive tastes but no bank account, took a back seat. I was a writer. There was my name in print to prove it, in the rarest avant-garde magazine published abroad! It was of course one of those freakish acceptances that sometimes happen to novice writers.

We were both changed persons when we descended the gangplank of the Cunarder that brought us back to New York. I was a "published" writer, Wendy was refreshed and marvelously alive, speaking the French I had taught her. We returned just before the stock market Crash and the beginning of the Depression. The Crash did not worry Wendy. She refused to be scared into selling her stocks and simply sat tight, her belief in American business unshaken. After all, I thought, business had made her, she knew its mysterious rhythms. Everything would come back, she said, given time . . . those frightened financiers who jumped out of Wall Street windows were men of little faith and fools besides.

We drove across the continent to San Francisco — Wendy to consult her financial adviser, I to visit my mother — while the country still rocked from the financial collapse. The transcontinental highways were almost empty of pleasure cars, smokeless factory chimneys punctuating the landscape, job-hunting hitchhikers thumbing rides between towns and on the outskirts of big cities, the beginnings of the packing-case shantytowns later to be dubbed "hoovervilles" were the early signs of distress. I refused to be intimidated by what I saw; I had a book on my mind which I intended to write, even though travel sketches of the souks and Sultanate cities of North Africa were not precisely what America needed at that point.

My mother had long since taken Wendy to her heart like an adopted daughter. She called her the "little Mad Hatter" and always brought out her old hats for Wendy to remodel, watching her expertise with feathers and bows with the same fascination I had experienced when I had first made friends with her through a looking glass. Once when my mother asked what Wendy would be doing while I wrote my book, I jokingly suggested that the mad milliner would probably open a shop in the midst of the Depression and doubtless make money, if for nothing more than to distinguish herself from the merchants of gloom.

This was exactly what Wendy did, in Los Angeles where we settled for the wait-and-see period before her unfinished travels could resume. She found a small vacant shop in the newly developing Wilshire district — a plaything compared to her earlier San Francisco establishment — and also two of her former apprentices. A calm came over her restless spirit as she went back into her role of creative milliner from which I had wished to "rescue" her.

My North African sketches were an amplification of my letters home. Wendy and I became the editorial "we," and, after eight months, they were in order with logical transitions. I sent the manuscript off to Brandt and Brandt, the literary agent I had called on during my brief stay in New York, fully aware that the book trade was sliding deeper in the Depression and that the odds were against me. Nevertheless, the young woman who had agreed to look at what I might eventually produce had listened to the description of my subject matter with encouraging nods, as if I were talking of the most timely material she had ever heard outlined, as if foreign travel for most Americans had not gone up the spout along with their paper profits in the bankrupt stock market. Her only suggestion at the time was that I not use "Sketches" in my title; it had no spelling power.

After the travelogue, I began a novel using the same Arab background, to see if I could pull through to completion a novel-length narrative. Eventually what I produced was the kind of thing a mature writer conceals — authentic background peopled by characters cut out of cardboard. (It was published but it still makes me blush.)

Acting as Wendy's publicity manager, I was also writing ad copy and opening announcements for the forthcoming shop. With Europe beyond the means of most travelers, Mexico was becoming fashionable. Wendy decided to give an Aztec tone to her new establishment, and off we went to Mexico to buy hand-loomed fabrics for the interior decoration of the shop and whatever we might find in the way of unusual native straws, jewelry and feathered ornaments for the opening collection. My shirtwaist-factory Spanish came back fluently as I haggled through marketplaces for the odd things Wendy pointed out and I thought: Nothing in life is ever wasted, every experience can be of use . . . even this trip with a Mad Hatter who gazes at heaps of handicraft on the adobe ground and sees millinery in them, stylish and highly original.

Outside the marketplaces, Wendy was again the wide-eyed traveler hungry for new impressions. We explored Teotihuacán's stepped pyramids dedicated to the Sun and the Moon, bristling with plumed serpents cut in massive stone; we climbed the SacroMonte at Amecameca to see a black Christ made of cornstalks and rode in a flower-decked canoe through the Floating Gardens of Xochimilco which gave a taste of what all Mexico City was like in the days of Montezuma before the marshes were drained. Then we made a jungle-hopping flight down to Yucatan to study the ancient Mayan temples restored by the Carnegie Foundation. In her teetery heels (I had never been able to change that) Wendy climbed the steps to the top of every temple in Chichén Itzá and Uxmal and there we would sit, talking about the mysteries of vanished civilizations.

Four months went by with no word about my book except my agent's acknowledgment of its arrival in New York. Then, precisely on the day Wendy opened her new hat shop, I received a telegram saying that *Arab Interlude* had been accepted by a Philadelphia publisher. The happy coincidence bowled me over, but not Wendy who said she knew all along it would happen that way. The horoscope she now confessed she had had secretly cast for me predicted success in "a field of art" while hers had promised profit for a business venture if started on a stated day. Both horoscopes foretold an ocean crossing within the year and a "very important encounter." I refrained from remarking that any astrologer who collected fifty dollars per horoscope from a pair of unattached women would have been a fool not to include ocean crossings and important encounters among all the other fortunes their lucky stars suggested. Wendy's belief in horoscopes, like her reliance on high heels for pyramid climbing, was an idiosyncrasy I had long since learned to leave alone.

Nevertheless we *were* off for France by the end of that year and the "very important encounter" — which was to end our terrestrial travels and send us inward on the longest journey of all — turned out to be the eventual meeting with Gurdjieff. In fact, it all happened exactly as Wendy's horoscope said it would. We were in the right place at the right time and, quite possibly, in the right receptive state of mind.

There were preliminary encounters that led up to the main one. The first, on our return to France, was with an American artist met aboard ship who became entranced with Wendy and sketched her as often as he could persuade her to stay still. She confided to him our plans to buy another convertible, finish travels the Crash had interrupted, then sell the car. He had two very special friends, American women who had lived for years in Paris, and were, when last seen, talking about buying a small roadster; perhaps in the end they might want ours. They lived quiet private lives on the Left Bank, seldom mingled with "outsiders" but would surely see us if we used his name. He wrote their names and addresses on his calling card — Miss Janet Flanner and Miss Solita Solano — and warned me to call them late in the afternoon since they were both hard-working writers. My heart jumped as I took his card. Writers! Two of them! I had never met a writer in the flesh.

CHAPTER FOUR

THREE writers were waiting for us in the Café Flore on an April afternoon. Besides the two who might buy the car, there was their friend Djuna Barnes. When the voice on the telephone had told me that, my excitement had mounted. The same issue of *transition* which had carried my story had reviewed Djuna's recently published novel *Ryder,* calling it "a work of grim mature beauty." Thirty years have not dimmed the memories of our ride up Boulevard St. Germain in the new Citroën roadster we were to sell. It was one of those Paris afternoons that songs are written about. Horse chestnuts in tender new leaf stippled the sidewalks with centime-sized shadows. Every café sported bright awnings and every bus-stop bench was loaded with lovers entwined. On the car seat I had Djuna Barnes's *Night Among the Horses,* a collection of short stories which Wendy wanted her to autograph.

We saw the three Americans before I stopped the car at the café curb. They were sitting in a row like three Fates beneath a slant of awning on the *terrasse.* They all wore black tailored suits, white satin scarves folded Ascot style and all were hatless. Three pairs of white gloves and three martinis were on the marble-topped table before them. It was like seeing in triplicate the sophisticated chic that only years in Paris could produce.

Janet Flanner of the *New Yorker* arose and put forth her tiny hand, introducing herself, then her friend Solita Solano for whom the roadster was destined, then Djuna Barnes who had come along to see it. I looked at their faces and felt as if I had come home to my kind. My great years in Paris had begun . . .

But the fruit of those years was to be even more than the lively friendships that knit our disparate quintet together in laughter and mutual admiration, in promises (mine to Janet Flanner that I would teach her friend to drive safely) and in personal anecdotes (Wendy's to Djuna Barnes about the first time she saw a Paris hat and almost got down on her "prayer bones" to study it — in a Wyoming horse town where she had stopped off for a season of work en route to San Francisco).

I suggested taking Miss Solano for a spin down the boulevard to give her a taste of the car she would own after we had broken it in on our forthcoming travels. Her violet eyes beneath black bangs followed my every move as I shifted gears, stopped and started at signals, taking me in as a part of the car, the talking part that explained the mysteries of its internal combustion engine as we rolled along. At the traffic halt before crossing the bridge into the maelstrom of the Place de la Concorde, I feathered the engine in neutral to show her how you kept it hot for a quick takeoff, and she turned to me suddenly and said, "Thanks for the lesson. I don't often have a chance to act in the physical center. I'm always in the other two." "The other two *what?*" I asked. "Centers of course . . . emotional, mental," she said. "Man

is a *three*-centered being. You don't have to live in just one,
like a beggar, as someone said."

Then the lights changed and I spurted forward in a splendid show of physical-center prowess while my uninhabited
mind echoed the exciting formulation. Man is a three-
centered being. *My Father's house has many mansions . . .*
was *that* the meaning behind my favorite Gospel metaphor?

I was unaware that I had just been given a first inkling of
the Gurdjieff ideas with which I was to wrestle for many
years. I credited Solita Solano with the striking statement.
She looked capable of any degree of original thinking, and
as I swung the car around Napoleon's Column I thought: If I
live through the driving lessons with this nervous high-
strung creature who speaks shorthand in gasps, maybe I can
coax her to tell me more . . .

There was no need to coax. Solita led us both, soon after
our return from Switzerland, Austria, Yugoslavia and Hun-
gary, to the place where, in her charged words, "the only
important thing in Paris" was going on. This was a study
group which Jane Heap (whom I knew only by reputation as
an avant-garde editor) was conducting in her Montparnasse
apartment, an introduction to the Gurdjieff ideas and meth-
ods of self-study.

Jane Heap in appearance was as formidable as her literary
reputation — a handsome heavy-set American with dark
cropped hair, that revealed the size and sculpture of a
remarkable cranium. Her warm brown eyes softened the
austerity of her masculine countenance, as well as the bright
lipstick she wore on her generous mouth. Her personal
magnetism was almost visible.

She had recently wound up some fifteen years of co-editing with Margaret Anderson a most adventurous small magazine published in the States — *The Little Review,* which had introduced to the American public such literary pioneers as Gertrude Stein, Sherwood Anderson, Ben Hecht, Ezra Pound and, in serialization, the *Ulysses* of James Joyce, for which their magazine had been put on trial by the Society for the Suppression of Vice for publishing "obscenity." Now she directed her energies to spreading the teaching of Gurdjieff.

Before that first meeting ended, I was taking notes furiously on the astounding picture of man as a habit machine, dominated and driven by any one of the multiple I's that composed him, a "sleepwalker" in short, who could live his entire life without waking up or even feeling the need to. Until he could uncover his *real* I, he was a helpless slave to circumstances, to whatever chameleon personality took the initiative with him for the hour, for the day.

"Man," said Jane, "is the highest possible development of the *self-evolving* form. Nature can do no more. All further development requires conscious effort." The Gurdjieff work she described as "a method of effort — conscious effort, not mechanical automatic effort." The start toward such consciousness was neutral scientific observation of one's self to discover from which center, physical, emotional or mental, most of one's reactions flowed. Re-actions, not actions. We must keep in mind that *as we were,* everything was done in us from outside, that we took no part in our activity because we had no unique central I, only a crowd of "personality I's" in continual argument between centers, fighting for their turns in the driver's seat. This, I realized, had been my state ever since I could remember, but I had thought it a condition peculiar to me — the writer who had to live multiple lives in order to understand Life. I had even thought it admirable to have such a capacity for varieties of expression.

Jane went on to speak of proofs (*if* we rightly read them) of a superior knowledge found all over the world — monuments Wendy and I had seen and been moved by. Temples, pyramids, dolmens, Mayan architecture and of course the Gothic cathedrals which had been built, said Jane, with a conscious purpose by conscious artisans, to elevate, if even for a moment, the vibrations of people. This ancient knowledge was lost to the mainstream of the human race, vast bodies of it having been wiped out by wars and calamities, as chalk off a slate, exactly as in our own personal lives there were great blocks of memory irretrievable to us in our present state incapable of self-remembering.

In the question period I gathered that several in the group were familiar with these Gurdjieff ideas. A few, like Jane, had studied with the mysterious teacher whose views on "sleepwalking" man tore the props out from under you as, I supposed, was intended. The people he drew into his orbit appeared to be mainly musicians, artists, writers, with an occasional doctor, lawyer or business tycoon — a serious eccentric elect in search of truth, in search of themselves.

I had hoped that some of the practiced disciples would speak of Gurdjieff the man, in brief reference of some sort, to help Wendy and me visualize the genie that had loosed all the anxious self-questioning. But no one did. It was apparently taken for granted that everyone there knew who he was and what he represented in terms of a teaching unique and revolutionary.

Solita of course had told us something about Gurdjieff. In

the late Twenties she had visited his Fontainebleau Institute. At that time he was teaching his method through sacred dances and had a considerable following, mainly French, British and Americans, with some Russians who had been with him since the days of his first organized teaching in Russia, before the Revolution. Though Gurdjieff had closed his Institute some years back, after a disastrous auto accident had all but demolished him, "his Work" (always pronounced as if capitalized) continued through such groups as Jane Heap's, "authorized" no doubt by him. There were blank spots in her briefing. Who exactly *was* Gurdjieff? How old was he? Where born? Where now?

I should point out that there was almost nothing in print about Gurdjieff at that time. Not a word of his own voluminous writings had been published and very little had been written about him, apart from newspaper accounts of his New York appearance with his dancing groups, back in 1924. My mother, curiously enough, had given me as bon-voyage present the *Letters of Katherine Mansfield* which contained the only personal report of him extant, as far as I knew. Some of her last poignant letters to husband and friends had been written from the Institute in Fountainebleau where she died in 1923. The famous short-story writer stated that Gurdjieff was "not in the least like what I expected. He's what one wants to find him, really." She believed implicitly that he could cure her tubercular body, and her ailing spirit "dying of poverty of life" and wrote warmly of the gentleness and awareness of his hard-working disciples whom she found to be "absolutely unlike people as I have known people."

Hers were intriguing glimpses of the man behind the ideas

that had captured my interest — the man nobody seemed to know (or if they did were unwilling to talk about), whom some even called "unknowable" although his reputation loomed in Left Bank conversations in a persistent hush-hush way, like a cloud enveloping a Jehovah.

Nowadays, with two series of Gurdjieff's own writings in print, a considerable collection of disciples' memoirs and above all the definitive interpretation of P. D. Ouspensky (*In Search of the Miraculous*) describing his years of study with the mystic he discreetly calls "G.," it is difficult to convey an idea of the peculiar atmosphere which his oldtime followers wrapped around him, turning him into a hermetic mystery.

It was to take me months to piece together a chronology that ran like this: He was born in the Caucasus in 1877, of Greek-Armenian parentage, received an education in both medicine and the priesthood; then as a young man, he formed a group called "Seekers of the Truth" composed of ethnologists, archeologists, physicians and religious specialists whose aim was to seek out the traces of a hidden knowledge which they believed was still conserved on earth by secret sects accessible only to the initiated. Their expeditions took them through Asia, Africa and the Tibetan Himalayas, visiting monasteries, temples and religious societies unknown to the contemporary world. With his knowledge deepened by religious and psychological instruction received in these places, Gurdjieff formulated his philosophical doctrine on which he based his practical method of inner self-development. In 1912, he founded a "school" in Moscow which he transferred to Tiflis after the Revolution broke out, then to Constantinople and Berlin, finally winding up in France in 1922. With the aid of his followers he purchased the Château du Prieuré near Fontainebleau and established his school descriptively named Institute for the Harmonious Development of Man. There he taught his method through sacred dances of great complexity, involving "gymnastics of the spirit as well as of the body" and an intense concentration of the mind. In 1934 he sold his château and moved into a Paris apartment near the Etoile. Here he received disciples and visitors at extraordinary dinners in the course of which, in his "humoristic language," he proposed toasts to the divers categories of "idiots" in which he classified his guests. "But beneath his attitudes deliberately singular," wrote one reporter, "Gurdjieff manifested a quality of inner life which made numerous intellectuals and artists consider him to be the only man likely to define the ways toward an authentic spiritual experience."

I had never before heard anything like Gurdjieff's formulation of man's dilemma — man the "unawakened," the "man-machine" imprisoned in the habit patterns of his likes and dislikes, his vanities and fears, his greeds and envies. I had never before heard that there was something one could do about this dilemma. I listened with the kind of attention Jane Heap spelled out as *at-tension* as she methodically unfolded a teaching that stretched the mind, and sometimes the credulity, until little arrows of truth applicable to me began to strike home.

The mystery enveloping Gurdjieff the man fascinated Wendy more, I suspected, than Jane Heap's exposition of his ideas with which, after the first month of meetings, she was having rough going. The old familiar restlessness took hold of her. One afternoon in the Ritz Bar where she had taken

Solita and me for a spree, she announced she would make a quick trip to California to sell her Los Angeles shop. She would leave me in Paris to go on with *"our* Gurdjieff studies," and the travel book on Mexico I was writing. She asked for copies of some of my notes, to "meditate over" en route, and assured us that she was not deserting the study group, only answering in person a business call. Solita flashed me a look that said, Let her go, she'll come back.

My emotional center worked overtime as I copied parts of the talks that had struck home — statements about Essence, Vanity and the Mask man wears to conceal his nothingness. On her last night in Paris Wendy announced that she would supplement my slender royalties — they totalled about $1800 a year — so that I could stay on and get more of "the Work," for us both.

Solita and I accompanied Wendy to Gare St. Lazare to put her aboard the boat train. In the station café we had a bon-voyage drink, talking as always of the "Gurdjieff ideas," our sole topic of conversation in those days of first exposure to them. I remembered something Jane Heap had said about the bolting of beginners, a familiar phenomenon in the groups she was filtering for fidelity to an Idea. Would Wendy really return to go on with the difficult work on herself?

Wendy answered my thought in a weirdly prophetic way. She was talking about the hush-hush atmosphere surrounding Gurdjieff. She thought it slightly ridiculous, possibly even a manifestation of "fear" on the part of his seasoned disciples. How else could you explain their reticence?

"When I come back," she said, "if I ever heard that Mr. Gurdjieff was in Paris again, I wouldn't hesitate to walk right up to him and ask him a question or two. I wormed it out of that Englishwoman in the group — Miss Gordon, I think — that he uses the Café de la Paix as his Paris office." She tossed her head, "Well, I'd go to the café. It's *my* Paris office too, for spotting new trends. I'd simply sit and wait until he came. Then I'd walk right up . . ."

Alone in Paris and counting each sou I lived the student life of the Left Bank. Place St.-Germain-des-Prés became *mon quartier* and the four-story walk-up hotel on rue Bonaparte, where Janet Flanner and Solita Solano then lived, was my home.

They had quiet top-floor rooms beautifully furnished with their own antiques. I rented an inexpensive first-floor room furnished with hotel bed, table and chair and a red plush sofa sprouting its springs on the under side. I could not envisage Heaven offering more, even including the room's appalling wallpaper — a cacophony of alternating stripes of dingy mustard yellow and bands of faded red roses.

I had always imagined living like that in Paris. I had always "seen myself" opening just such a French window directly over a busy narrow street (so directly indeed that I could have leapt from balcony to bus top each time the big green A/M autobus roared down the one-way Bonaparte en route to the Opera via the Tuileries), and standing there in its tall frame, looking down enraptured on Paris's neighborhood life.

Across the street was a small fruit shop that featured in their seasons California oranges and Oregon pears and leaning out from my window, I could see the Divan Bookshop on the corner of Place St.-Germain-des-Prés; just beyond, a bit of the façade of the Benedictine church, which was the oldest in Paris. The part visible was a wall of the Abbot's residence where, in a niche, stood a white stone bust of the Benedictine monk and scholar, Jean Mabillon, who was buried in the abbey in the same chapel with the bones of his fellow savants Descartes and Montfaucon. At night when the stones of the abbey darkened, the snowy bust of Mabillon appeared to float in the shadows like a living presence.

The weekly lectures of Jane Heap, given freely to all who came with real interest, were the intellectual food on which I was growing. In my Left Bank life, I dined most often alone in a little bistro behind my hotel, the Petit St. Benoit. Their menu, a five-franc *tout compris,* featured whatever was cheapest in Les Halles that day. As I ate, I reflected on the immense concepts of this "work on one's self" we were trying to do, while I stared at the plain wood buffet that displayed the evening's choice of desserts, usually *crême caramel* or one small fruit. Jane repeatedly referred to the cinema of one's life, that it was on record th. t people drowning had a complete memory of everything that had happened in life. Could we use this power consciously? she asked. "Everything that has happened to us, every experience, is within us. The impress is in some one of the three centers, never to be eradicated, but generally forgotten. *Everything is there."*

She told us how to get at it — by beginning with the day's events, picturing oneself as the central figure, but impersonally, so as to leave the emotional center free with its pictures. This method of seeing oneself pictorially in all one's daily activity was a way of keeping one's life from slipping into oblivion. "It has been called 'a specific against mediocrity' " she said and my mind leapt for her phrase while my pencil underlined it in my notes.

After doing the day's cinema, she suggested we try the cinema of our lives, unrolling all the reels. If we could do these things, if we could teach ourselves to see impersonally, uncritically, we should gain a mastery over the three mechanical centers. There was "an inviolate completeness" which could become the property of the human being. We were only approaching the outskirts of it . . .

But I had a wonderful time on the outskirts. I learned how to add seltzer at widely spaced intervals to one vermouth-cassis and make it last for hours on the *terrasse* of the Deux Magots café directly opposite the Church of St.-Germain-des-Prés. Against that beautiful backdrop I would unroll the reels of my life, especially the early ones of a crop-headed tomboy tongue-tied with adoration for her sardonic father who could puncture a dream with a word. Now and again when he was on scene, my inner projector stopped turning and I would think about him deeply in terms of my newly learned ways of evaluating. Was that father predominantly a "physical center" man?

I recalled how he loved rich foods, fast cars and glamorous women. And wool, of course, being a wool merchant . . . but it had to be only top quality fleece wool, only "first-clip" — long-fibered and resilient with crimp. I discovered that when the father's shadow loomed in thought nothing in me then stood apart like impersonal witness. I wondered if I could "write him out of me" in some sort of self-remembering exercise. In the years since college, I had drifted far from him and knew of his whereabouts only through occasional references to him in my mother's letters.

One afternoon, in the café chair I now thought of as mine, I tried to get in focus on my screen pictures of myself as a tongue-tied child yearning for her father to come home. His

woolen mill panned into the picture, a place of magic always
to my brother and me, and I let those happy reels roll away
while I began writing . . .

The woolen mill had teasels to work the wool after
scouring, hooked brown bracts on stems, strange to see
among all the great machinery, especially if you knew they
had once been blue flowers. I always wondered if my father
knew their origin, if he had seen them standing stiff and
defiant on the hills beside the Golden Gate, not bending
to any wind. They were like him in a way. I could have
talked to him about teasels, but was afraid. Mooning again,
Tom, he would have said, and something in me would
have curled up the way my bitten nails curled into my
palms whenever he asked: Well, Tom, how are the nails?

I stared at my paragraph of self-remembering then closed
the notebook. I had forgotten until that moment that I used
to bite my nails, often down to the quick. I recalled how
vanity had cured me of the habit, in my university years when
I fell in love with a fellow chemistry student who had green
eyes and red hair . . .

We were making tests for saponification, shaking our test
tubes back and forth as we chatted, when I saw his eyes
widen with shock. He had looked at my test tube to check if
any fats were saponifying in the alkaline solution and had
seen the bitten nails of my right hand exposed down the side
of the tube. There was of course no way to hold a test tube
without exposing the fingernails. He backed away from me
ever so slightly and that was the end of my romance. I never
bit my nails again.

Had that been my first triumph over the "tyrant body,"
that abrupt cessation of a nervous physical habit fixed by

eighteen years of gnawing my fingers? I regretted the absence of Wendy who was missing too much. Often I wrote to
her from the bistro, transcribing in simplified language my
latest notes from the group, especially anything new I picked
up on Gurdjieff.

One thing I heard fascinated me but I did not relay it to
her mainly because I would have had to tell her first about
"the scale" and Gurdjieff's "Law of Seven" which had
excited so many of us as we diagrammed it in our notebooks
under Jane's guidance. It was like a cosmic blueprint of the
way up the scale of man's possible development from sleeping state to consciousness — all too difficult to paraphrase.
As the implications of this Law had dawned on us, there
arose in our emotions, as so often but never before quite so
sharply, a clamorous desire to know more about the teacher
who had formulated the wondrous scheme that hitched
man's wagon to a star. And someone had ventured once
again the plaintive wish, If we could just *see* Mr. Gurdjieff,
just once when he passes through Paris . . . why, Miss
Heap, do you always discourage the idea?

I don't remember her exact words. I was too mesmerized to
take notes. I recall only the surprise of her opening: Because
he might disappoint you, throw you off entirely from his
Work . . .

He might, for example, choose on your approach to play
the role you detested most in humans (which possibly you
yourself exemplified unaware). He would know looking at
you which one that was. To a woman flaunting allure (and
proud of it) he might imply that the way to learn more from
him was via the conjugal bed. To a man displaying self-
esteem for intellectual achievements, he might choose to play

the ignorant rug merchant with leering look and spots of spilled coffee on his vest. To one whose god was money or material possessions, he might very well convey by words and gestures that the only way to him was through the pocket-book. He could play any role with consummate artistry. He would play the one that would shock you most . . . to test you, of course. To test the depth of your desire to learn more. It was genius screening, obviously. He had not time to waste on dilettantes or, as in our case, on novices still green with illusions and false ideas about themselves. Apparently no one who had ever met him emerged from the encounter unimpressed, one way or another. Nor did any two give similar reports of him beyond of course the exterior description which any camera might record: shaved cranium high and rounded like the dome of a mosque, magnetic dark eyes and "handlebar" moustaches thick and virile, curled up at their ends like a ram's horns. I put a Cossack cap of black astrakhan on the massive head as I pictured it, after someone mentioned casually that that was his winter headgear.

Meanwhile I was earning what I hoped might be my future living. I wrote every morning in my hotel room. Against the hideous wallpaper I made my memory recall its pictures of Mexico. I would stare at them until every detail sparkled clear, then write.

The narrow stairwell outside my door echoed the faint clackings of the typewriters three floors above where Janet Flanner and Solita Solano earned their current livings from "Letters from Paris" for their respective magazines. The clacking echoes inspired me with the hope that one day — if I kept at it and copied their disciplined writing habits — I also might achieve the status of a selling author. Occasionally I showed a finished piece to Solita for I always learned something when she edited. One day I handed her my story of Chichen Itza's pyramid topped by a circular limestone tower called the Caracol — the Mayan observatory from which that ancient race had studied planets and stars. Secretly I was proud of the piece; it evoked the mystery of a vanished civilization, of signs of forgotten knowledge over which the jungle had drawn its protective green mantle of wildness and kept intact until discovery.

I held my breath as I watched her poised blue pencil. She turned a page and began reading with awesome intentness. Suddenly she looked up and cried, "What's this, Katie?" She flashed a page that had got into my manuscript by mistake — the paragraph of self-remembering, about my father's woollen mill. Abashed I told her what it was — just an exercise in "unrolling the reels." She picked up my Mexican travelogue and tore it crossways twice under my startled eyes.

"*This,*" she said shaking my woolen mill paragraph at me, "is what you're to do. Right now. Drop everything else. Forget about Mexico . . . my God, can't you see this is good?"

No, I couldn't. I had a blind spot in relation to my work, no judgment of it before, during or after composing. Besides, I said, that woolen mill bit was only intended as private exercise.

"Then go on, *do* it as exercise . . . call it anything you want but *do it!*" She reread my half page and said, "You just might get a book out of this if you keep up the quality. Show me pages each day. I'll clean them up as you go."

So began the book that was to be my first real attempt at

creative writing, under the guidance of a merciless editor, in the ugliest room in the most beautiful city on earth. I was writing about divorce — my parents', not mine, yet with my own chagrin showing through. For auto-encouragement I called it a book rather than an exercise in self-discovery turning over the old pain of my own divorce as I remembered my fatherless childhood. It took me years to do that deep spading and when it was finally accepted by Alfred Knopf and published under the title of *We Lived As Children,* I was speechless with joy. I have always believed that if an unknown man named Gurdjieff had not told someone, who told someone else who finally told me, how to unroll the reels and look at the shadows of forgotten selves buried in the unconscious memory, there never would have been that start. Until I had begun hearing about the buried "I," my previous and current condition on earth had been of less interest to me than the life of any passing stranger with a story in his face.

Before Wendy came back, Margaret Anderson and, subsequently, Georgette Leblanc joined our study group. I had read their recent books — Margaret Anderson's *My Thirty Years War* (her literary adventuring with *The Little Review*) and, in French, Georgette Leblanc's *Souvenirs* — her memories of twenty years of life with Maeterlinck, which Janet Flanner later translated into English. But those memoirs of two extraordinary beings scarcely prepared me for their actual presences. Margaret Anderson came into Jane Heap's salon like a Valkyrie, a warrior in search of challenge. Our sessions sparkled when she was there. She, with Jane Heap, had attended the Fontainebleau Institute when Gurdjieff was still teaching his Method through sacred dances, so she knew how to load the questions she fired at

Jane, how to bait her to reveal more than perhaps was intended for beginners.

Of all the people who had been drawn to the Gurdjieff ideas, Georgette Leblanc seemed on first sight to be the most improbable. I must confess that my first meeting with her was also improbable. It happened on Christmas Day of 1931, in the Château de la Muette at Maisons-Lafitte outside Paris, which she and Margaret Anderson had rented. The occasion was a musical reception for their friends in the art world. I have an old newspaper clipping describing the event:

> Madame Georgette Leblanc gave a musical reception on Christmas day in her Château de la Muette at Maisons-Lafitte. The frame is truly worthy of this high-priestess of art.
>
> The Château de la Muette was one of the hunting rendezvous of Louis XIV, built by Mansard, restored under Louis XV. Voltaire came there frequently and the presentation of Marie-Antoinette to Louis XVI (15 and 18 years old) took place in the salons of la Muette.
>
> Under the name of "the follies of Artois" la Muette was long owned by the Count d'Artois. Later, Napoleon gave great hunt breakfasts there. Benjamin Constant and Madame de Staël also met each other there.
>
> The lighting, uniquely from candles, harmonized with this ancient dwelling and brought about a lovely confusion of candlelight reflections from the mirrors and crystals.
>
> In the Louis XVI rotonde, very high and all white, a Christmas tree decorated in silver tinsel and white plumes stood. A young American pianist of great talent, Allan Tanner, played Bach, Gluck and Lulli.
>
> Among the invited guests were Luigi Pirandello and his interpreter Marta Alba, James Joyce, Jacques Chardonne, Darius Milhaud, Philippe Heriat . . . Germaine Dulac,

Osso and the Princess Murat, the Princess of Cystria and
Monsieur and Madame Philippe Berthelot . . .

I looked out on the sparkling scene from the shelter of
"the American room," an exquisite library adjoining the
salon where Margaret had assigned me to preside over a
small cocktail bar set up for the Americans. The arched
doorway framed my view of the *rotonde* filled with beautiful
people holding champagne glasses. I kept an eye on the
candles in ornamental brackets — over fifty, Margaret had
told me; I was to replace any burning low. Reflections from
the antique mirrors set into the circular walls multiplied
them into hundreds. Opposite my viewpoint, a great log fire
leapt red under the white marble mantel. The mirrors picked
up its glow and then suddenly, in the midst of the burning,
Georgette Leblanc made her calculated entrance.

She was a Tanagra figurine dressed in scarlet. She stood
before the leaping fire to receive her guests. She wore a
strange *moyenâgeux* gown of antique material soft and cling-
ing and a matching scarlet turban twisting above a stylized
crown of blond hair. The train of her gown arranged in
swirls about her invisible feet made her seem to grow out of
the floor, fragile and ageless, like a statue.

After the guests departed, Georgette Leblanc invited the
Americans (whom she obviously adored) to spend the night
in the château — Allan Tanner, his friend Pavel Tchelit-
chew, Solita and me. Everything was, as she expressed it, *trop
beau* to come to an end. *Trop beau* . . . too beautiful
indeed — but what followed was even more so.

With the candles burning low and the fire leaping high, we
sat about the vaulted salon and listened to Allan Tanner play

the Débussy music of *Pelléas et Mélisande*. Under the spell of his piano the château became the castle of the Maeterlinck poem, isolated and eerie on the edge of a grottoed sea. The forest of Maisons-Laffitte surrounding us, white under December snow, became the enchanted summer woods of the legend and, as the first gentle notes of the Mélisande theme were sounded, Georgette Leblanc — without sound or motion — began acting again the great role she had created in the Boston Opera House nineteen years before.

Over her marvelously expressive face emotional memories flowed and her green eyes glistened and darkened with the mood of the music, her gaze on a distant point outside of our circle, outside our experience. I felt like a trespasser as I watched. When Allan Tanner came to the end, the death of Mélisande, it was almost unbearable to see the little princess dying alone in her big bed . . .

I stayed over in the château for several days, sitting in Georgette's paper-stacked apartment under the mansard, reading chapters of the new book she was writing, walking the glorious *allées* of the forest arm in arm with her, with her German shepherd dog snuffling at our heels, and listening, fascinated and beguiled, to the voice that had sung Thais, Carmen or Salome, now talking of the Gurdjieff ideas. How long was the reach of that Russian mystic, I thought, to have caught the mind and heart of this extraordinary woman whose life, until she met him, had been lived for art and love alone, like the "Vissi d'Arte" aria from *Tosca* which she sometimes sang.

Jane Heap came to the château one day while I was there. Then I saw the touching communication within a trio — Jane, Margaret and Georgette — whose friendship was more than a decade old. Margaret, who seemed to read Jane's thoughts, did a simultaneous translation of her talks for Georgette (who understood no English) in a queer abbreviated French that sounded like a patois, while Georgette sat motionless between them, her magnificent eyes moving from face to face, taking it all in.

Shortly after the New Year of 1932, Wendy cabled that she would sail from San Pedro aboard a French freighter, through the Canal to Le Havre, bringing with her a two-ton Packard roadster with Dietrich body and convertible top.

It was well she gave me a month to prepare for her return. I ran out of the hotel to send an answering cable and threw away my purse somewhere along the rue Jacob on the way to the *poste.* Every document I owned, except mercifully my passport, was in it — *carte d'identité,* French driving license — everything needed, in short, to resume my job as Wendy's driver-companion. I told the police that I must have dropped the purse in the excitement of certain *bonnes nouvelles* just received, but I knew that I had probably opened my hand and let it fly as I had hurried along, talking to myself like a Frenchman and making palms-up gestures in the air . . . *Mon Dieu!* A two-ton Packard in these narrow streets . . . is she mad? I could not see myself doing this but knew it must have been so. Months of stoic self-observation had flown out the window on receipt of that cablegram.

As I filled out the request forms for duplicate papers, I thought: You lost yourself completely in that purse-flinging moment, *what is all this fancy talk about self-observation?* You haven't even made the *first step* in that direction . . .

Wendy's freighter emerged from the Channel fogs at four o'clock on a February morning and warped in slowly to her mooring at the far outer docks of Le Havre where I had been waiting since midnight with seagulls and stevedores for company. Twelve heads showed over the bulwarks of the forward deck. I looked for the one with the fanciest hat and began to wave to it as her voice fluted down, "Katie, Katie . . . oh, I *knew* you'd be here, no matter what!"

She felt like a bag of bones which even her new fitch fur coat could not pad out to human proportion. The Packard roadster lifting out of an aft hold looked like the entire ship's engine being removed from hull to dockside. We talked through the dawn while the rest of her baggage came off. And presently, as I had arranged, a representative of the Royal Auto Club drove up with gasoline for the car and all necessary papers to admit it into France. A sleepy Customs agent made a token inspection of the smallest bag, chalked his clearance on the rest and we were off, soon after sunrise, on the *grande route nationale* that led to Rouen, 56½ miles to the south. The Packard made it easily in an hour, getting us into Rouen just as the hot croissants from the town's bakery appeared on the breakfast tables of the Hotel de la Poste.

We loitered the rest of the way to Paris, talking about Jane Heap's study group, the fascinating new people in it whom I had met and who now were waiting eagerly to meet her, and what we would do when the sessions ended. Wendy confessed that there was still a lot of travel she longed to do if, she said wistfully, it would not conflict with the book in progress. I told her the so-called book was actually an exercise of sorts which could continue anywhere since all its material was inside me. Not listening, she launched on our future itinerary . . . Vienna, Budapest, Warsaw, perhaps later the Holy Land . . .

I'll never know what whimsical notion made Wendy plead for a stop in the Café de la Paix before going to the Left Bank hotel where a cozy suite awaited her. The notion caught her in the maelstrom of the Place de la Concorde when I was trying to maneuver the huge car over to the right, toward the bridge that led to Faubourg St. Germain. "No, no, *keep left,*" she cried. "We go first to Café de la Paix!" I battled my way back into the vortex to head toward the Opera and the sumptuous old café on the corner of the square.

There was, unbelievably, a Packard-sized parking space just before the café's main entrance, and I backed our two tons into it with two turns of the wheel. Wendy said, "Bravo for you Katie!" We pushed through the revolving doors into the warm splendor of the world's most famous café and saw, unoccupied at that crowded aperitif hour, our favorite banquette table in the second *salle* that faced out on Boulevard des Capucines. "It was waiting for me," Wendy said.

The whole café as a matter of fact seemed to be waiting for her. Newspapers were lowered and monocles adjusted as she passed by in her elegant coat of fitch. The only male in the section who did not look up was a shaven-headed writer bent over his work at a table opposite. The waiter remembered Wendy. He gave her a welcome back to Paris and said, "Amontillado sherry *comme toujours,* Madame?" I ordered a café cognac to pick me up from my predawn vigil.

After our refreshments, I relaxed and café-gazed with Wendy. She ticked off every chic woman in view by the name of the couturiere who had costumed her and the modiste who had hatted her. I always enjoyed her specialist side and the amusing way she took women apart, exhanging the hat of this one with that one to make both look lovelier. Her musical voice tinkled on like a fountain while she looked around at the gold Corinthian pilasters upholding lofty ceilings frescoed with sky scenes and cherubs, at the busy murals in wall medallions aglow with indirect lighting and at the gold-draped show window giving out onto the crowed *terrasse* and the boulevard beyond. Then she turned her big eyes on me and asked: "However could Mr. Gurdjieff concentrate in a place like this?"

I saw she wanted an answer. The man on the opposite banquette was still busily writing. I nodded toward him and said, "Some can. That one for instance. I don't believe he has looked up once since we came . . ."

He looked up as I spoke and I saw the countenance I had pieced together fancifully from Jane Heap's words — dome-like shaved cranium, large black eyes and handlebar moustaches curled up at their ends. My whole inner being froze to attention. Presently he found the phrase he sought and bent again to his work. On the green velour banquette that sagged slightly under his weight, I saw folded beside him a black winter overcoat with Karakul collar and a Cossack cap of the same tightly curled lamb's wool.

"But that must be Gurdjieff!" I could have bitten off my tongue, for Wendy pushed out the table, arose and said, "Come . . . we'll go right over and speak to him."

CHAPTER FIVE

WE stood before his table waiting for him to look up. He made us wait for an interval that felt like eons, then slowly raised his head and gazed at me with the most beautiful eyes I had ever looked into — even slightly angry as they were, scowling.

"Excusez-moi, Monsieur . . . êtes-vous Monsieur Gurd-jieff?" My voice dwindled as I hurried on to explain that we belonged to a small group meeting each week in Montparnasse to study his teachings with Miss Heap. His eyes narrowed as if regarding something very small, then his glance moved on to Wendy standing taller behind me.

"Geep?" he rumbled. "Mees Geep?" It took me a moment to realize he was repeating Heap with a hard G for the H which his Russian tongue could not aspirate. I said *"Oui, monsieur"* with my last breath. Then he nodded and said "Sit," in English. He thrust aside his overcoat and made a place for Wendy beside him on the banquette, indicated any old vacant chair for me to pull up and invited us for a coffee with him or whatever else we might prefer.

Wendy did most of the talking. She told him how we had stumbled, so to speak, into Miss Heap's circle, how she had made notes (she had copied mine) and had always wanted to meet him since she believed in going direct to a source. She was a businesswoman, she said, as if that explained everything. Hands as well as voice conveyed her delight for the unexpected encounter. He studied her as she chattered confidingly. Did he understand a word of her rapid breathless English? He offered her a long Russian cigarette and placed one in his own short holder made of some sort of briarwood, dark and knotty. He accepted a light from me without looking my way, then said, "Business, aha! I also am businessman."

I know now that we must have caught him in a moment of weariness after writing for hours in the blankbook that lay on the table beneath his brown fingers flattened at the tips like a musician's. Unknown and uninvited, we must have appeared when he needed what he was later to term for us "idiot relief" — a most useful expression for anyone toiling to communicate through the written word. I marveled at the way Wendy chattered on unabashed, then listened to him, seeming to understand his abbreviated English which was not pidgin (as some reports had suggested) but simply nouns without articles preceding verbs without adverbs.

Presently he said to Wendy, "You have car?" and she pointed out the window to the Packard parked at the curb, directly behind his mud-splattered sedan. He looked at the long lowslung roadster, then turned directly to me and said, "You are chauffeur?" I meant to speak up brightly and naturally like Wendy but the full force of his regard caused me to blush and stammer.

"He invites us to go to Fontainebleau with him this afternoon," Wendy said across the table. "We are to follow his car." Gurdjieff turned his eyes away from me for a moment to study Wendy registering pleasure at the prospect and I got my voice back firm and strong in time to answer his next query: "You *can* follow?" "Yes Sir," I said, looking straight into his wonderful eyes, "I am very good at following."

He instructed me to come to the café at three o'clock exactly. With night bag in the car. "And bring the Thin One," he added, giving Wendy the name which summed her up for him.

We arose, thanked him for coffee and walked from the *salle* as if emerging from a royal audience. At the revolving doors I looked back. I had to see Gurdjieff once again to believe that the encounter had really happened. With one leg pulled up beneath him Oriental-fashion on the banquette, he looked from a distance like a broad-shouldered Buddha radiating such power that all the people between him and me seemed dead.

In the car we sat for a moment to catch our breath, laughing nervously together for no reason at all. Then I told Wendy to memorize both number-plate and rear-end contour of the black sedan in front of us which, in exactly three hours, we would begin following through the congested boulevards to Ponte d'Orléans and thence south for thirty-eight miles to an unknown destination in the forest of Fontainebleau.

The perfect timing of that first meeting with the renowned teacher, right on the heels of Wendy's return to Paris (when I was hoping for something to highlight the ideas that had absorbed me during her absence) did not seem strange in the least. Compatible coincidences were daily events in her life. She seemed to draw them to her like a poltergeist.

I drove with redoubled caution toward the Left Bank, listening to her speaking my own thoughts over and over. "He's not anything like what I imagined . . . absolutely not anything. He never once mentioned one thing we ever heard in the study group. He talked business, fancy that! Says he wants to sell that château he has in Fontainebleau . . . Do you suppose he thought I might be a buyer? Why did he up and invite us . . . out of the blue . . . just like that? He's simply not anything like what I imagined," she said again. "Thin one . . . I suppose he has a terrible time with American names. He pronounced it Theen like a Frenchman!"

I had taken a suite in Hotel de l'Université, around the block from my former haunt; Wendy flew about the apartment unpacking suitcases and repacking an overnight bag with accessories for us both while I studied on a road map the several routes one could take to Fontainebleau. I wished Solita had not gone to the country for the day. It would have been so exciting to tell her of our encounter.

We had a snack lunch in the Café Flore, then we were off down Boulevard St. Germain heading again to the Opera and Café de la Paix. The black sedan was parked in a different space. I pulled into a restricted taxi area for the momentary halt and walked into the café — the good courier reporting on the minute of three. Gurdjieff said "Aha!" when I stood before him, then put on his Karakul cap, picked up overcoat and briefcase and preceded me out of the café.

He started his car with a race of the motor that belched smoke from the exhaust and I swung out behind him into the boulevard traffic, galvanized by the single fixed purpose to let nothing get between us for the next thirty-eight miles. I lost him a dozen times before arriving on the outskirts of Paris.

He drove like a wild man, cutting in and out of traffic without hand signals or even space to accommodate his car in the lanes he suddenly switched to . . . until he was in them, safe by a hair. Black French sedans exactly like his seemed to fill the streets. I learned to watch ahead for the one being driven the most erratically, then — gripping the wheel — to try to follow it. In the breathing spaces at red lights, I sometimes saw him off to the right or the left, black fur cap set at a jaunty angle, puffing tranquilly on a cigarette. He always got away first on the green light even (so it seemed) when he was one or two cars behind the starting line.

Outside Paris things were a bit easier but not much. I could keep him in sight for longer stretches on the *route nationale,* but the chances he took overtaking buses and trucks were terrifying. I watched with suspended breath each time he swung out around a truck and headed directly into another coming toward him on the narrow two-lane road.

Somewhere midway or possibly beyond (memory retained no data of village names, route markers or mileposts passed) the black sedan on which total attention was riveted appeared to be slowing down. Presently it pulled off the cobbled road to a halt beneath some trees. Gurdjieff got out and walked toward the Packard pulling in behind. He gave us an enchanting smile and said, "Here we make pause . . . we listen to *grenouilles.*"

Grenouilles . . . frogs! I stuttered to Wendy. We got out and listened. Frogs were singing somewhere off in the marshes beyond the trees, a chorale of splendor issuing in chirps, croaks and trills from hundreds of amphibian throats.

Seeing Gurdjieff smoking, I lit a cigarette with shaking

hands, watching him warily over the tip of my lighter's flame. He held up one finger, cocked his head toward the singing and said, "You *hear?*" with a possessive smile as if the frogs had turned it on for him alone, knowing he would be passing that way at that magical sunset hour . . .

After a while we climbed back into our cars and drove toward Fontainebleau. Within the town Gurdjieff circled slowly around the crowded *carrefours* and I believed with a rush of thankfulness that he was watching us through his rear-view mirror, wishing (for God knew what reason) not to lose us in the last mile. From the railroad station we followed him down a hill to Avon, a small village with a church that looked to be very old. We came to handsome wrought-iron gates; the sedan halted and klaxoned. A young lad swung the gates open and we followed the sedan into a courtyard enclosed by pinkish stone walls and, beyond a circular fountain splashing gently, the façade of the Château du Prieuré where, in the Twenties, Gurdjieff had conducted his Institute for the Harmonious Development of Man. We took our night bag from the car and entered the silent château on the heels of our mystifying host.

A woman with a beautiful, composed face emerged from one of the darkened salons, spoke in Russian for a few moments with Gurdjieff, then turned to us and said in French she would show us to our rooms on the second floor. I did not know (until our next meeting with the Paris group) that we were housed that night in the wing for VIP's which American disciples had once called "the Ritz," in the actual room that had been Madame de Maintenon's boudoir when the château belonged to her.

I was only vaguely aware of the luxury of the Louis

Quatorze room with its canopied beds and fine old mirrors set into painted walls. I gave all attention to the quiet-voiced Russian who treated us, not like two strange creatures the master had picked up in the streets of Paris, but rather like expected guests whom she wished to put at ease. I remembered Katherine Mansfield's words about the people who surrounded Gurdjieff in her time — "absolutely unlike people as I have known people." This woman of gravely beautiful countenance, so completely in possession of herself, must have been one of his earliest followers. She seemed to know our inner states of blank astonishment, to read our nervous thoughts about what comes next. She smiled and stated the simple schedule. Dinner would be served on trays in our room; afterward, around eight o'clock, we were to descend for a visit to the Study House which Mr. Gurdjieff wished to show to us. After coffee in the morning, we were free to leave at whatever time we wished. We would probably not see Mr. Gurdjieff in the morning since he had many things to attend to in the town.

With a friend, in the spring of 1962, I revisited the Prieuré when making an Easter pilgrimage to Gurdjieff's grave in the nearby cemetery of Avon. A taxi took us from the railroad station to the iron gates of the château, now a sort of convalescent home run on state *assurance* and union welfare funds for the benefit of the aging and infirm. We had come on a day when no visitors were allowed and could not go beyond the locked gates.

I peered through the bars at the château with its gray slate mansard from which seven little dormer windows protruded. There were the same lovely wrought-iron lanterns hanging on curved hooks at the main portal and the big circular fountain was still there but no longer splashing its musical jet from upper to lower basin. A small bronze plaque set into the wall at the right of the gates noted that Katherine Mansfield had died here in 1923. That was what brought the tourists, said our driver.

But I was peering back thirty years, trying to revive the memory of the other celebrity who had once inhabited that château and of the one night I had slept in it — a night which had afterwards seemed like a dream, singular and inexplicable, a vision of trespass through a haunted house.

I realized that it *had* been like a haunted house when Wendy and I had stayed there. Had that been the reason why Gurdjieff had asked us to accompany him? To offset in some way with our two human presences manifesting excitement the ghostly quiet of the great Study House that once had hummed with the striving of disciples practicing movements of sacred dances? I could not see if the Study House still stood at the edge of a grove on the other side of the château but I remembered, like a yesterday's experience, how Wendy had clapped her hands and cried, "Oh how beautiful, Mr. Gurdjieff!" when he had led us into the Persian-carpeted enclosure — a large hall out of *The Thousand and One Nights* with painted windows, divans and a fountain before a stage at the far end . . . and how he had looked at her in the colored gloom with a peculiar expression and had said, "You *feel?*"

Despite the stagy furnishing there had been a holy feeling about it which came over us after the first moments. I could not remember how long we sat beside our host on a carpeted divan in the silence, or what he said that made it seem to come alive with white-robed dancers turning slowly in movements of dervish prayer. I didn't even know if he was telling *us* how it was, or simply reminding himself of a time in his teaching that gave him satisfaction to recall. I was so overcome with the strangeness of the experience that I failed to remark the motto painted over the Study House door; years later one of the men who had helped to build it told me that it said: *Remember that you came here realizing the necessity of struggling only with yourself and thank anyone who helps you to engage in this struggle.*

We said our farewell to Gurdjieff under the lanterns at the château entrance and tried to express thanks for his extraordinary, if enigmatic, hospitality. He waved away our conventional phrases and thanked us instead . . . "For company," he said with an edge of humor to his unexpected words. Then he turned away and walked off through the gardens with a slightly rolling gait, hands clasped behind his back. With one of my sudden uprushes of emotion which no amount of work had yet managed to anticipate or quell, I thought that he looked like the loneliest man in the world.

We did not see him again for over a year. He vanished from Paris but not from our minds. His powerful image had impressed us so profoundly that we continued to see him in bits and parts in every swarthy Oriental countenance seen in cafés, in every fur-capped figure encountered in the White Russian tea rooms around the Rue de la Boetie — parts, but never the whole man.

Then we met him briefly and again by seeming chance in the very last place we, the uninitiated, would have expected to find him — in the clattering, tiled and chromium interior of a Child's restaurant on New York's upper Fifth Avenue. Through friends of the Paris group we had learned that he was in town and meeting disciples there. We could hardly believe it — (the contrast of Child's with the plushy elegance of the Café de la Paix was so surprising) — but we went and saw him, for the first time, in an American frame.

In that antiseptic white setting with its look-alike New York business crowd, Gurdjieff stood out with stunning singularity — a monumental Moses dropped like a museum piece into the midst of it. He sat at the head of two or three tables that had been dragged together on which coffee cups were scattered and Danish pastry, ordered but uneaten.

Gurdjieff appeared to remember us when we advanced to shake his hand, and motioned us to the foot of the tables to an unoccupied place. I looked with envy at the people who "belonged," pioneers of the group A. R. Orage had organized when he preceded the master to the States in 1923. They were sitting very quiet and attentive, awaiting their turns on the chairs to the right and left of Gurdjieff who talked with each one singly, in a low rumbling voice not meant to carry beyond the listener's ears.

It was beautiful to watch the teaching being given live, so to speak. I thought of the Old English root of teach — *tǣcan*, like token, and saw the token being passed like a visible object from teacher to pupil.

When would my turn ever come in that exclusive receiving line?

CHAPTER SIX

I HAD been a follower of the Gurdjieff ideas for almost four years when at last in Paris my turn for direct teaching came. It was not exclusively "my turn" but that of a small group of Jane Heap's students left high and dry when she finally moved to London. Yet I call it mine, as must each who passed through Gurdjieff's hands. No two of us had the same soft spots in our undeveloped selves; no two received the same treatment. The mark of Gurdjieff on each was as unique as one's thumbprint.

Through the intervening years since I had first been drawn into Jane Heap's circle, I had carried with me everywhere like two life rafts my notebook of the Gurdjieff ideas and the unfinished script of my childhood rememberings, which I still worked on and secretly hoped might turn into a book. Meanwhile, Wendy in her sphere had had a disillusioning experience with yet another hat shop (opened in New York's fashionable East Fifties), a repetition of her old life pattern which had brought none of the inner satisfactions she once had known and believed could be repeated. After she had had a year of battling the red tape of Roosevelt's NRA, which she interpreted as "idiot government" trying to tell *her* how to run a business, I had helped to extricate her from a formidable $50,000 lease by the simple expedient of finding a buyer for it, as well as for her costly shop fixtures and workroom facilities.

Now, in the late summer of 1935, I was in Paris again and Wendy planned to join me in a month or so and make a real try at settling down in France. I moved promptly into my old Left Bank hotel room, resolved, during her absence, to get on with my own life.

Our special time with Gurdjieff began with sessions of studying him from a discreet distance across the *salle* from "his place" in the Café de la Paix, to which he returned unheralded just before Jane Heap left for London. We were three Americans in her liquidated Paris group — Solita Solano, Louise Davidson and myself — who refused to take No for an answer. No, he is *not* organizing any new groups . . . No, he will *not* teach again, except through the medium of his books on which he has been engaged for the past six years . . . No use hoping, he is in another phase of his work now.

We passed the café every morning, looked in to see if he was there. If so, we went in and sat opposite, quietly watchful, disturbingly wishful. When he looked up from his writing he could see us (but never seemed to) like three blackbirds sitting in a row, sipping coffee the way he drank it — with a section of lemon squeezed into it. Occasionally Margaret Anderson and Georgette Leblanc, on a visit from their lighthouse in Tancarville, joined the watch. Then there were five highly vibrating beggars waiting for a crumb from the master's table.

We did not think this activity strange in the least, although

I realize that in today's faithless world my picture of our preoccupation must appear bizarre, suggesting that Gurdjieff was some sort of god in our eyes. He was, in the sense that any genius is godlike. We believed quite simply that we were in the presence of a great teacher who had formulated for the modern mind a sublime cosmogony with ladders in it to help mankind out of its caves. One day, we were sure, he would acknowledge our persistence. One day, perhaps, he might help us out of the underground dens we inhabited, like the deluded humans in Plato's famous analogy the Myth of the Cave which we were then reading.

Jane Heap left for London on October eighteenth — a Black Friday for us who went to the station to see her off on the boat train. She had brought us into the Gurdjieff work, had given us a taste for the indefinable vastness of its aim. I remembered as I fought back tears (for which weakness she would have chided me) one of her statements that had really put the fear of God in me: "We in this Method are like Lucifers, cast out from the mechanical heaven in which we live." In the stress of emotion my mind flew off in hyperbole, presenting pictures of us falling through empty space, drifting and falling . . .

Her train pulled out, and our group dispersed in different directions. I stood alone for a moment, then a self I had never seen or heard, the self that Gurdjieff was to name Crocodile that same evening, propelled me to the Café de la Paix, through its heavy revolving door and directly to Gurdjieff's table.

He gazed up at me without a trace of recognition. My heart pounded as I recited my sketchy credentials for the intrusion, reminding him that I had once driven behind him to Fontainebleau, later met him in a Child's Fifth Avenue and now had come from Gare St. Lazare after seeing Miss Heap off for London. His boring eyes seemed to be sampling my inner state as I chattered; then, when I had come to the end of my rope, he mercifully invited me to sit for a coffee.

After a period of easy-feeling silence he looked at me and remarked that I had changed; I was "thin in the cheeks," he said. "Now I think you smell my idea, you smell so-o . . ." he inhaled deeply. "You can change ten times like that, each time more strong. Then maybe the next change is not *it* changing, but *you* changing. Maybe perhaps," he added thoughtfully.

Raptly I watched him squeeze lemon into his black coffee and frugally shake the yellow rind for its last drops. Presently he continued talking in another vein. He had been sitting there thinking. Now I must have rest . . . and I had come in and *I* was rest. Did I know what he meant by rest? he asked. I imagined he meant "idiot relief" and nodded. Then he asked me if I had ever heard of his "crayfish club" where he took people and "sheared" them. Shearing, I knew, was his colorful term for getting contributions toward his Work. Would I like to be a "candidate for shearing" that night? he asked, and I was nodding in advance of his statement of what it would cost me. Had he read my mind (as some on the lunatic fringe claimed he could do) he would have seen my readiness to pay for a trip to the moon if I could tail along in orbit behind him.

The coffee finished, he gathered up his notebooks and told me to come with him to his hotel. It turned out to be the famous old Grand next door to the café. He had a small room cluttered with books, manuscript, and a vintage type-writer at which a male secretary was working. Gurdjieff slipped off his greatcoat, looked over a mass of manuscript and handed me some twenty pages, explaining that it was a new English translation of his work which he wished to hear read aloud.

I was agonizingly aware of the author sitting opposite me on a sofa, one knee drawn up beneath him and immense head hung forward, listening with a concentration that seemed to burn up all the oxygen in the air between us as I labored through pages of allegory incomprehensible to me. I read from word to word, sentence to sentence, as if feeling the way, halting before tongue twisters of proper names com-posed chiefly of consonants, which the master occasionally pronounced in a low tone. He knows every word of his massive creation, I thought.

After a half hour of this breathtaking exercise, my intro-duction to his labyrinthine prose, Gurdjieff said *"Enough!"* and I stopped reading midsyllable. He went to a huge armoire, took from it a bottle of vodka, some jarred herring, a piece of smoked sturgeon and a block of white goat's milk cheese. The secretary brought bread from some other unex-pected place — a bureau drawer as I recall — and we sat for lunch at the typewriter table. Gurdjieff talked Russian with his secretary, save once when he caught me staring and cried, "Eat . . . *eat!"* Right after lunch, he indicated I was free to leave and escorted me to the door. He reminded me of the crayfish dinner that night to which, he said, I could invite one friend and he would invite one. We would meet in the café at seven.

I sorted out my excited thoughts walking home to the Left Bank faster than a bus could have taken me. Was this possibly the end of our long siege of café sitting? I heard every word he had spoken to me, exactly as spoken, rumbling, meditative or jocose, heavily accented. How quickly one got used to his extraordinary simplified English when one listened to it with head and heart! I rehearsed his words for Solita and Louise as I flew through narrow streets lined with picture galleries and antique shops where formerly I loitered for hours. Though he had said "one friend," I intended that both of them accompany me to that crayfish dinner.

We were in the café promptly at seven, as instructed. Gurdjieff was alone at his table and appeared glad to see three of us. His friend had not come, he said without regret. We sat with him until his waiter brought his bill. To a generous tip he added, from his pocket, a handful of small wrapped candies which the gray-headed waiter gathered up with a pleased expression.

"Like a small boy," Gurdjieff said as the waiter went off. "Always I take bonbons in my pocket, chiefly for children. They call me Monsieur Bonbon. Even here in café by such name I am known. So I *must* give, always. They *expect* . . ." A sound of deep inner mirth escaped him as he repeated the name by which the innocents identified him. "Monsieur Bonbon!" . . . but *we* knew the real name of the man we followed out of the café to a taxi stand. His name was Rama, Krishna, Hermes, Moses, Pythagoras, Plato. His name, in latter-day descent from those great teachers, was Gurdjieff.

Later in our time with the master, the Brasserie Excelsior became a familiar testing ground, for us as well as for the many subsequent hopefuls, notables and nonentities, who came to Paris in those last golden years before World War II because the master was known to be there and teaching again. With more educated eyes, as our understanding stretched, we were to watch what Gurdjieff deliberately made for us to watch — pretensions and vanities sheared away from the pretentious and the self-proud, like wool off a sheep . . . in short, the human psyche stripped bare as only this master of the psyche could strip it. And I was to witness those later strippings with a kind of holy retroactive wonder that we, the initial threesome in his ever-widening circle, had been let off so easily on our first visit to his "crayfish club."

Everyone in the brasserie knew the master. The *patron* himself hurried forward to show him to his table already set with service for four. The little Frenchman kissed his finger-tips as he described the excellence of the *écrevisses* he had found that morning in Les Halles, fresh-caught in the ponds and streams of the neighboring provinces. Gurdjieff cried *"Oie, oie!"* when the huge platter of crimson "river lobsters" was set before him steaming in a thin reddish sauce which he ladled out like a soup into the dishes the waiter held. Then he forked a heap of crayfish into each and our main course was served.

There was a pause while Gurdjieff poured Armagnac into the six glasses he had ordered set before him — four for himself and party, one each for the *patron* and the waiter. He told us about his *"science d'idiotisme"* which he had studied seven years to create, putting into it all his knowledge of human typicality, polarity and so forth. He then lifted his glass, instructed us to drink half on the first toast and the magnetized *patron* and waiter to drink all, and gave the first of his famous ritual toasts: *"A la santé de tous les idiots ordinaires"* . . . To the health of all ordinary idiots.

With the Gascon brandy scorching one's throat, we followed his lead to the crayfish, peeling off the bright pink shells and eating the delicate meat of the crustacean from our fingers, then dipping bread into the devil's-brew sauce and eating that. On the second toast — "To the health of all superior idiots" — I began to memorize the sequence which, I presumed, described the progression (or the retrogression?) of the human state. The next toast was to the health of "all arch idiots" and our second glass was to last for three more toasts. I saw that keeping up with Gurdjieff was in itself an exercise in control, measuring and, above all, remembering, and became so excited with this small discovery that I inadvertently sucked some of the peppery sauce into my windpipe.

I began to choke and cough. Gurdjieff cried, "Bread . . . take bread!" I thought he said "breath" and worsened my state by trying to inhale. Then tears of fury for the stupid paroxysm stung my eyes. He watched the display, nudged Solita to watch also — a phenomenon of physical strangulation and emotional constriction not to be missed. When it was over, he nodded toward me and said to my companions, "I could write her diary!"

I believed that he could. Under the gaze of that master of the human condition, I knew that I must be as transparent as glass. The realization shocked me but only for a moment; then I felt a flood of relief that there need be no more pretending . . . at least, before this one man on earth who read me like a book. I watched my all-or-nothing nature hand myself, the composite of all my mutually antagonistic selves, over to him totally, in perfect trust. It felt like a deliverance.

I didn't care that he saw me making a mental note of the brand name of his preferred Armagnac — Château de Larresingle. Later, when the bottle was empty and he called for the bill and paid it, his mocking glance in my direction — as if he knew I had borrowed from my hotel *patron* what I thought would be enough to fulfill my promised obligation — did not dismay or disturb. He could write my diary. He could title it Diary of a Sleepwalker.

We took a taxi to the Café de la Paix for after-dinner coffee. This was a lyrical hour in that night's adventure. We sat outside on the café *terrasse* under the October stars. Gurdjieff studied the faces of boulevard strollers, seemingly as relaxed as any café idler; but presently he turned his great thoughtful eyes on our faces, looking from one to the other, weighing, measuring, identifying. Then he began talking in a low rumbling voice about man's "inner animal" — how he saw in each one of us the different creatures that typified for him our inner natures, the creatures with which we had to contend, had to keep friends with, always, so they would help us to achieve the aim of his Work . . . "Help, not hinder . . ."

In Louise, for example, he saw Sardine, not the sardine in its native element, but at that moment when it leaves the water for the sand to die, throwing its body over and over in perishing somersaults and long after that great thrust of energy was spent, continues quivering, gasping and flipping its tail.

Solita flashed me an excited glance; in our readings of the Greek esoteric schools we had found some disciples named after animals. Was it in Plato? in Zeno? I shook my head, I couldn't remember — not while Gurdjieff's hands were turning into sardines, twisting, arching, then flattening out to die while his rumbling voice told something to our gentle New

England friend (was this perhaps suggesting the risk of the leap out of mechanical life into his Work?) that held her transfixed, blue eyes popping wide.

Solita gave a gasp of admiration. He looked at her and said, "You *like* my formulation?" She nodded, too overcome to tell him how much. Then her turn came.

"And you, Miss . . ." he paused to brush up his moustaches, watching her eagerness, the pleading in her eyes that *her* animal be something strong and beautiful, something rare and if possible symbolic of the hidden knowledge which impassioned her — a unicorn, a phoenix . . .

"You are Canary," he said.

It was so perfect for her that I lost his next words. I was shot back on the word canary to my childhood home and my detested chore of cleaning the cage of my mother's Hartz Mountain Roller — the most costly, fragile, seed-scattering bird that man ever thought to pamper for the reward of its song. (Costly? Fragile? I knew she was always scattering seeds of thought . . .)

"Canary? Oh, Mr. Gurdjieff . . . *not* canary!" Solita's dismay made him laugh. I had not heard him laugh before. It was a contagious sound. I looked at Solita's face of woe and began laughing with him, though I knew she was simulating some of her distress to lead him on to say more. And when he refused, she pointed a finger at me and said, "And what is *she?*"

"She is Krokodeel," Gurdjieff said without preamble.

It was my turn to be stunned, but only for a moment. I thought of the mud of sentiment I lived in, of the crocodile tears I shed so easily, reviewing every wearisome aspect of myself as the name of the most unlovely beast in creation echoed through my mind. But was I *really* so tough-hided? So somnolent? So voracious? My own picture of myself as thin-skinned, sensitive and alert at all times suggested more the lizard than the crocodile. *What* did he mean? Crocodile, my God!

He watched my discomfiture, then said: "I give you one analogy. Crocodile meat I do not like, never eat, but crocodile I like, I can send ahead of me to swallow enemy, can be *useful* to me. *Now* you understand?" I was farther at sea than ever and shook my head, hoping for more, something perhaps about the inner fortitude I believed I had. But he was finished with the subject. Presently he looked at his watch and told us he had an eleven o'clock appointment in the café.

We rose to go — a Canary, a Sardine, a Crocodile — a peculiar little animal kingdom he had brought into being there on the city's most sophisticated *terrasse,* to show us something about ourselves. We thanked him for our dinner, for our names, and started to walk away when I heard my name called . . . *Krokodeel!* — a crackling command that spun me about instantly. The master invited me to meet him in the café next morning at eleven, to accompany him to Fontainebleau.

In a small café around the corner, we stopped off to review our night's adventure, to make notes on every word Gurdjieff had spoken, pooling our memories, squabbling amiably . . . "The way I heard it . . ." "Nonsense, he would *never* have used that word . . ." beginning then the documentation of the master's spoken words which was to run to over a hundred typescript pages before it ended, utterances stranger (and, to the uninitiated, more incomprehensible) than anything to be found in the new school of surrealist literature that flourished in Paris at the same time.

We called each other by the names he had given us, trying them out, seeing unwillingly how they fitted . . . *Wish or not wish,* as he had expressed it. From the superbly illumined portals of the Opéra across the street, the audience that had witnessed Borodin's *Prince Igor* began flowing out after the final curtain. Limousines drove up to the foot of the wide-curving staircase, paused to receive animated bundles of satins and furs, and drove on. We watched the glamorous pantomime without envy. We had our own Russian prince.

I kept the eleven o'clock rendezvous with Gurdjieff next morning in the café. He had brought one of his books for me to read, since we were going to Fontainebleau by train and therefore could work. In the rattling old local, I sat opposite him on the hard bench of a third-class compartment. He had marked the chapter in his manuscript which he wished me to read — the Epilogue, entitled "From the Author."

"Since you smell my idea, I think this best for you to read first," he said, then opened his Russian newspaper and vanished behind it.

I plunged into the opening paragraph which described the three essential tasks he had set himself in the writing of his three series of books, the aim of the first (which I had) "to corrode without mercy all the rubbish accumulated during the ages in human mentation." Occasionally I remembered to observe myself as I labored on. One part of me yearned to gaze out train windows at the lovely autumnal scenery slipping by; one part tried to escape into the daydreaming that train motion always induced; and yet another made impudent

comments about what it was like to travel with Gurdjieff
. . . No mooning, no idle talk, *no* talk . . . just work, *his*
work . . . just what you prayed for once, remember?

I discovered that by keeping at it with disciplined attention, I grew accustomed to his involved prose, even became
agile over the hurdles of hyphenated phrases such as
"receivers-of-the-many-quantitied-vibrations." How had I
ever managed to read aloud such tongue-twister matter
. . . only yesterday? The train slipped into the small station
of Fontainebleau-Avon in what seemed to have been half its
usual running time down from Paris.

We rode a trolley to the house of Gurdjieff's brother,
Dimitri, who was not expecting him but who managed, with
the help of his handsome wife, to put together an excellent
meal by two-thirty in the afternoon. It was strange to be in
the family circle of the man who to me seemed too extraordinary in stature to have any earthly counterparts. His beautiful young nieces had his eyes, black and flashing, his brother
his Slavic cheekbones but more delicately formed. Gurdjieff
was obviously the Big Stick in his family. Only the sister-in-
law spoke easily in his presence. She called Gurdjieff by his
first name in the Russian familiar — a sound of endearment,
Georgivanitch.

We caught the last late afternoon train back to Paris. In
the rattling hard-bench compartment Gurdjieff said, "I am
very very sleepy," pulled his hat over his eyes and appeared
to sleep most of the way back. I felt as if I had been traveling
with him for years.

The next morning, without instruction or invitation, Solita,
Louise and I reported to the Café de la Paix in midmorning,

sat at a table near to Gurdjieff's and waited for him to summon us or to ignore us. Subsequent events suggested that we were already tied together in his mind as a small group with which he could work; but that thought was as far from our imagination as a space probe was then. We were simply waiting for another crumb from his "idea table," if such might be forthcoming. An invitation for another crayfish dinner that night was the reward for our enterprise. And after dinner, said Gurdjieff, we would all go back to my hotel room and read his book.

This was our group's inception — on a Monday night, October 21, 1935, in a Left Bank hotel room one flight up from the noisy street, with extra chairs brought down from the higher and better rooms (to which Gurdjieff did not wish to climb) and Perrier water and ashtray set out for him beside the sagging sofa that he occupied completely, like a Buddha on a pedestal, listening to us read aloud in turn the opening chapters of his First Series entitled *An Objectively Impartial Criticism of the Life of Man* or, *Beelzebub's Tales to His Grandson.*

In the beginning, the manuscript readings dominated our nightly sessions and seemed to be their *raison d'être.* The supposition that Gurdjieff was using us as sounding boards for his massive composition was borne out by the way he watched us. Like an author measuring audience response, he hung his great head toward the reader while his roaming eyes played like searchlights over the listeners' faces. To test our capacities for attention — the readings would go on for two hours — he sought constantly to distract us, with chuckles over comical passages or even outright guffaws that interrupted continuity.

For the uninformed, I should explain that this famous First Series comprised the tales told to his grandson by one Beelzebub — a benevolent and wordy old raconteur who had been banished from his "place of arising" in the center of the Universe and was now traveling through our Solar System in a "transspace" ship named the *Karnak,* dropping in on Mars, Venus or Earth and, for the edification of his young grandson, commenting on the kinds of life found on the various planets. Within this deceptively simple story scheme Gurdjieff had concealed the body of his revolutionary teaching about Man's place in the Universe and the plight of the "three-brained beings" inhabiting the far-out planet Earth.

In those mid-Thirties when only science fiction writers had dreamed of manned spacecraft, Gurdjieff's literary invention of a vehicle that could flit from planet to planet and eventually return to its home port in outer space made unbelievably weird reading. There were passages outclassing Jules Verne, written with a factual realism that tempted one to wonder if this were the autobiography of space-pilot Gurdjieff masquerading under the pseudonym Beelzebub. To discover the teaching in such a context was like hunting the proverbial needle in a haystack.

Yet we kept at it doggedly to get as much as we could while the going was good. The belief then prevailing, that this strange manuscript would never be published, never be permitted to circulate outside the elite of Gurdjieff's own selecting, gave it the aura of holy writ and us the sense of being chosen. The knowledge that half the literary Paris we knew would give its eyeteeth for a glimpse of those worn typescript pages added a kind of worldly luster to their content.

After our first weeks of probation under his critical eye, Gurdjieff occasionally left the manuscript with us. We copied excerpts from it in the intervals between reading sessions. We rolled paper and carbons into the typewriter and the Canary dictated, the Crocodile typed, while the Sardine hovered watchfully by the door. We had no pangs of conscience about copying for absent friends (Margaret and Georgette in northern France and Wendy in New York); only a slight anxiety that we might be caught at it by the author himself. But this nervousness vanished after our hotel *patron* (who called Gurdjieff *Monsieur le Professeur*) obligingly consented to signal his approach by three quick warning rings of the house bell.

CHAPTER SEVEN

I NEED a *World Almanac,* now, to discover what else, be-- sides our meetings with Gurdjieff, went on during the last months of '35 and all of '36. Western society was in visible dissolution, every headline ominous. The fascist bombing of a Swedish Red Cross unit in Ethiopia, the Nazi reoccupation of the Rhineland, the abrupt resignation of Pierre Laval's cabinet — the ninety-ninth to fall in the sixty-five years of France's Third Republic. I know that I must have read each day's threatening news, but I have no memory of reacting to anything that happened outside the magic circle of our group where Gurdjieff was preparing us for another kind of war. He himself seldom spoke of outer-world affairs. If perchance he mentioned Mussolini or Hitler, it was to underline what "man-machines," asleep in their dreams, could lead their sleepwalking peoples into — all of them, leaders and the led ("As *I* see them with the inner eye," he would say) operating like well-ordered machines under the power of external influences beyond their control. To stop being a machine geared to such a "wheel of circumstance" was what he was teaching us to desire.

Our venturesome trio expanded. Miss Elizabeth Gordon, a prim British follower from the Prieuré days whom we had

already met, came into the picture acting as Gurdjieff's secretary and as a sort of self-appointed Mistress of Novices over
us, the demonstrative newcomers to his Work. A gentle-
woman of independent means, she was reputed to have made
substantial contributions in the past to the Work, but appeared to have derived little practical benefit from it. In the
presence of Gurdjieff her emotions sometimes got out of
hand and became visible, in the form of quick flushes or
small livid angers (when he publicly spoke of her short-
comings) ; but it was touchingly obvious that she worshipped
the ground he walked on, even when she seemed half-afraid
of him. Our own inquisitive and acquisitive attitude toward
him and what he represented often struck her as quite
disrespectful.

Then Wendy returned to Paris, paid her respects to the
master and was invited to the nightly readings to which she
listened with head thrown back, eyes closed and her usually
gesturing hands folded in her lap, slightly overplaying her
anxious act of undivided attention. Watching Gurdjieff studying her the first night, I discovered a change that had taken
place within me during her absence. My former obsessive
protectiveness for the little Mad Hatter had vanished; I no
longer saw her as a soul in search of a new life, linked to me
as the guide (and how presumptuous, I realized) who could
help her find it. We were both in the same boat now. Before
Gurdjieff, each one of us stood absolutely alone.

On what turned out to be our last meeting on the Left
Bank, Gurdjieff admitted Wendy into the exercise-work he
had taught us before her return. He instructed Solita and me
to pass on to "Thin One," in his exact words, the steps of this
first "work on the self" that had changed our activities under

his guidance from listening to doing — or, more accurately, *trying* to do.

It is not relevant to this personal memoir (nor would it be within my competence) to describe the Gurdjieff exercises for beginners. I believe that anyone who has struggled to shut off the mechanically racing mind through a sleepless night, or who has tried to pray for even half a minute without having associations drag one's attention away, has had a taste, however small, of the kind of self-discipline into which he initiated us. It was a basic "spiritual exercise" aimed to help us build inner energy.

His final admonitions had touched me deeply and they moved Wendy, as I had hoped they would, when we related them to her. "Be simple like a monk," he had said, "a monk given a task. You do this exercise with *faith*, not with *knowing* . . ." he had touched his forehead, "but with *sure-ing* . . ." his expressive hand had dropped to his solar plexus. *"Not knowing* . . . but *sure-ing*. Not with the mind but with the feeling." It was a language Wendy seemed to understand.

A few days later, Gurdjieff moved into a flat on Rue Labie back of the Etoile, just inside the old fortifications of Paris. This was our meeting place for the next year, the testing ground to which he summoned us for Lucullan meals which he cooked himself and consumed with us, at the head of the table, teaching, exhorting, attacking, sometimes (but rarely) mollifying our injured vanities, making of our dissimilar materials the kind of "soil" he could work with for his kind of sowing the seed.

In his at-home attire — shirt sleeves, baggy trousers and carpet slippers, with tasseled red fez tilted back on his great shaved head — he appeared the paterfamilias, a deceptive impression unless rightly interpreted as high priest of his family with unlimited powers to punish or expose its members. His table talk was as deceivingly simple as his paterfamilias exterior. Often we wondered why he insisted on truths we believed we had heard before, or on ways of conduct we thought we had always followed . . . until we pondered his advice and realized we had done the exact opposite all our lives.

"When you do a thing," he said once, "do it with the whole self. *One thing at a time.* Now I sit here and I eat. For me nothing exists in the world except this food, this table. I eat with the whole attention. So *you* must do — in everything. When you write a letter, do not at the same time think what will be the cost of laundering that shirt; when you compute laundering cost, do not think about the letter you must write. Everything has its time. To be able to do *one* thing at a time . . . this is a property of Man, not man in quotation marks."

In his objective eyes we were all "man in quotation marks," with only a possibility of becoming otherwise (becoming "part of God") *if* we would work unrelentingly on ourselves and open our eyes to our essential nothingness. Only from that point of awareness could there be a beginning. "Man must die to be born again" was what he was saying, but he selected words calculated to rouse resentment on first hearing, as if trying to put us off the track along which he goaded us.

Our nothingness he called our *"nonentity-ness."* To see this for ourselves was our primary task. "To know the insignificance of yourself is extremely difficult," he said. "It is, for example, like trying to imagine one's own death. You can imagine Mr. Smith being killed, but never can you imagine yourself being killed. So it is with insignificance, with nonentity-ness. You can know this about another person, but not about yourself."

In early January of '36, he drew four of our company together — Miss Gordon, Solita, Wendy and myself (four of the most contrasting types one could have handpicked from all Paris in those eccentric Thirties) — and formed us into a special work group, mutually supporting. In allegory he explained: we were going on a journey under his guidance, an "inner-world journey" like a high mountain climb where we must be roped together for safety, where each must think of the others on the rope, all for one and one for all! We must, in short, help each other "as hand washes hand," each contributing to the company according to her lights, according to her means. Only faithful hard work on ourselves would get us where he wanted us to go, not our wishing.

"For wishing and doing," he said, "man is made in two separate parts and such is the law concerning the operation of these parts that the more he may wish to do, with one part of him, the less he can do in the doing part — even with constant struggle. For a young person, Nature will help in the effort *to do,* so that person will not have to struggle as will a person of responsible age. After a certain age, this effort is very difficult, often impossible . . ."

He gazed at the quartet he had tied together on a metaphorical rope — a Canary, a Crocodile, a Thin One and a British spinster who always kept her hat on. We called our odd foursome "the Rope" among ourselves. We knew, I believe, even from the first day what that invisible bond portended. It was a Rope up which, with the aid of a master's hand, we might be able to inch ourselves from the caves of illusory being we inhabited. Or, it was a Rope from which, with sloth and lip service, we could very well hang ourselves.

Another aspect of this Rope I discovered later. It was stronger than any bond I had ever felt before — for any man, woman or charity child who had ever crossed my zigzag path on earth. And it tied me now — not only to a restrained Englishwoman I hardly knew and a guardian-angel editor I already loved — but to Wendy once again, more tightly than any of the strands of affection, compassion and admiration which had bound me to her a decade before when I had led her out of a hat shop to see the world.

The Rope had a table in the Café Flore, our assembly point where we often met, an hour or so before the trek to Gurdjieff's apartment, to discuss the exercises performed in the privacy of our rooms, what we thought we had observed going on within ourselves as we had striven to achieve even the first step of them — to "make all quiet inside" — and to rehearse the reports to be made to the master, which at first were mainly confessions of chaos within. Associations were the thieves, vandals and wreckers of our efforts toward total concentration. Gurdjieff had told us not to try to shut them off.

"You can *never* stop association," he had said. "As long as you breathe, there are associations. These are automatic. Therefore, in this task, you must not try to stop them; let associations flow but *not be active*. With the *other* part of your mind you work at this new task, and this is active. Pretty soon you find you have the beginnings of a new kind of brain — a new one for this kind of mentation. And then, that other one becomes entirely passive. Very important that you know the body *as a whole,* for this work, very important . . ."

With our heads together and the coffee growing cold in our cups, we talked of our trials. Hats always invaded Wendy's meditations, magnificent creations on which she could have made a fortune had she thought of them while she still had a shop. Words chattered into mine . . . Would I ever finish that book? Would people read it? I forget the obstacles that made Solita groan and Miss Gordon blush. Friends outside our struggling circle thought we had all lost our minds. In one sense, that was exactly what we were trying to do by emptying them of their machine-made contents, their vainglory and false conceptions — an Augean-stable cleanup in its truest meaning.

The hardy among us walked across Paris to the Rue Labie apartment, not only to work up appetite for Gurdjieff's rich meals, but also to keep our figures trim after consuming, for example, a special rice steamed with apricots and raisins, roast baby lamb, *fraises des bois* with fresh cream, Latvian chocolates and Syrian *loucoum.* Our route led down Bonaparte to the Seine, over the Carrousel Bridge, through the flowering Tuileries to the Concorde, then up the sparkling slope of the Champs Elysées to the Etoile. Our destination was, quite literally, out of this world.

In Gurdjieff's apartment, with all window shades pulled down (as he always kept them for reasons we never asked) and only one salon lamp lighted over his rug-covered divan, we were chambered in a strange kind of place-time neither night nor day, an ambience completely dissociated from the world outside the shuttered windows.

We always arrived punctually, dropped coats in the hall-way, took our places in the small salon and read from his manuscript while he interviewed us singly, in a room apart, about progress with the exercises. My reports often faltered under his comprehensive glance which read my state of self-disgust while I was still hunting words short, simple and rooted in truth to describe it. Once, after a particularly barren confession, he nodded gravely and said, "It is not *easy*, Krokodeel . . . what we wish to do."

What *we* wish to do . . . His use of the plural pronoun threw me into a momentary tailspin. It was as if he had implied that he too was tied to our earthbound Rope, striving with us step by tottering step toward the higher consciousness he already possessed to a degree that even my eyes could perceive. Was that "we" a calculated kindness to us in the beginning, to help us over the first hurdles toward detach-ment from our mechanical world — the only one we in-habited, the only one we knew?

Another day he used the first person plural while telling about a worldly problem that confronted him. We were aware how often his seemingly jocose remarks lifted sud-denly to another level of understanding and listened atten-tively to his tale of a brand new car he might be able to get with no down payment whatsoever — a deal so unique that he thought he should have some help to see it through. He asked if any of us had a special saint to whom he might burn a candle, looking first to Miss Gordon, our senior, for a suggestion. She named a saint noted for granting requests, but the master shook his head. He knew all about that one. "No," he said, "it must be a saint who would be indulgent *for one of us.*" One of us in the Work . . . you, me . . . Canary, Thin One . . . his eyes searched our blank faces, then he shrugged.

"If you cannot suggest such a one," he said, "I could just as well take my own saint — Saint George. But he is a very *expensive* saint. He is not interested in money, or in merchandise like candles. He wishes *suffering* for merchandise, an *inner-world* thing. He is interested only when I *make something* for my inner world; he *always* knows. But . . . such suffering is expensive . . ."

We did not need a post-meeting discussion that time, to understand exactly what he meant. We knew through dismaying experience. The cost to one's ego and vanity of discovering the inner emptiness seemed sometimes unbearable, even with such self-discovery coming, as it did, only in briefest flashes, only after intensive efforts with the exercises. Flashes white-hot and blinding, like lightning, that left you shaking in the dark afterwards, glad they were over.

I believe that Gurdjieff, out of his own powerhouse of consciously accumulated force, must often have fed us some sort of strength that helped sustain us in our first attempts. To reach the "inner world of Man" was the goal he made us desire with impassioned intensity. Once, he painted it for us:

"Man has three worlds. One — the outer world, world of impressions, of everything that happens outside us; two — the inner world of the functioning of all our organs, the totality of organic functioning; and three — the Soul, that is . . . the world of the Soul which was called by the ancients the World of Man. Three worlds Man has . . ."

(and you can choose which one you wish to live in, his glowing eyes seemed to say). "This exercise is exercise for the *inner world of Man,* the world of the Soul."

By May of '36 we were going every day to the Rue Labie apartment, occasionally twice daily for the double gastronomic ordeal of a prolonged midday dinner and late evening supper that often ended near midnight, especially when there were visitors. The new arrivals at Gurdjieff's table were seldom introduced to the Rope, but we quickly learned through the master's reception of them which were curiosity seekers and which sincere seekers of his teaching. For the former he often played one of his humoristic roles exploding mirth around the table, revealing himself as the eccentric old magician they had come prepared to find, precisely as some rumors had depicted him. The serious guests he frequently complimented by attacking them, "stepping on their corns," as he expressed it, making them squirm and see things about themselves (vanities, prides, mental pretensions) they had never realized were part of their makeup. We on the Rope watched with fascinated attention what he had made for us to watch — revelations of the human psyche. There were also some oldtimers in the Work who came now and again, stayed for several days, then vanished. They could be recognized at once. Gurdjieff was working with some of these, as individuals or possibly as representatives of groups existing in other countries, we surmised.

Wendy sometimes wondered aloud to Canary and me about all the "other people" who had crossed Gurdjieff's path in the past, now no longer in evidence. What had *happened* to them? Why so few *working* pupils like us around him now? The seeming exclusiveness of our Rope foursome, to which no new members were ever added, looked, she suggested "just a wee bit odd," didn't we think? It was not until many years later, when Ouspensky's book came out, that I found the answer to her skeptical queries, or what seemed to be a likely answer to them. Ouspensky had also been mystified by the unconnectedness of the Moscow groups, until Gurdjieff had explained to him that he never mixed groups, but occupied each with a different work, "according to the state of their preparation and their powers . . ." The master explained that by the very nature of the work he could not have many pupils — presumably at any one time.

In early summer of that year Margaret Anderson and Georgette Leblanc returned to Paris and joined the company around Gurdjieff's table, now his principal teaching site. Though we had sent them our diary notes of his table talks, we had not quite prepared them for the peculiar atmosphere enveloping that table. The long silences during eating, the ritual toasts suddenly declared, Gurdjieff's salutes to our Idiots as they came up in progression (Sardine's on the Hopeless, Canary's on the Compassionate, Thin One's on the Squirming, and so forth) and his mock-ceremonious comments upon our current states which we had learned to take without flush of shame or pleasure, depending . . . caused the eyes of the new arrivals to widen. Watching their surprised expressions, we took the measure of our own small progress, if not in our inner worlds, at least in that outer world of conflicting impressions which Gurdjieff generated at will. We had become habituées of the incalculable.

Gurdjieff named his enlarged family of listeners "Knacht-schmidt and Company" — a term which always made him smile when he said it. He finally explained that in "old Russian" Knachtschmidt had comical connotations; it referred to groups of peasants, shoeless and shabbily clad, who, after the day's work was done "came together to *make something.*" Although it suggested an unflattering description of us as perhaps he saw us, the more we thought about it, the more apt it became. We had certainly come together to "make something," though we still had only a vague idea of what that "something" might be. The Rope foursome, however, through the exercises (which were not given out to the others in the company and forbidden to be discussed with them) was beginning to get a taste of what this eminently practical work-on-the-self might eventually lead to . . . a taste, I thought, of what oneself with a single I might be . . . a taste of what the Matthew gospel preached esoterically in its passage about the "single eye": *The light of the body is the eye: if therefore thine eye be single, thy whole body shall be full of light.*

After we became a company of seven more or less regular daily boarders at Gurdjieff's table, he established a "kitchen box" into which we dropped a specified sum of francs each time we went. The meaning of these contributions (which would hardly have paid for one course at his luxury-laden board) was perfectly clear. His Work was not a charitable enterprise; it was not meant for people too unsuccessful in life to be able to pay for the kind of teaching he gave. Also, he had often observed that people never valued a thing if they did not pay something for it — therefore the "kitchen box," a symbol of his students' valuation of the Work. Apart from those small daily contributions, we on the Rope had our own individual obligations, each according to her means. Wendy and Miss Gordon made the most substantial contributions to our intensive program since they were obviously in a position to do so; Canary and I gave what we could whenever we could. We never discussed among ourselves the amounts or the frequency of our donations to the Work, but we knew that whatever its total might be, it was only a drop in the bucket of the master. His extravagant scale of living — deliberately exaggerated to show his scorn for money per se — indicated nevertheless sources of income of considerable magnitude. Certainly the individuals he was "curing" at this time — of alcoholism, psychic depressions or of visible maladies like a crippling arthritis — accounted for some of it. These patients, men and women of obvious means, became part of "Knachtschmidt and Company" for the duration of their "cures," sitting at table with us, listening to the talks, being drawn out of themselves by Gurdjieff's skilled reading of their troubled inner states — for us a visual education in applied psychiatry of the highest order.

My abstinence from cigarettes during the whole of the first year with Gurdjieff was a subjective experience in self-denial which taught me to say "No" to my inner animal and netted for our entire company some memorable teaching on this kind of suffering. My personal war with myself began in the Café de la Paix on January 12, Gurdjieff's birthday. We had all gone to the café to greet him, to find out what his plans for us might be on that day. By an association I have forgotten, he began talking about the things to which man is a slave, and of how these slave impulses took the initiative with us because we had not one strong central aim with one strong corresponding impetus, but many aims, many sources for impetus. He read our inquiring looks, perhaps overheard Wendy murmuring that her "slavery" was for beautiful fast cars. Man was slave only to *big* things, he went on, only to powerful things such as alcohol, sex, drugs and (he looked at me smoking) tobacco.

I knew, because my childhood story was going surprisingly well in the midst of my concentration on the Gurdjieff work, that the habit of smoking while writing had increased. But I never thought I was a "slave" to cigarettes — or slave to anything for that matter (which is the way all slaves think). I even had the temerity to state aloud that I did not believe such a "slavery" applied to me; I could quit at any time.

"Why not try . . . and *see?"* Gurdjieff smiled.

"You mean *now,* Mr. Gurdjieff?" I looked at my half-finished cigarette.

"Why not?" he challenged. And under his eyes faintly glinting with mockery, I pressed out in the ashtray the unfinished cigarette. Thus, on a passage of words which at first seemed to have no relevance to my own condition, I was caught in the trap the master had artfully set.

I fed on self-esteem for the first few weeks; then all the nicotine slaves that had lain down at my command, rose up and turned into wild animals. I dreamed so realistically of smoking that I often awoke in tears for having failed to keep the pledge. My concentration was reduced to that of a monkey's, even when trying to do my exercises. It was difficult to formulate this for the master but I knew that I had to tell him. I chose a day when only our Rope was with him, no outsiders to hear what could sound to the unattuned ear like the babbling of an idiot. I told it in terms of my suffering animal that gave me no peace, no respite, not even for *his* work. "I can't even *begin* to make all quiet inside, Mr. Gurdjieff . . . not even the preparatory step is possible any more . . ."

He listened gravely until I ran out of metaphors, gestures and breath. Then he leaned back and gave to us all an instruction that sounded like prayer. "This can be a thing for power," he said. "I will tell you one very important thing to say each time when the longing comes. At first you say it and maybe you notice nothing. The second time, maybe nothing. The *third* time . . . maybe you will notice something. Say: I wish the force of my wishing be my own, for Being." He thought a moment, then shook his head. "No. Better another way. Force, such as this, has special results, makes chemicals, has special emanations. Better to say — *I wish the result of this, my suffering, be my own, for Being.* Yes, you *can* call that kind of wishing suffering, because it is suffering. This saying maybe can take force from your animal and give it to Being . . . and you can do this for many things. For *any* denial of something that is a real slavery."

A few weeks later, in a seemingly by-the-way association that flowed from a totally different subject, Gurdjieff referred again to my smoking denial. He had driven to Rouen that day, making the one hundred sixty-eight-mile round trip in his customary record time. He was back in the Café de la Paix by seven-fifteen that evening where the Rope was waiting for him. He dropped to the banquette with a sigh of pleasure and began talking about "roses, roses . . . ," how he felt. He had consummated a successful business transaction which put off for one week a certain financial reckoning. Then, he told us, instead of "roses, roses . . ." there would soon be "thorns, thorns . . ." But thorns in one's outer world were good, because then there were roses in the inner world.

"It is law," he said. "For one dissatisfaction, *always* there must be one satisfaction." Over his coffee he asked us which we thought he would rather have — roses in his inner world, or in his outer world, then decided he had posed too complicated a question. "Better that I tell you one thing," he said. "This will make you rich for life . . ." He raised his index finger, held it pointing up in the teaching pose.

"There are *two* struggles — inner-world struggle and outer-world struggle, but *never* can these two make contact, to make data for the third world. Not even God gives this possibility for contact between inner- and outer-world struggles; not even your heredity. Only *one* thing — you must make *intentional contact* between outer-world struggle and inner-world struggle; only *then* can you make data for the Third World of Man, sometimes called World of the Soul. Understand?"

One of us, Canary as I recall, said, "Not quite, Mr. Gurdjieff, but I get the taste . . ." I shook my head when he looked at me. He put a cigarette in his briarwood holder, smiling to himself. Then he looked around our circle.

"That is too far ahead for you yet," he said, "but I can give you a small example which maybe will give you a *taste* of this Intentional Contact. You, Krokodeel, for example . . . your cigarettes. You have outer-world struggle — not to take, not to buy, remembering always that you wish to break the habit . . . and also you have inner-world struggle about the same thing. With inner world you imagine how it was when you smoked; you imagine in a different way —

more keen, and with more longing, and it seems with this inner-world imagining even more desirable than it ever could be. You have made this cigarette the Intentional Contact between the two struggles, and even by this small thing you will make data for the Third World, for the World of the Soul as is sometimes said. I have a chapter on Intentional Contact in the Third Series . . . but this is enough to give you all a *taste* of what it is."

It was more than enough. He had given us something too dense in meaning to be taken in and understood there on the spot, there in a worldly café at the rendezvous hour, where the very sight of him with teaching finger pointing up was an anachronism. The sound of his voice was exactly pitched to reach our ears and not a breath beyond. Later, at our Left Bank round table, we reread his words that had gone directly from the pool of our immediate memories to paper. We analyzed, interpreted and synthesized, each according to her lights, and came together with something we could grasp.

(There was a finale to this cigarette denial which I shall skip chronology to record here, since it indicates, I think, not only one of the ways of Gurdjieff's teaching but its remorseless drive toward a Next Step. I had crawled through a year of abstinence, and had become quite thin-skinned as that year progressed. Things seemed to get through to me faster as if I actually *had* shed some of those metaphorical crocodile skins with which the master had endowed me. Occasionally, when he greeted me — "Well, Krokodeel . . . and how are the skins today?" — I demonstrated my suffering with a pantomimed shivering act that evoked his Olympian laughter — a reward, incidentally, which compounded the value of losing one's skins in his Work. At the end of that year I told him I believed I had conquered that slavery [which he sometimes called Man's "dogs"] and could now go on indefinitely. He nodded: "Yes, for you, this makes a source for force." He looked quite benevolent as he studied me; then he added in a casual voice: "But at the same time, *any* man can *not* smoke. You do not wish to do what *any* man can do?"

"Oh no, Mr. Gurdjieff . . ."

"Smoke then . . ." He offered me one of his Russian cigarettes. The first puff made my head swim. Through the smoke Gurdjieff's face was a mask of cunning. I knew exactly what he had done as the dizziness subsided and pleasure expanded. He had attached me again to my "dog," to be now its master, not its slave. He had set my feet on the harder path, the golden middle way between abstinence and excess. (Total abstaining was much too easy.)

In the summer of '36, Gurdjieff abruptly declared a three-months' cessation of work, during which time we could go where we chose, providing we returned to him in the fall to resume. We had come to a midway point on our "inner-world journey." Now he was sending us away, possibly to see how well we could keep the fire burning on our own, or (what seemed afterward the most likely reason) to give us the shock of discovering the meaninglessness, the absurdity, the spiritual bankruptcy of what we sometimes referred to wistfully as "our old lives."

In the final week at his table before the break, Gurdjieff concentrated his fire on Wendy and me — the two going the farthest away, to the States. Though well aware that the main aim of the trip was to enable Wendy to shift some stocks and raise the sum of money she had promised as her contribution to the work — "each according to her lights, each according to her means" — he would pretend at times that she and I were runaways from everything he represented. He needled us about the "starvation" we would experience in America — starvation for his ideas, of course — but he presented the famine always in terms of food while expressing his great pity for us.

Once when he had prepared a wonderful hot-spiced dish of lamb which he named *karavanpaschi* — "food for the king of the caravan" — he told the company that he had composed it expressly for Thin One. "To crystallize, in her, data for remembering," he said, "so that when she is far from here in that other world — America *can* be another world — she will remember how she eats here and come back sooner. For her I composed this because she is not so much in my centrum as you all . . . and I *wish* her to be. So I composed this special thing for making quickly."

Wendy obviously did not enjoy hearing she was not so much in his "centrum" as she imagined she was; she bridled under his pinprick reminder. He watched the manifestation with a peculiar smile, then his expression changed. "No, in truth . . ." he said, looking at all about the table, ". . . I hope only in memory will you suffer for my food, but that with the *other* parts of you, you will wish for the *other eating* at my table. Let the food you eat here stay in memory only, but the *other* kind of food . . . *carry with you!*"

We were to have several partings from Gurdjieff before the real separation of his death. But none save the last would be as deeply affecting as that first one when he sent us forth with our uncompleted work. Again and again he stressed the importance of remembering our exercises, of doing them daily no matter where we would be or in what condition. "Not *once* will you do them," he said, "not one hundred times will you do them . . . but *one thousand and one times* you will do, and *then* perhaps something will happen. Now it is imagination, but sooner or later it will be *fact,* because your animal is *law-able*." He prepared us for our journey as if the spark he had kindled would snuff out with the first breeze of American air. But we believed otherwise, and told him so at our last conference. Even before leaving Paris we were having a taste of how strange a return to the old life would be. Friends outside our circle were giving us bon-voyage parties. Unable in those gatherings to talk about him or his work, we had found we had very little to say.

"Yes, it is so," Gurdjieff said. "You both will feel strange. As you are now, you are like the players in that game . . ." (The game of Musical Chairs, his favorite analogy to drive home to disciples the uncertainties implicit in the Work, the risk of losing one's place, of being left standing and ultimately counted out.) "You are out of one chair and have not yet the data for sitting in another chair. All that you will do in America will seem like a pouring from the empty into the void . . . all meetings with people and so forth. Later, when you *have* the data, you will go back and do the same thing and *then* it will mean something."

He came with our "Knachtschmidt" company to the Gare St. Lazare to see us off on the boat train with a string bag of Persian melons for us to eat en route. In his "station café" at the far end of the cavernous *salle d'attente,* he had final subjective talks with Wendy and me, separately, at a table apart. Wendy preceded me to his table. I watched her sensitive face, enhanced in beauty by its new look of seriousness, taking in his final advice. Possibly because he detected in her a certain nervousness about fulfilling the tasks he had given, he began his talk with me by speaking of her state:

"One thing you must know, Krokodeel. Nervousness has a momentum. The mind cannot stop nervousness, it must go on until the momentum finishes. It is important that you remember this. When you see Thin One nervous . . . let her be. Soon it will pass." He reminded me again not to lose myself in any situation, not to let the emotions lead me into self-forgetting, even for a moment.

"You must know," he continued, "a most important thing about Man. Man cannot stay long in one subjective state. The subjective state depends from a thousand things. You can *never* know the subjective state of another. It is typicality of man that no two such states are ever the same; they are like thumbprints, each different. When you see her," he indicated Wendy at another table, "in some subjective state, you must not try to understand what causes it. Even she cannot know. If, for example, she is angry with you, you say — *She* is not mad with me, her state is mad with me. *Never reply with your interior. Never* have revenge associations . . ." Turn another center, his eyes commanded, and suddenly I understood the meaning of that puzzling gospel about turning the other cheek. He nodded and gave me his final command in a voice so low I had to lean across the table to catch his words: *"Keep the fire burning."*

He walked with us down the long quai to the railroad coach placarded Le Havre. Our companions — Georgette and Margaret, Jane Heap on visit from London and the remaining members of the Rope — formed in a semicircle beneath the train window with the master standing forward alone. As the train moved slowly out, he raised his right hand and gave us a blessing, lifting and lowering it thrice for Wendy, thrice for me — the first time either of us had ever been blessed by anyone on earth. It was as if he were setting a seal of safety on our spirits. We stood mute and transfixed at the open window until the train pulled us out of view around a curve.

I remember almost nothing of our sojourn in the States beyond our constant referrals (when alone) to something Gurdjieff had said, done, clarified or obscured, and the cunning we both developed when pressed for particulars of our long stay in Paris and our plans to return soon for more. ("More of *what*, for heaven's sake?") We discovered early that it was wisest not to mention Gurdjieff's name among friends who knew a little about him, gleaned mainly from a recently published book (*God Is My Adventure*) which presented our teacher as a modern Rasputin endowed with peculiar hypnotic powers. The distorted picture, in such sharp contrast to our own personal experiencing, was flashed back at us from the most unexpected quarters in New York and set the tone of strangeness that hung over the whole of our journey home. Exactly as Gurdjieff had predicted . . .

Old activities passed before our eyes, as in a dream sequence, when we crossed the continent in a Pullman. Wendy reviewed her past going West the first time; I reviewed mine from the opposite direction. Wendy talked about the pompadoured young milliner who had stopped over for a season in Cheyenne and had made hats for ranchers' wives, putting her whole soul into making them look lovely for once. "I lived then," she murmured, "only to make women feel pleasant

. . . the right hat always did it." Every factory smokestack across the plains evoked for me a preposterously self-assured collegian setting out to conquer the world. *What world?* "I used to talk about how the other half lives," I said, "as if I already knew all about the one half . . . imagine that!" We communed like ghosts in passage past the landmarks of former lives.

Yet we were far from feeling like ghosts, especially after arriving in San Francisco, the city we both loved above all others — Wendy for the love as well as the money she had earned there; I for my tomboy childhood coasting down its hills, roaming Twin Peaks for wildflowers and sailing in imagination on every freighter tied up along its wondrous waterfront. My taproots tugged when I was with my gallant mother (looking a little older now) and Wendy's when she saw, and was tearfully remembered by, the same little Italian from whose flowerstand on Grant Avenue she had always bought foxgloves and gladioli for her shop. It was a little more difficult to do our exercises there, it took much more time to "make all quiet inside"; but we persisted faithfully when alone in our hotel. We stayed a month, then turned our faces eastward. In the Pullman our exercises were easy to do, seeming again to be a functional part of us, like breathing.

Looking back on that long journey, it does not strike me as strange that neither of us recognized the inner transformation the Gurdjieff work had already wrought — an intensification of inner-world awareness which, save for our month on the home soil, reduced the outside life to shadow play. We obeyed our teacher's strict and frequent injunction — *never* to look for results, *never* to "philosophize" about what we were doing, but simply to *do* — with faith. Even his words, visible in the notebook we often read from, did not prompt us to put two and two together and see what was beginning to happen in us. About the very exercise we practiced en route, he had said in summing up: "And this will gradually make clear for us the difference between inner and outer worlds, will teach us to keep the two separate from each other so that when we look at something — for example, some object, we will *not* look like monkeys with our *all* going out to object. *We will not identify.* We must try *not live* in the outer world."

We were back in Paris on November second, exactly three months to the day from the day of our departure. We had barely escaped the nationwide shipping strike that tied up the port of New York soon after we sailed, as earlier we had seen it immobilize San Francisco's harbor. It had seemed like pure luck that we caught the last ship out before the transatlantic shutdown, but I was to observe in later separations from our teacher that always when one was on a mission concerning him or his Work, one always got through — over, under or around whatever obstacles blocked the way.

We went directly to Gurdjieff on the evening of our return. Though neither of us confessed it aloud, we had an inner anxiety about how we would be received. Would his omniscient eyes discover any inner-world depletion, any evidence of backsliding in us? Then wrath might welcome us like a thunderclap. This was a "first" for us, this return to the master as a bearer of his Work, of even the smallest fragment of it.

Gurdjieff had moved to a new apartment during our absence — Six Rue Colonels-Renard, near the Etoile. Miss

Gordon had telephoned that we would come on ahead and he had left his front door on open-latch as always when expecting his people. We entered quite silently; sounds from the kitchen told of his whereabouts. We found him in the midst of preparing a pheasant dinner for the Rope and stood in the doorway waiting until he would look up from his work. Presently he raised his eyes. At the sight of us, a slow smile spread over his dark face, growing in radiance like a gathering of suns as he surveyed us. Then he opened his arms straight out like a bear's and we rushed into his welcoming embrace that was wide enough to hold the two of us at once. He spoke the names we answered to in his world, *"Theen One! . . . Kroko*deel*!"* then he stood us off from him to have another long look at the state of our souls.

On November 17 we began a Third Series of exercises under the master's guidance. The new work was complex and required a sustained inner attention beyond anything ever before attempted. The kind of "being efforts" we struggled over, he told us, had been called "self-beatings" by the adepts of an old monastic order he had visited in the days of his searchings. "Self-beatings" perfectly described our intensified efforts to dominate the recalcitrant selves. There was never any feeling of masochism, such as "self-beatings" seemed to imply. There was, to the contrary, the deepest inner satisfaction any of us had ever known — the "earned pearl," as Gurdjieff expressed it, that lay in the center of our beings after each session of work. A work on the self that now went beyond the self . . .

Gurdjieff had given us a pledge to say each time before beginning the new exercise — that we would not use this for the self, but for all humanity. This "good-wishing-for-all" vow, so deeply moving in intent, had a tremendous effect upon me. For the first time in my life, I felt that I was truly doing something for humanity as I strove to make my own molecule of it more perfect. The meaning of this Work, which at first had seemed quite egotistical and self-centered, suddenly blossomed out like a tree of life encompassing in its myriad branchings the entire human family. The implications of it were staggering. By my single efforts toward Being, I could help sleeping humanity one hairsbreadth nearer to God. I believed this. Every time I said the pledge before beginning my exercise, I believed that if I made something for my own inner world, I would be making it for "all humanity." It was my first experiencing of the Mystical Body of Christ of which I knew nothing then, but would encounter many years later like a familiar concept though always shrouded in its immense mystery.

Our daily life with Gurdjieff continued unchanged while the outside world seemed heading toward disaster. On Armistice Day of '36 the French Foreign Minister announced that the world had nearly two million more men under arms than it had in 1913. A few days later Franco's Insurgents drove to within the city limits of Madrid. The Red Army air chief drew cheers from the All-Union Congress of Soviets at Moscow with the news that Russia now had more than seven thousand planes. And at Fort Belvedere, in the presence of his three brothers, King Edward VIII renounced his English throne.

One day Gurdjieff gave to each one of us on the Rope a chaplet made of large black beads of some curious substance, upon which we were to do a special sensing exercise as we

passed the beads between thumb and index finger. He told us
how in the old times such chaplets were known as the
Inanimate Helper and that many kinds of inner-world work,
far more difficult than our current exercises, were done with
their aid. "You see men — Turk, Greek, Arab, Armenian —
sitting all day in the coffee house with such chaplets. To you
they make a picture of the lazy man, but what they do with
these beads creates an inner force you cannot imagine. Even
some special holy men, initiate, of course, could move mountains if they wished, just sitting still, working with their
chaplets, seeming half asleep."

He advised us to carry the chaplets with us everywhere,
but not to make spectacles of ourselves doing the exercise
visibly in public. "Carry in your pockets," he counseled.
"Such exercise as I have given, you can do anywhere in
life — while sitting in café, theatre, on autobus . . . but do
not let people see you do it. They do not understand." So
now we were doing the Work in the outside world, wherever
we went, missing no opportunity to finger those beads hidden
in purse or pocket, as if every minute counted. "Why waste
our dear Time?" Gurdjieff said once.

A fortnight before Christmas, he put us to work packing
the gifts, foods and candies he bought each year for the many
families, besides his own, who depended upon him. These
totalled forty in all and he wanted that number of boxes, all
alike. Wendy undertook that task and came up with forty
hatboxes glamorously colored pink and mauve which she had
inveigled one of Paris's leading modistes to contribute to *un
bon oeuvre.*

The forty hatboxes completely filled one end of Gurdjieff's
entrance hallway; the remainder of his apartment became a

Santa Claus workshop. The mantel in the reading salon was populated with dolls and toys. Sacks of wrapped candies, nuts and dried fruits stood about, ready to be divided and repacked into small paper bags, forty for each category of Christmas treat. Our entire company, including any transients who happened by, sat cross-legged on the salon floor around the mountains of edibles Gurdjieff spilled from the sacks into our midst. He stood over us watching to see that we did not simply scoop up but counted pieces exactly. So many liqueur-filled chocolates in each paper bag, so many caramels, so many striped peppermint balls, so many marzipans moulded in diminutive shapes of vegetables and fruits . . . I had data for such mass production; it was like the old factory days for me.

For the backbreaking work over sweetmeat piles, the master rewarded us handsomely with gourmet dinners, enthralling table talk, and, above all, with the music he played for us afterwards on his small hand accordion. This was the music of prayer — haunting, disturbing, indescribably beautiful, a music calculated to arouse the deepest longings hidden in the heart of man. I remember the night he played the music he composed for the last chapter in his Second Series (which we were then reading), the chapter devoted to Professor Skridlov, the "essence friend" with whom he had traveled to an Asian monastery to meet an ancient adept who had given them the formulation that differentiated Knowledge from Understanding: "Only understanding can lead to Being, whereas knowledge is but a passing presence in it. New knowledge displaces the old and the result is, as it were, a pouring from the empty into the void. One must strive to understand; this alone can lead to our Lord God." I knew the formulation by heart after many readings aloud. I repeated it to myself while Gurdjieff brought from his small "squeeze-box" its companion music that seemed to go on after it ended. We sat like statues watching our master lay aside his harmonium and light a cigarette. He looked through the smoke at our motionless forms, then gave us our signal to depart, saying *"Why do you sit?"*

CHAPTER EIGHT

THE Christmas of 1936 was the only one I was ever to spend with Gurdjieff, a celebration that made all subsequent ones seem lusterless and routine. I gathered impressions that holiday season as if I knew it was to be a once-in-a-lifetime experience in which Gurdjieff seemed to have invented Christmas.

In the preceding days I acted as his chauffeur, for he had developed a bad infection in his right thumb which, for a time, prevented his driving with a swollen bandaged hand. The first time I went to the café to offer my services, he refused me. But the second time he accepted, grumbling about getting around Paris in a taxi driven by an idiot who knew only three place names — Etoile, Opéra and Montmartre. "When I drive my own car," he said, "I can always go directly where I wish, finding even the smallest streets."

"You are like the American Indian for direction," I said. "Our Redskins could go through the forest reading signs no white man could see."

"Not for forest am I specialist," Gurdjieff replied, "but for *sand*. Never can I get lost in desert. You know . . . how to travel in desert depends from two secrets which pass from father to son, a legomonism [his word for any transmitted knowledge]. One I can tell. For example, always big ridges lie a certain way in relation to the wind. Before you start across, look how these dunes lie. If they lie across your path, then always you must keep them traverse, with the sun over the shoulder and making slight changes for the changing sun. These great dunes never change for an ordinary small storm; only a big storm can move them and make them different. This, you see, is very important to know because once you are fifty meters from the starting point, there is no right, no left . . ." Just as in his work, I thought. Was that why he told this simple piece of desert lore which any Saharan traveler knew? I drove him that day to Hédiard, the famous spice shop behind the Madeleine, where he purchased the rare spices and out-of-season fruits which, at his table, he vaunted as having been sent to him from the "Planet Karatas."

On Christmas morning I reported to his apartment at eight-thirty to see if he still needed me, and drove him to the Café de la Paix for breakfast. I watched him select from the kitchen cooler a large piece of cheese, wrap it and thrust it in his pocket; then we were off.

In the café, he ordered butter for me. "You, being American, have a habit for butter," he said, "and in truth it is a very good thing with this cheese. I do not order for self only because I have not such habit." We ate in silence, then he pushed back his breakfast plate and said: *"Now we can service Nature again.* You know, Krokodeel, this is what food is for, for servicing Nature. In truth we are slaves, such poor slaves. Nature does not give this food; all his life man must work for it, and, when he eats, it is not for him but for servicing Nature. Nature gives only *one* thing; he gives atmosphere, this air. This is all he gives. For all the rest, man must work his whole lifetime." He looked at me with a grin. *"Only air* . . . and that Old Idiot who created such, he swaggers now. Imagine . . . swaggering for having created such an absurdity!" I knew better than to interrupt with a pointed query about the breathing exercise he had given us, aimed precisely to take from that absurd air the "being food" it contained, as conscious man had done since the beginning of conscious time. I sat like a yogi doing the breathing exercise while he tried to bluff me out of my belief that an instructed man could take more from air than the oxygen the lungs required.

Presently Wendy arrived at our table, and seeing that the master was in a most genial mood, she began chattering about the big news of that day — the first Christmas the Dionne quintuplets were allowed to spend with their family. I saw Gurdjieff's puzzled expression and explained: "Before this, the quintuplets were kept apart, Mr. Gurdjieff; scientists wished to study them. They think some valuable scientific elucidation might result."

"Study?" Gurdjieff mocked. "How study when scientists come from the same barrel? Such nonentity, all of it. With such thing as five from the same birth, there can be nothing to study. Five take what was meant for one. No individuality can be there." He talked about the money the parents had made; in his Russian newspaper he had read the arrangements. "Now, many people are jealous because these parents are rich, and many people try for the same thing. But if people understood what this *really* means, then they would cry. *Now man begins to breed like mice.* Never before in history was such thing as this — four, five at a time. Twins

even were a rare thing. Soon now, five will not be notable.
People will speak only about six, then of seven. Nobody sees
what this means . . . *quantity destroying quality.*" He dismissed with an angry wave of the hand the stupidity of that
day's headlines, the stupidity of the outer world of man.

Our entire company, including the exquisite Georgette
Leblanc, dined with him that Christmas day. Georgette came
seldom to his table, unable to "eat with honor" the vast
meals he served, but she was often in his reading salon, to
which she had access at any time, to read from the French
translations of his books. When she graced his table, he
treated her like a member of the Rope — a mixed blessing
for those not inured. This day, a melon for dessert sparked
his attack and led, finally, to one of his most enchanting
formulations. It began with a struggle to find a corresponding word, in French, for something he wanted to express for
Georgette, after she had asked if the melon came from the
French colonies of North Africa. Possibly her social tone,
seldom heard at his table, prompted him to expand, for the
benefit of all:

"I *never* eat anything French, Madame," he exclaimed,
glaring at Georgette over the basket of French bread still on
the table, over the French Armagnac still in our glasses. "All
French food is for me like *soupe à l'oignon,* as is all French
mentation. As all English mentation . . ." his glance of
feigned scorn swung to Miss Gordon, ". . . is like frozen
meat." He asked the Rope for the French equivalent of
frozen. We suggested *congelé, glacé, réfrigèré* . . . none
suited him. In the French language, he scolded, *never* could
you find the *exact* word. He knew seven hundred and eigh-

teen words the French language lacked. "I am a god of languages!" he cried. "Except for such idiot things as this 'frozen' that anyone can learn. I speak scientifically, very simply do I speak. Why learn idiot words good only for idiot talk? I do not have the time . . ."

Miss Gordon said quietly, "What a picture of God that is. Speaking scientifically, but every word exactly understood, every word known like the leaves on a tree that stem from a common root." And this, of course, was what the whole matter was about — the philological question so dear to the master's heart — the tower of Babel in which man lived linguistically, ineffectually.

"Such idiot words," Canary observed, "*you* need not know, Mr. Gurdjieff. Such a nose you have for roots." This opened the way to his memorable formulation.

"Yes, this can be," Gurdjieff agreed. "Except that the nose is no good in an alien country, is good only where *in general* the land is familiar. Imagine yourself in a foreign country where not one syllable, not one word, has any association for you. Such is how I am with your English." He smiled. "But *one* thing I notice . . . *always* you can make yourself understood anywhere with the *language of the smile.* Anywhere on earth you can get what you wish — grain for horse, water, bread — with a smile. Because the smile corresponds exactly with what the other man feels."

The *language of the smile* . . .

He celebrated Christmas by the Orthodox calendar, on New Year's eve, and turned it into a combination Russian Fair and surprise party. He invited all seven of us, giving no hint that it was to be anything special.

Forty or fifty people were already crowded into his apartment when we arrived — in bedrooms, kitchen, dining room and hallway, and in the Christmas-tree salon, the center of gravity for the occasion. Only eighteen adults at a time could fit into it to admire the immense fairy-tale tree hung with rare glass ornaments, colored lights and small Russian costumed dolls. Viewers could stay for so many minutes, then had to pass along to make place for others. Children, exempt from the time limit set for grownups, sat cross-legged beneath the glittering boughs, staring up and piping with delight.

The forty hatboxes we had helped to pack were stacked at one end of the hallway. As reward for our labors, we thought, Gurdjieff was going to allow us to see the distribution to "his people." We were familiar with many present — his Fontainebleau family and in-laws, his Russian friends, Dr. Stjoernval, Rachmilevich, the chauffeur and his family, his publisher, the apartment-house manager, all the nieces and nephews and Gabo, his handsome Russian aide-de-camp and faithful kitchen helper for big occasions.

There was an ebb and flow to and from the Christmas-tree room, an undercurrent of excitement as if a large supporting cast were trying out the stage before the star performer appeared. Presently Gurdjieff entered and the hubbub ceased instantly. He held a notebook in which were listed the forty names of those who were to receive a Christmas box. His eyes outsparkled the tree's lights as they swept the room. "Tonight, just now," he said in English, "arrived the milk lamb and baby pig and while we wait for these to cook, we might as well make business." He called in Russian for Gabo to put the first box on the table. The party had begun. Like all imperishable memories that live in the active present the moment they are summoned, this one flows into the present tense as I recall it from my old notebook.

Gurdjieff reads the box number and consults his list. "Aha, a-*haa!*" he exclaims as if he did not have the list already fixed in his fabulous memory. He calls forward our senior, Elizabeth Gordon. Her shock of surprise is shared by all in our company. His disciples in the Work come first, ahead of family and friends.

"For our dear esteemed, Our Reverence, Miss Gordon," he says with his embracing smile. The next box is Wendy's. "For our dear delicious Thin One." Gabo then brings two at once — Solita's and mine. "For our dear dear sing-ing Ca-nary!" . . . "For our dear and terrible Krokodeel!" Louise's and Margaret's boxes are presented next with appropriate remarks, and finally, with a twirl of his moustache, he bows to Georgette Leblanc and says, "For our dear esteemed so-so-so, so-so-so *Madame!*"

He instructs us to carry our boxes at once from the salon to make room. We are torn between two desires — to look into them in his bedroom where our coats are piled, and to hear the rest of the presentations. We decide that our presents can wait and hurry back to the crowded salon. The Russians now are shouting, waving aloft Gurdjieff's personal gifts and saying some very funny things in Russian which make him laugh. The commotion increases with each presentation. Ikons, underwear, toys and perfumes are plucked from the boxes and waved aloft, then thrust safely back amid flurries of thanks in Russian . . . *Spasiba,* Georgivanitch! *Spasiba, spasiba!*

Now he comes to the disposal of the unfinished boxes, the

most fascinating to watch. He has two or three opened before him on the table, each with a last small corner to be filled. He looks from them to the mantelpiece loaded like a gift counter with silk scarves, bottles of vodka and brandy, perfumes, Russian dolls, soaps and toys. From a box he takes one wrapped object, holds it, intense and concentrated, recalling its content; he seems to be reviewing the entire subjective life of the as-yet unnamed recipient — what like? how like? how much? For a second or two he stands thus, weighing his souls. Then he quickly takes a bottle or a doll from the mantel and tosses it in. Or else, from his pocket he takes his bankroll, drops a fifty franc note in each corner of one box, a thousand franc note squarely on top of the next. The box cover is held open so the recipient can see at once what he gets, so we can study his face as he accepts it.

So much, how much . . . each of the uncompleted boxes receives this final personal touch. One Russian character doll holds a balalaika, another a basket with a tiny rabbit in it; Gurdjieff weighs the problem of choice between even such small differing details. It is spellbinding to watch, like some operation of impartial justice. Gabo gets a thousand francs in his box, so does Dr. Stjoernval. A sister and sister-in-law receive a thousand franc note between them. Everybody is poking about in his box to discover treasures hidden in corners. The publisher is ordered to put on his bathrobe and show it to all, and hold up the bottle of brandy also in his box. "Once," Gurdjieff tells us laughing, "I was sick and he gave me a dressing gown and bottle . . . now he waits for me to be sick again!"

For the last of the children's boxes, Gurdjieff has a toy he must first exhibit to everyone, the treasure of treasures, the unique of uniques, in his eyes. It is a small celluloid baby naked in a crib with infant clothes around it, a miniature doll to be dressed and undressed. He carries it around the room on the palm of his hand, then goes into the dining room to show it to an old Russian lady sitting there. His face shines with delight.

Presently the boxes are all distributed and carried to hiding places in different parts of the apartment, to clear the main rooms for dining. But the presents are not quite exhausted. Gabo enters with stacks of Greek bread in his arms. It is an old Greek custom, he explains. In each loaf there is a coin. You must have all your family with you when you divide the flat loaf and whoever finds the coin in his piece will be the richest for the coming year. Gurdjieff tosses a loaf in each of our laps, then to each of his Russians sitting, standing, kneeling or crouching in corners, so tightly packed that the addition of the brightly wrapped loaves seems to swell the room to bursting point.

It is after nine o'clock when at last the master sits to table with his doctor on the right and his publisher on the left. Somebody calls out, "All the English to table!" and we take our places thankfully at the main board, a sanctuary of relative peace and elbowroom after the joyful agitation of the Christmas-tree room. In unjostled perspective we can see it now through the salon archway and we can see Gurdjieff's face watching also, very beautiful and patriarchal as he regards his flock settling down to food.

Our own plates are before us, all prepared — a cleavered segment of suckling pig and one of milk-fed lamb, a mound of *kasha* steamed with apricots, a pickle, a Russian pastry stuffed with spiced meat — small plates, enormous servings.

Gurdjieff calls on Canary to give the first ritual toast, then we begin. In the tree room the families are mostly standing to their food around the small center table and in front of the mantelpiece. Some mothers sit on Gurdjieff's divan with Christmas boxes stacked like tables before them, feeding their small children. Loaded plates go arm-high over the crowded heads, passed to someone pinned plateless in a far corner. People are eating in the hallway, bedrooms and in the kitchen.

Watching all from his place at the head of our table, Gurdjieff finally arises for a closer look. He enters the tree room and stands among the young ones, seeing what they eat, how they eat — the functionings of his lesser cosmoses. His beautiful niece from Fontainebleau cries a toast for him in Russian and before he can stop the young ones, there is a rah-rah-rah, followed by his roar and a thunderclap of rage, and such a dressing-down for her who proposed the toast that even we, the chosen sitting at his table, put forks down and cease swallowing, immobilized by his wrath.

"No one in my house *ever* proposes my health," he cries. "*Never* do I drink a toast outside of Idiot toasts and only he who can drink to number twenty-one can propose my health!"

Miss Gordon is brave. She speaks up for the stricken niece in her clipped English voice. "But once a year you used to allow, Mr. Gurdjieff. Like tonight . . . at the Prieuré."

He comes back to the table grumbling. "At Prieuré . . . that was other place, other kind of people." The dessert melon is cooling to the throat.

After Turkish coffee he summoned Wendy to the bathroom to help him bathe and rebandage his infected hand. The children were bundled into coats, their hats sought, their

boxes tied with twine. Many families left but the rooms
never seemed to decrease in population. Then Gurdjieff
reappeared carrying a gift necktie in his left hand, holding
up his cleanly bandaged right hand to announce a trick. He
had just shown Thin One how he could tie a four-in-hand
with one hand, he said; now he would demonstrate for us.
He swung the cravat quickly, causing it to fall into loops
around his bandaged hand; then he plucked the ends through
and showed us a perfect knot. *"Many* such tricks I have. This
is only a small thing. For example, one other I can tell . . ."

We knew by the glint in his eyes that this was to be a racy
story; he glanced at Miss Gordon registering in advance her
disapproval of his Rabelaisian anecdotes which I, incidentally, relished. He decided to be *"bon ton"* and switched to
Russian. His compatriots roared as he told his joke, his eyes
on the favorite niece he had scolded so tempestuously as if
wishing to restore the laughter he had blasted from her face.
Playing his role of eccentric old uncle with a bag of scandalous tricks, he succeeded of course on the instant.

Scold with one hand, spoil with the other . . . how often,
in his year of patient teaching, he had done this to us, I
thought. As he saw us out the door he told the Rope that *if*
we wished, we could wait for him in the Sans Souci, his Rue
Pigalle café, a bit later. "For one five minutes at midnight, I
must be one place; afterwards, I will come there. Maybe we
can have one *bouteille champagne* . . . but only for you. I
will take Vittel water." *If* we wished . . . as if anything in
Paris on that New Year's Eve — opera, ballet, Folies Bergère
or balloon-bursting parties in smoky *boîtes* — could hold a
candle to one more hour with Gurdjieff, even if he said
nothing at all!

"We will come, Mr. Gurdjieff," we said on one voice.

We had to take two taxis back to the Left Bank with all our boxes and had time to examine them before meeting the master in Montmartre. I made a list of what I found in my box:

1 Georgette crepe kerchief hand-blocked
1 pound-sized box of Turkish *loucoum*
1 "exact arrangement" box of candied fruits
1 tin of Smyrna *halva*
1 roll of apricot paste pressed thin like parchment
1 bag of pistachio nuts
1 bag of currants from Corinth
1 box of Deglatnour dates on the branch
1 glass jar of special marmalade
1 small Russian character doll, an accordion player
1 large Cossack doll authentically costumed
1 hand-painted postcard, a sleigh scene in Russia
1 package of dried white Smyrna figs
1 pink silk slip, lace trimmed, every stitch handmade
  ("Not only must you put it on," Gurdjieff told me
  afterwards in the café, "but also you must *feel inside*
  how you look outside!")

We reached the Sans Souci before him. The café was filled with platinum-blond chorus girls still in heavy makeup, relaxing after their midnight stints in nearby *boîtes*. A few minutes before one o'clock, Gurdjieff looked in the door to make sure we were there. Over the heads of the blond chorines, his black eyes, black moustache, black astrakhan cap and fur-collared greatcoat looked twice black.

Every eye in the café was on him as he walked toward us

like a dark sultan showing pleasure because we had managed to capture and keep a corner table for him. Nobody but ourselves knew, or could even have remotely imagined, that he had been up since dawn of the previous morning (we were now well into New Year's Day of 1937) sorting gifts for nearly half a hundred people, listing them and the contents of the boxes destined for them, distributing them with dramatic ceremonial and remarks appropriate to each one's age, sex and state of being — then feeding his flock — all this accomplished with a badly infected hand and a perennially flat pocketbook. He sat down among us with a deep sigh.

"Another *swallach* year [*swallach,* Russian for garbage pail] is ended," he said. "I deserve a rest. *Truth,* Miss Gordon?"

She could not answer without having her emotions too revealed. He had come to us to unwind, trusting our disciplined company to provide the only thing he needed just then — a bit of "idiot relief" after his long labors. He ordered Mumms champagne for us and Vittel for himself, and watched the waiter's practiced hands uncork the champagne with the interest he always paid to an expert doing his special job. We told him we had had time in the hotel to investigate our Christmas boxes, how we had run up and down the stairs comparing gifts, filling the darkened corridors with excited whisperings. "Truth, like small children," he said approvingly.

He gazed at the dazzling chorus girls while sipping his Vittel; their coarse vitality as they greeted each other seemed to amuse him. Then his attention swung back to us. Rubbing his bandaged hand ruminatively, he began speaking about a

château on the Marne which he had inspected, renting for
some twelve thousand francs a year, an appropriate place to
see the people he soon must be seeing.

"Such a place we have now," he said, "is not convenient.
We must have a more *solid* place. From this perhaps can
begin the actualization. We will see what future will flow
from this . . ." His use of the "we" touched us, sparked the
hope that we could always go where he would go. I looked
across the table at Wendy and said with my eyes, *You* could
make this dream come true for him, hands down . . . this
dream of a more *solid* place . . . and I had launched myself, unaware, in what was to be my last act of passionate
striving to ease the rugged way of a master who asked no
easement, who in fact deliberately created situations to prevent it.

"But first," Gurdjieff went on, "there is one special business to attend to." He put out his bandaged hand and told us
of his need to cure, once and for all, the poisonous germ
within him. He was going to try to make his kidneys pass it
off. "This is a shorter way — two weeks, more pain, but
strong kidneys I have."

"And if you can*not* pass it off, Mr. Gurdjieff," Miss
Gordon asked anxiously, "is there any *other* measure you can
take?" He told us there was a special water at Vichy he could
drink, along with injections and plenty of rest. But he
preferred the overtaxing of the kidneys with some new drug
he had, and pain, and a short time for his cure. He saw us
wince from the thought of pain self-induced and possibly
dangerous and told us a long story about how his body had
been like a small boy's since his accident, how it was vulnerable to many germs that only small boys have . . . "cold

germs and many another kind that not for years have I had."
This new microbe was more strong than all the others. He
would let it go through his body and *eat* all the others, and
make him clean of everything except *him*. "Now when *him* I
kill," he regarded his swollen hand as if he saw the staphylo-
coccus through the bandages and knew it personally, "I can
begin from new. You see? This has one very good side!"

At two-fifteen on that New Year's morning we persuaded
him to go home and rest. *"Why do you sit?"* we said to him,
in his own words, with his exact mocking intonations, as he
had said so often to us. He smiled as he rose from the table.
Over his shoulder as he walked away, he said, "Come tonight
for dinner at eight o'clock."

We had had our playtime. Now we would soon go back
to work.

The night of New Year's Day with Gurdjieff was also
unforgettable. He was sitting on his divan and nodded as we
filed past him and found places around the Christmas tree.
He seemed rested; possibly he had managed to have without
interruption his customary siesta. He asked Canary to put out
all the lights and to plug in the contact that lit the tree. We
sat in silence for several minutes. Then Gurdjieff said: "This
I like. Such tree makes you quiet, peaceful inside. It is like
sitting before an open fire. *Coziness.*"

The mirror over the mantel reflected the tree's colored
lights. Wendy whispered, "I see two trees . . ." and started
our master talking about reflected light, a chapter out of his
unknown past.

"It would be better if it was candlelight," he said.
"Candlelight blends better; electricity does not blend. But the

most beautiful light *I* know, is the light I saw many times in Persia. They make a clay cup, fill it with mutton fat, put twist of cotton in, and this they burn for holiday, fete, wedding. This light burns longer than any other kind of light — even for two days one such small cup will burn. And *such* light — the most beautiful for blending. For Mohammedan fete, once I saw a whole house lit by such lights . . . such brightness you cannot imagine, it was like day. You have seen Bengal lights? This I speak about was even more bright. For man, it is the best light for reading . . ." A note of nostalgia for the Near East came into his voice. "In Persia, they even arrange rooms for such light. Once I saw one I can never forget. They hang mirrors everywhere, even floors and ceilings have mirrors — then around, in special places to make decoration, they put such clay cups with mutton fat, and when you see — it makes the head spin. Wherever you look, you see lights, endless, thousands. You cannot imagine how it was. Only, one must *see* — and when you see you would never imagine that such a beautiful sight comes from such small idiot thing as this clay cup of mutton fat. Each house has its own clay cups, sometimes painted, sometimes with names on them, expecially if for a wedding — the names of ones who marry. Or, the name of some special event . . .

"One other thing about such lights," he went on, "is most original. When they make them with frozen fat, this they put together in layers, each layer with special perfume, with separations between layers so that when they burn — first you smell, then the room fills with *one* perfume; after half an hour with another, and then another — *all planned exact!* Such knowledge they had before . . . such candles they made *consciously* and everybody had them. *Such was life then!* Now . . . they make them automatically . . ."

A sadness settled over our spirit after he had spoken, as so often happened when he made a glowing picture of how man once was — simple, unspoiled, aware of his soul and its needs. The strident mechanical life of our time always seemed doubly monstrous in contrast; and now, in the beginning of 1937 with Europe moving automatically toward another war, doubly dangerous. *Such was life then . . .* such was what it still could be, if only Man would learn, as Gurdjieff taught, to conquer himself instead of his neighbor.

In the colored glow from Christmas-tree lights, Gurdjieff's powerful torso was humped forward like Rodin's Thinker, his ponderous pondering form was contracted and contained, its mysterious force unknown, invisible. He meditated often like that in our presence, especially after playing his sacred music.

As I watched this "man without quotation marks," I remembered the thrilling statement he had once made about such initiates, the "Peace on earth among men of good will" gospel dated in Gurdjieffian terms.

"*All* men without quotation marks are the same," he had said. "By every proof of science, by every test, all such men are exactly the same — same tempo, same vibration, same polarity, *same understanding* . . ." These unifying words were of thunderous significance, words that forecast the future of Man, of all humanity on earth. *Same understanding* . . . same understanding instead of thousands of tongues and dialects — words I was to hear myself repeating over and over again in a personal future that was nearer than I knew . . . when I would be in a California Babel, swinging from a scaffolding, welding Liberty ships for the North African landings in a war that was now only a poster on the Paris walls, a portent to follow the Spanish Civil War bombings . . . and, in a later version of Babel, when I would be salvaging human beings from the postwar Displaced Persons camps, beings who would remind me so poignantly of our vanished master — White Russians, Poles, Ukrainians, even the old Nansen-passport refugees called "Stateless," left over from the '14–'18 changes.

Since I could not then, on that January night of 1937, even remotely imagine the coming horrors which were to separate us all from each other and from our master, I continued to gaze at Gurdjieff with a naïve "Where you go I go" emotion, as I waited for his next words.

His next words sent us back to work. He began talking about the staircase (up the scale of consciousness) and the stairs which for us, in the beginning of the Work, had been artificial. "Fantasy stairs," he called them. Now they were becoming real. Now we were at a definite place on those stairs which symbolized his "scale" — up which we had the possibility of progressing, or down which we could swiftly slide back to where we had started.

"A scale will always involute back to its beginning note, *do,*" he reminded us, "unless you carry it to the *do* of the next scale. *Nothing remains halfway.* This is *Law* . . ." He was referring to his Law of Seven, the "fundamental cosmic law" described in one of the most difficult chapters in his manuscript, (and also in Ouspensky's) embracing everything from solar systems to man, from man to atom, in a panorama of an ordered universe evolving consciously or involuting mechanically. Under his brooding gaze we had read that brain-cracking chapter innumerable times, groping for the knowledge it contained and trying — without any help from him — to see its application to us in the Work, to fit ourselves into it, as it were. "There are seven times seven scales . . . the formulation of forty-nine is you in yourself!" The cryptic formulation, hinting possibilities of development beyond conjecture, certainly beyond the powers of any of us even with a lifetime of trying, seemed to hang in the air like luminous writing, the words understandable as words, the meaning of them too vast to grasp, except by emotion only. Then Gurdjieff spoke his "language of the smile." "But this is already very far," he said. "We cannot now speak of this; anything we say is only titillation. Now we must eat . . ."

He unfolded himself from the divan and led the way to the dining room, adding in a tone pregnant with warning, ". . . If we do *not* eat now, then our animals will make revolution!"

That night we drank a toast to our Squirming Idiot, Wendy. As the toastmaster announced it, Gurdjieff raised his glass to her. "May God help you to transform into Ordinary Idiot which is very high . . . Next after Unique when the sequence begins again."

Wendy bowed her thanks for his words. "I hope I fulfill your wishing, Mr. Gurdjieff."

"*Not* hoping . . ." he picked her up quickly. "Hope in my opinion is an evil thing, is why man is nearly not man any longer. Man must *use what he has, not hope for what is not!*"

His words were meant for the entire company. To *use what we had* . . . Before this new year ended, we were all to discover in our varying ways how little we had, now that we were standing alone.

CHAPTER NINE

I WOULD have had that life with Gurdjieff continue indefinitely. But I knew that in the very nature of the Work, those high days of association with him must eventually come to an end, that we must all return to our former lives to use what we had learned from him, even to find out what that "something" was. We often felt that he seemed to be preparing us to go it alone. At the turn of the year, in one of a series of our private talks, he said: "This is a most important day for you. After you assimilate what I am giving, you will be responsible for all your acts, even for your unconscious acts. Beginning then, you will take a *position of responsibility*. A record is kept for each. All you do is written in red or black in the Angel Gabriel's book. Not for everyone is this record kept, but only for those who have taken a position of responsibility. There is a Law of Sins; now you are subject to this Law. If you do not fulfill all your obligations, you will pay. For every satisfaction, you must accept so much dissatisfaction . . . if you do not so acquit yourself with this Law, you will pay . . ."

Thus, I imagined, with similar somber warning, had he sent away from him many former disciples, after having brought them as far along the way as their individual capacities could accept. How far along the way had he pushed us? How much of what he had given had we been able to understand and assimilate?

In early February of 1937 he announced a trip to the Riviera for the Rope. Though we did not know it then, this was to be our last trip with him as a group. A radiance envelops the memory of that sortie out "into the world" as it were. When Gurdjieff took us on his travels, he taught directly from the "book of life," a marvelously enlightening aspect of his teaching which left us without a shred of illusion.

We would be gone from Paris some five or six days, he said. We could go in our own cars, at our own speeds and tempos, and meet him on a certain day in Cannes, at the Hôtel Splendide where he would reserve our rooms. Miss Gordon, with stoic indifference for life and limb, agreed to ride with him in his Buick, with his brother Dimitri whom he planned to pick up in Fontainebleau.

Many former disciples had accompanied Gurdjieff to the Riviera in the Prieuré days before his grave accident. They rode in his swaying sedan, taking notes he dictated while steering, then reading back to him in Russian or Armenian the material that was to be the basis for his Three Series of writings. References to those hardy souls crop up in current memoirs of witnesses, but nothing I have read tells what it was actually like to be *on* the Riviera with him, to stroll the boulevards of earth's most celebrated play place beside a "man without quotation marks" who saw nothing of the gay façade or, if momentarily he remarked color, sound and a human swarming bent on pleasure, reduced it to dust with a single comment.

On our first night in Cannes, Gurdjieff gave us a formulation that embraced all the Riviera habitués. "Paint them, and then with ceremony, throw them into the sea. Like old automobiles, you paint them and make them look like new; but *still* they are good only for throwing into the sea. But, of course, with ceremony . . . *big* ceremony!"

Throw into the sea the painted dowagers made up to look like debutantes, the beach-tanned gigolos masquerading as young gentlemen of leisure, the veritable old gentlemen of leisure brushing up their whiskers and undressing with rheumy eyes every pert English nanny tripping past . . . We seldom missed a meeting on the hotel *terrasse* when our master was there to comment on the passing parade. Sometimes he sounded like a professor of scatology observing some new form. About the cocktail dancing he was ruthless. Wendy came late to the group one afternoon after watching the dancing in which she took innocent delight. "They are dancing out there, Mr. Gurdjieff!" she said gaily, even (to my remembering ear) a bit wistfully.

"*Everywhere* they dance," said our master. "But you know what it is, Thin One? It is practice for passion. This is how *I* see it with my special eye. They practice publicly, you can see it in their faces. Some can even no longer remember what passion was . . . on their faces you see '*Please,* memory *please,*' while they *hope* for an association that will take them back to the days when they had such a thing. Never can I look on dancing — only when both partners are young. But this you never see here . . . only old woman with young man, or old man with young woman."

After two days of enlightening studies of the fleshpots, Gurdjieff proposed a picnic. We innocently supposed that he had in mind some sun-drenched cove along the Côte d'Azur, a bijou of Nature no one else had ever seen. Instead, he drove straight away from the sparkling Mediterranean, from the mimosas and the sunlight, up into the Alpes Maritimes as far as he could go without tire chains, farther than any of us would have ventured *with* chains. Bundled in the back of his Buick, we shut our eyes as he negotiated the switchbacks out of Grasse, climbing in groaning low gear up into the snows where, as he proclaimed, there was "a feeling of wide." The Buick decided the picnic spot by refusing further ascent; it suited Gurdjieff perfectly.

In a great virgin snowfield that had not seen a footprint, possibly since Napoleon had passed that way, we prepared the cold lunch which we had shopped for enroute. Gurdjieff broke apart the loaves of French bread while Canary and I twisted open tins of anchovies, tuna and sardines which the master forked onto the bread chunks with the tip of his jackknife. All about us was snow and silence. Gurdjieff was in his element. The happiness in his face almost made us forget our frozen feet and fingers and the fish oils on those fingers which would have to be washed off with snow. Then, when he spoke, he shot warmth into us with words that touched our hearts:

"Ah," he sighed, "if only I had my accordion up here. I would play for you. It is a *different* thing, music high up. So fine and clear are notes in the mountains. The vibration is more fat. If I could play for you up here, you would *know* *something about the divine!*"

The next day he drove us to Monte Carlo, the "other end of the stick" from our rugged alpine outing. This day he went deluxe all the way, giving us a practical example of his favorite aphorism — "When you go on a spree, go whole hog . . . including the postage."

He led us to the most stylish restaurant in Monte Carlo — "his" café in the Place du Casino, just in front of the columned gaming halls. He found trout on the menu, ordered it for all, cooked in fresh butter, the only way he would eat it. Then he told us we had exactly one half hour before the platters would arrive at the table. With a smile he announced how we would spend that half hour:

"One custom I have, always in Monte Carlo. To all the children I give money and they must play *all* in the Casino, and after — give me half their winnings. So now . . ." To those of us deemed children — Margaret, Solita, his brother and me, he gave one hundred francs each and waved us off to the roulette tables.

Years before, Wendy and I had visited the Casino. With the writer's acquisitiveness for detail, I had studied the fascinating machinery of Chance and the unlikely people it fascinated — young and old, bejeweled and poverty-frayed, regal and plebian, a cross section of humanity such as I had never seen packed together in one place, obeying with identical gestures a single voice, the croupier's calling on all to place their bets. As I had watched the gamblers' faces spellbound by the gyrations of a small steel ball it did not occur to me that I was looking at the faces of slaves.

Now, on the return, the familiar scene had an aspect of real terror. The same people seen years before seemed to be there still. With a shock I thought I recognized one or two of the more eccentric-looking players. They were in their same places, at their same preferred tables, placing their same careful bets on the red or the black, the odd or the even, the "saddle" or the *carré,* and writing the table's winning plays in the same tally-keeping diaries (slightly thicker books now) that lay beneath their fingers. As I stared with my inner eye at the faces of slaves who had died to everything in life but the turn of a gaming wheel, I understood why Gurdjieff had sent us into the Casino, the best-equipped laboratory on earth for the study of dead souls.

I understood something more as soon as I placed my first bet. My objective eye almost ceased to function. I fought not to identify with my lonely chip standing rashly on a single number; but I watched it, as the zombies around me were watching theirs, as if it was a piece of myself laid out there on the green baize. *We will not identify,* I commanded silently. I felt a slight perspiration break out on my forehead when the croupier swept in my losing chip. I tried to tell myself that this was because I was gambling with Gurdjieff's money (which I madly hoped to quintuple at least) but I knew in my inner world that only a hairsbreadth of self-possession separated me from my green-faced neighbors around the table, reflecting the baize at which they stared.

At the end of the half hour, our gaming foursome met at the door of the Casino. Solita had two hundred fifty francs, I had a hundred fifty and Margaret and the brother were cleaned out. The winners paid back to Gurdjieff the half of the take which he accepted with a great act of blank-faced astonishment.

Accustom yourself to forget nothing, he had told us once. My recollection of that Monte Carlo lunch will endure until memory gives up its ghost. Our table seating seven had center place in the fashionable scene. The Mediterranean sun directly overhead played down like a spotlight on the vast platters of trout, the baskets of bread to be eaten with it and the wine glasses filled not with the conventional white wine that accompanies fish, but with amber brandy — a scandalizing deviation in the eyes of the French *beau monde* surveying us. The first "idiot toast" sent shivers of shock through our judging audience trying in vain to place us in some recognizable conventional category. I borrowed their eyes, looked at our master through them and saw the aspects of his unique unconventionality.

When we had eaten the pink-fleshed fillets off both sides of the trout, Gurdjieff told us now to go on to the "best part" — the brain and eyes in the head where most of its "active elements" were stored. Very delicately he picked up one of his trout heads and showed us how to suck out its essential matter. Some of us could follow him, some could not. Those who could not passed their fish heads across the table to him at his request. Only parvenus — "jump-up people" as he called them — would waste such activating goodness.

He chose the Grande Corniche via La Turbie, the highest road back to Nice and thence to Cannes. As the seven-passenger sedan swayed around hairpin curves, he announced the views coming up — crags, precipices and sudden sweeps of blue sea miles below — calling on all to take notice of what he had brought us up there to see and sense: his cherished "feeling of wide" on the grand scale. Down in Nice he drove the back alleyways through the town to avoid the Mardi Gras festival on the beachfront esplanades. We heard the faint blaring of brass bands without regret. We had had our carnival . . . and with the master . . .

The next day we drove back toward Paris in a two-car procession heading north into rain. Gurdjieff's sedan in the lead, with Miss Gordon and his brother, resembled a great flower basket on wheels, stuffed to the roof with golden mimosa which he was taking for friends in Vichy, the proposed overnight stop. "Scent alone should keep me on his traces," I said to my companions, and then quite suddenly I lost him in a torrential downpour somewhere in the Rhone Valley before Lyons. The bright yellow bouquet on wheels vanished as if washed off the earth, with not even a trace of windblown blossoms along the soaking highways to show that it had ever passed that way. We checked every major hotel in Lyons and the parking lots around them in a vain hunt for our leader, then turned in for the night since the rain was coming down in solid sheets. At five next morning we were off for Vichy, subdued and anxious, identifying totally with our nightmare visions of a black sedan lying upside down in a ditch with mimosa spilling out from shattered windows.

In the Vichy hotel a message awaited us, telephoned in from some unnamed place. "Monsieur Gurdjieff will arrive at two o'clock this afternoon." Something prompted me to go out in the street and watch for him. Possibly it was love and relief, possibly it was the writer's urge to witness the finale of a trip with the master which had had everything in it, including a mysterious vanishing behind a curtain of rain. I was rewarded for my vigil by an unforgettable picture.

A few minutes past the arrival hour, the high sedan with plumy mimosas nodding out of all its open windows, entered the head of the street up which I gazed — ostensibly a carnival car, home from a spree. The only head visible was

Gurdjieff's behind the wheel. With fur cap set at an angle, moustaches twisted smartly up and black eyes sparkling, he bloomed with vigor. Miss Gordon slumped like a rag doll, sound asleep beside him, and the brother was nowhere visible until Gurdjieff stopped the car with sudden application of brakes before the hotel. Then the mimosas heaped on the back seat parted and Dimitri's white face appeared like a death mask; he groaned *"Je suis mort!"* as I lifted off his flowery shroud and gave him a hand out of the car.

Paris in the spring of '37 presented its immortally beautiful exterior — tulips in the Tuileries, chestnuts budding up the Champs Elysées, a springtime light cast over its gray stones soaring in cathedrals, arching in bridges, riding the sky in sculptured monuments. But its interior seethed with anxiety and unrest. In March the warships of France, Great Britain, Italy and Germany began policing the coasts of Spain, presumably to uphold the neutrality agreement, while their nationals on land took sides in Franco's revolution.

Gurdjieff had a formula that fitted the times, though he used it mainly in relation to individuals, a sort of handy rule-of-thumb by which to assess new arrivals at his table. *Auspicious* exterior, *sus*picious interior . . . or vice versa! At table he never mentioned the deteriorating international scene, only the deteriorating human scene, the leitmotif of so many of his talks. On a trip before Lent when he took the Rope with him to Vichy (where he royally fed his Russian flock who lived there huge dinners of trout and chicken, topped off with platters of tropical fruits brought down from Paris for the occasion) we told him, after the festivities, that we had had a lesson in hospitality, watching him entertain his hungry compatriots.

"Hospitality, yes," he said. "Man does not have it any longer; in him it is atrophied. Hospitality now is only cunningness. *Organically,* man does not have it. As, for example, in that place — Turkestan — there still exists *humanity-ness* . . . from the heart. Friendship there means when two people buy something together, one sells his part and makes money and this he divides with the other fifty-fifty. Two times he does this and friendship is established for always."

I told him about some striking men from the Kirghiz steppes we had once encountered on a ship out of Constantinople bound for Mecca via Piraeus, Port Said and the Red Sea. They had all come aboard in flowing robes, embroidered skull caps, teapots in one hand and umbrellas in the other. Were they like the men of Turkestan?

"Kirghiz, yes," Gurdjieff said. *"Also* such people they are. Moreover, they go to Mecca which proves what holy men they are, simple people with heart. Those places — Turkestan, Kaffiristan, Kirghiz — are centrum of humanity-ness . . ."

His original phrase described what he created at home, on the road, in hotels and cafés, wherever his great thoughtful presence presided. A centrum of humanity-ness. It embodied, exactly as I felt it, what we would be leaving soon.

Gurdjieff had earlier announced a plan to visit New York that fall. He concurred with Wendy's notion for us to sail some three months ahead of him, so she could find a flat and get "settled in" before he would arrive. He had even handed over to us, to take in for him, some presents for American supporters which would have weighed too much in his own luggage. Despite this reassuring sign that he intended to sail for the States that same year, I had mixed emotions about our earlier departure.

I observed myself during that last Easter with him, gathering up every word of his teaching like an instinctive animal preparing for a long hard winter, possibly two.

The Rope was in Vichy with him on Palm Sunday, in his Café Gambrinus, and he was talking about the holy places he had visited as a boy. "Of course, I was psychopathic then," he said. "I received impressions differently. Later, I saw such places again — Echmiadzin, for example, a holy place in Armenia, like Jerusalem — and the last time I went, I remember how different it was. All changed — people, faces, all. All goes so fast now, no time to assimilate. In last fifty years, the customs of one thousand years have gone. *What takes a long time to come, stays a long time;* short time to come, it passes quickly. Now in Armenia even small boy reads newspapers. You can imagine what idea of Life he receives . . ."

After dinner in the hotel restaurant, he invited us to his room for coffee. "In exactly fifteen minutes you come," he said as he left us. Despite our long experience with his tests for exactitude, despite careful clock-watching and estimates of how long it would take us to mount the flight of stairs to his room, we managed to arrive two minutes late, for which he scolded us. I tried to take the blame, telling him that I had been timekeeper for the group, but he brushed me off.

"Not to only one do I speak," he exclaimed. "Small or large, you all come from the same barrel . . ." and there we were, back in the hated herring barrel of his favorite analogy which described the location and state of all undifferentiated humanity, looking alike, smelling alike. "And now . . ." he waved us into his room, "the coffee is cold."

He had brewed a special Turkish coffee he had brought from Paris. To my taste it was perfect and I had the temerity to say so, to continue talking in the face of his seeming anger. "It is very good, Mr. Gurdjieff. Not cold . . . just right," I said, which drew his scornful glance my way with another sharp fragment of his teaching meant for all:

"This is how *you* like it, Krokodeel," he said witheringly. "This you must not tell among many. For *you* it is good, but spoiled for another. *You must enter into the situation of another . . . see* what it is and *put words in your mouth to correspond* with what you see. Even your *bon ton* books tell this . . ."

Back in Paris he spoke again and again on his twin themes of humanity-ness and our need to become real Man. For the smallest forgetfulness, he drove us unmercifully as if he knew that time was running out on our group labors. Jane Heap came over from London for a short sojourn at the source. When she was with us at his table, he drove us harder for every inattentive slip. One grave and terrible luncheon stands out in my notes and memory. Gurdjieff appeared that day to be in some kind of hidden pitying rage about all of us.

The first part of the luncheon was eaten in total silence.

Wendy, who a few weeks earlier had been appointed Cellar-esse in charge of the Armagnac bottle, refilled the glasses for the ritual toasts and passed over a few who had signaled her to skip them if she could, unobtrusively. Our master of course saw the maneuver. His face darkened — not for the weaklings attempting to falsify their drinking at his table (which he always measured with expert knowledge of our individual capacities) but for Wendy, their foolish accomplice, moreover one on the Rope who should have known better.

"Thin One," he cried, "your obligation you do not fulfill. You do not see all around you, only ones near you like me, Miss Heap, Crocodile. I gave you small obligation, but you do not fulfill. If you cannot do this, then all you do will be false — *even hats! You must feel your subjects around you* — you for them must be king. King with all his objects — house, people, your checkbook even. Yet . . . all this is a *cheap thing* beside real Man. One Man without quotation marks is worth all your kings and all their objects."

Wendy looked away from him to hide her quick tears as he upbraided her. "Why do you look at Sardine?" he asked in gentler tones. "Look on Miss Gordon. She is much higher . . ." and he tried to pull her back as she bolted from the table to powder her nose in the bathroom and cool off. Later, when she slipped unobtrusively into her place behind the Armagnac bottles, Gurdjieff ignored her. He was passing the dessert to Jane Heap — some kind of strange oranges dark and ancient-looking with rough pebbled skins. "This is food for Man," he said to Jane, *"real* Man, not man in quotation marks. Nature *hates* man in quotation marks. For him, Nature does not give such things. But here, if you are real

Man, you can have all the time. Here is quintessence of all
good that exists . . ."

Here in this room, here at this table, here with me . . .
The echoes of the words he might have added seemed to
shout out of the silence after he finished. He brooded over
his coffee as if alone in the room. We tiptoed about our tasks
clearing away the plates, washing up in the kitchen. I realized as we went out the door of his apartment that I had been
close to tears throughout the entire meal. Perhaps Jane Heap
knew what she was talking about down in the street when
she said gravely: "Today he is sorrowing because of us, what
we've done . . . we haven't been able to take enough of
what he gives. We've failed him somewhere."

It was a thought that had often entered my mind during
the year of trying to take enough of what he gave. I knew
that we must have failed him, not only when he had roared
at us and told us so, but many another time when it had not
been worth his while to point out the obvious. And, I
thought, we would fail him again and again, despite all our
unrealizable efforts.

Yet I believed (because our "animals were law-able" and
our inner-world work a daily undeviating practice) that some
of Gurdjieff's teaching must surely have become a part of us,
even organically. So that later, though we might appear to be
running wild in forgetfulness, I believed there would always
be the warning note from the small inviolate place he
established within us to hold the single "I" we struggled to
unify — a place no one could touch, the place to retreat to in
times of stress . . . "Like a small dog house," Gurdjieff had
once described it — belittling, amusingly, to diminish purposefully any premature sense of achievement we might have

entertained. Dog house or (as I envisaged it) ark, and I believed that such a sanctum now existed in the depths of my being.

April was Wendy's and my last month with Gurdjieff before sailing. Though I knew my place was with the Thin One, and that one of my tasks was to "keep the fire burning" in her as well as in myself, I felt a painful depression at the thought of leaving. I fought to conceal my gloomy state from Gurdjieff's knowing eye, but he detected it instantly as if I were made of glass. One night after dinner he called me to his bedroom at the end of the hall, where we always went for personal talks. He stood me before him, looking into my eyes and, without any preamble or questioning, he said in the gentlest voice I had ever heard from him:

"Krokodeel, we will not be separated as long as *with inside* we have the same idea. This going will not touch your inner world. Soon again we will meet . . . ." I don't remember by what method of locomotion I left his room. I remember only how he turned me around by the shoulders and sent me forward toward the door with a slight push.

We had our last lunch with him on May third. Wendy and I had visited that morning the Russian Orthodox Church in the Rue Daru to watch the superb Easter ritual. When we told Gurdjieff where we had been, he nodded approval and said to our companions, "I am very glad that these two, in their last days here, went to the Russian church to participate in such a good thing, for *feeling* experience . . . Now the Russians feast for forty days until that day, Ascension, when He goes up . . . such a custom they have. For everything in life there is custom. Only in America custom is not known. America has custom only for fox-trot!"

Through his own Easter feast he continued talking about churches, telling us how all Christian services derived from the Greek. "Once, in Jerusalem, I saw nine different kinds of Christians all together in one place for Christmas. In the center was the Greek, on the right was this very old people Italy now makes war with — Abyssinia — and so forth. I watched all this very impartially and I saw that only the Greek was the real thing, and this I do not tell because I am Greek. When you see this Greek Christmas, it *opens up all your feelings.* You forget why it is, even for whom . . . such knowledge they have for composing ceremony for the psychology of people."

Someone asked him if the New Testament also came from the Greek.

"Yes, of course," he replied. "Everything Christian came from the real old Greek . . . then was spoiled. All, all comes from Greek even before there was Bible. Your Testament is *new* book, composed four, five hundred years after, by fishermen. This was how fishermen saw. Fishermen today are exactly the same as they were then. You know fishermen . . ."

"But before the fishermen, Mr. Gurdjieff, what happened to Knowledge?" Wendy asked.

"Nothing happened . . . it was always with initiate people," Gurdjieff said. "All goes in one stream; you remember initiatism? *Still today flows that stream.* You see, Thin One, *you* ask questions from one stream, I answer from the other, then you go back to your stream with my answer. You remember the two streams I wrote about? The difference in the two streams is the difference between interpretations of events on earth. Events have two interpretations — one for mankind, one for me. *My stream is initiatism.* What hap-

pened before, as you ask, does not interest me. Remember my
chapter on Maralpleicie . . . this is what happened before."

Seldom was he so indulgent with a question from the
Rope, so expansive in reply. *Still today flows that stream*
. . . it chanted in my mind like a doxology. Miss Gordon
leaned forward, resolved to carry on.

"But there have been *messengers* before, Mr. Gurdjieff
. . . like you," she said.

"Many such messengers there are!" Gurdjieff ignored her
personal reference. "Even you have them in America. For the
English and Americans they are something, but for me . . ."
he made a grimace . . . "in the objective sense, they are
manure."

A week earlier, he had not been quite so categorical.
Wendy and I had accompanied him on a trip to Fontainebleau and Vichy. In some café halt en route, he had talked
about early Christian words and their real meanings before
spoiling corrupted them. This had prompted us to bring up
the subject of America's "hot gospelers" and the extraordinary manifestations of their vast following. He had listened
with interest to our account of Aimee Semple McPherson's
preaching stage in Hollywood, full orchestra, harvest-moon
backdrop and revolving colored lights. His comment on such
theatricalized religion had been the opposite of what we
expected: "This shows how people are hungry for *something
more,*" he said gravely. "Every year on earth there appear
such — last year was one in Russia. Not a bad thing. *Even*
with such misunderstanding, is better than your fox-trot. No
matter how *little* it has, already it has *some* reality for
people . . ."

A bit here, a bit there, a long memory and an aptitude for

putting the bits together like a mosaic — this, I reflected, was how the teaching was apprehended. Nothing ever made easy, nothing ever given out wholly, every scrap of illumination worked for . . . as Miss Gordon was working now, for herself, for the Rope. Not put down, or out, by Gurdjieff's rebuff, she pursued her messenger theme stubbornly.

"But Christ," she went on, "He was not . . ." she refused to repeat Gurdjieff's excremental word, ". . . *He* was a real Messenger, was He not, Mr. Gurdjieff? Once you told how He had been brought up by the Essenes and initiated." We had all heard that statement. We had waited nearly a year to have the amplification Miss Gordon pressed for. In my eagerness for one more bit, I almost forgot this was my last day, for a long time, at his table.

"What I told, that is another question," Gurdjieff said. "*You* believe what you *wish* to believe. For such things, I have no interest." Yet he had. With his next words, he gave us a glimpse of its real depth. An undertone of world sorrow accented his summing-up: "*Nobody* now believes in the Christian thing — not with the *inner world*. Especially young ones . . . especially in your England and America. In general, man does *not* believe . . ." *Not with the inner world,* his dark eyes repeated, searching our faces, communicating their sorrow for Man's religious state as *he* saw it — an emptiness echoing lip service before altars.

In silence we ate his delectable *pascha,* the Russian Easter dessert. *Nobody now believes* . . . In my mind's eye, I saw again the mound-shaped *paschas* carried in processional three times around the Russian church, then brought into the golden interior and laid for a blessing on a dais wreathed in incense smoke. The sanctuary screen of Byzantine ikons separating the holy of holies from the believers facing it slipped into my thoughts like a lantern slide as I looked to the head of the table. Then I saw our master sitting before it, a strange, yet (to me) perfectly appropriate double-exposure. Against the ikons depicting Creation in traceries of gold and jewels, his heavy human form had an Atlantean density and power.

Deliberately, purposefully, aware that (had he known of it) he would have excoriated me for such fanciful "philosophizing," I held the picture until it imprinted itself in afterimage that I could later bring back at will. He had taught me how to do this. He had also taught me, I realized in a sequential flash of thought, *how to believe*. Exactly as he had just said nobody now believes . . . with the inner world.

Wendy and I went separately to his bedroom to say our goodbyes. Once again he stood me before him and put his hands on my shoulders. He said, "Let the vow be your left-shouldered angel," and told me to close my eyes. I heard his big voice reduced to a murmur saying something that may have been prayer, or invocation — in Russian I could not tell. Then I felt his thumb trace the sign of a small cross on my forehead.

When I opened my eyes he was smiling. "Now go," he said gruffly. He made it easier for me to move by turning away to examine some papers on his bedside table.

CHAPTER TEN

I WAS not to see Gurdjieff again for more than a year, and then in Paris, not in New York as anticipated. By that time I was a Crocodile in name only, skinned nearly bare by the excruciating experiences which fate had had in store for me.

The beginning months of the long separation were auspicious. I had finished my book at last, and my friendly agent, in whose judgment I had such confidence, told me she liked it. The momentum of life with Gurdjieff I knew would endure, and I took the distracting noisome backdrop of New York as merely a change of scene for a continuing work. The inner world I was determined to keep intact seemed more solid than Manhattan's cement and glass-walled canyons. As I put to the test everything learned at the master's table, I discovered capabilities within myself which seemed to be inexhaustible.

I took a job doing what I had once sworn never to do — write advertising copy. I went to work for a travel service, selling the experiences of my travels in every *Where to Go, How to Go, When to Go* booklet I composed. Consciously, I made a special task of my work ("Man must use what he has . . . not hope for what is not") and observed myself knuckling down to ad copy without any self-pitying lament for my unsold book manuscript which was making the rounds of the publishers.

Living in the inner world while working in the outer world, and the constant struggle to keep those two worlds separate was a psychological adventure of first magnitude — two levels to live on, two lives to live. That I made a quick success of my advertising work was no surprise. I had a formula for such in-life activities and training under an expert in applying it: "When you do a thing, do it with the whole self . . . one thing at a time."

From my office window on the thirtieth floor of Rockefeller Center, I could look out on the Hudson River piers where two or three times weekly the French Line ships docked, bringing long letters from the Paris Rope in the elliptic communication of adepts, about our "being-work." The master's table never seemed far from my office desk in those first months of absence from it.

Often in my lunch hour I crossed the Avenue and went into St. Patrick's Cathedral to do my exercises in the silence of the rear pews. I used to watch nuns coming into the cathedral for their devotions, bound together in their way as we on the Rope were in ours.

Our work with Gurdjieff had created an inner-world intimacy, a kind of caring for the soul of another such as I had never experienced before in any human relationship. He had predicted such a "brotherly love" when telling us that whether we loved or hated one another, we would always have this special feeling for the other on the Rope because we had made a common aim together. "Common aim is stronger than blood," he said.

I fancied that the veiled Sisters knew about that exalted bond. As they passed my pew, always in pairs, I remembered Gurdjieff had described the kinship of persons who worked for a great common aim as "the arisings-of-a-homogeneous-causality," and the jawbreaker phrase well described my transformed relation with Wendy.

She, meanwhile, seemed to need little help from me to "keep the fires burning." She had rented a flat near Washington Square and sent for her French furniture in California. In the familiar setting of the little milliner whose main aim had once been material success, she referred to Madame X in the third person and past tense, as one speaks of a vanished friend. I heard no undertone of nostalgia when she recalled that former self whose grace and gaiety she still possessed as well as her love for hats. Now she made hats at home for friends, using her knee as a hat mold, stretching felts over it, stitching and patting, while expounding in her own odd way the teaching that had changed her.

By the questions she asked, I knew she was doing his exercises as conscientiously as I did mine. When unable to clarify some problem she had met, I passed it along to Gurdjieff in Paris, through Canary, who was now his secretary. He always replied, through her, to any question touching on the Work. It seemed mysterious and wonderful to me how, at such a distance, he knew exactly what we were doing wrong, and what was to be corrected.

Wendy had also taken up her reading of the little magazine of spiritual guidance which had been her comfort through all her Madame X days — the nonsectarian *Unity*. It helped her, she confessed, to understand certain aspects of the Gurdjieff teaching which in my notes often sounded merciless and harsh, almost too difficult to accept. However she padded them out, those notes were nevertheless the words we lived by, communicated with, spurred each other with — consciously and remindingly, "hand washing hand."

The knowledge that many former disciples, who had been much farther along in the Work than we were, had fallen by the wayside after separation from Gurdjieff's magnetic field did not disturb my conviction that we could keep to the path. How strong was the Rope? How long could it hold? As long, the master had said, as *with inside* we had the same idea and invincible aim. That meant forever for me, I believed with the strength of my Crocodile nature.

August was the month when Gurdjieff was due to arrive in New York. Instead we had a cable from Canary that his brother Dimitri had died. We cabled "Your brother is our brother," and sent money to help him with the funeral expenses, sure to be enormous, since the master never did anything halfway. I began to fear that Gurdjieff might not be coming to the States in 1937 and that there would be other events to detain him, for crises attended his passage through life like satellites around great Jupiter.

With all thoughts centered on Paris, I was unaware of the crisis rising up in my own affairs until it dropped like an axe on our analogical bond more real to me than the steel elevator cables that pulled me daily to my skyscraper office.

Wendy fell ill with shocking suddenness in September and all but lost her life during an emergency operation that lasted five hours. I got to the hospital just in time to see her wheeled away, prostrated by an intestinal obstruction, to hear the surgeon's prognosis given frankly because I looked "strong enough to take it." Then the mind I had trained to stand guard like a policeman over my emotions abdicated and the old die-hard mechanical self climbed into the driver's seat.

At the nearest cable office, I composed a message for Gurdjieff; then cables poured in from the "Paris family." A friend outside our group but close to Wendy in spirit suggested asking *Unity* in Missouri for the help of their prayer circle of which I had never heard until then. I worded the wire as directed, giving name, age and malady, and felt less alone. I was in company now with some unknown people out in the middle of Missouri who were praying for an unknown woman on an operating table, and with our master, whom I saw clearly with my inner eye "making something" with all his will for a distant disciple in peril.

I had seen Gurdjieff do this, not once but several times in Paris, and the memory of it gave me belief in what was coming in from him to sustain the Thin One. Was it telepathy, assistance from "higher forces," or simply something out of his own great powerhouse of inner strength earned through remorseless work on himself all those years in Tibet? Whatever, however . . . it was a fact I accepted without question, as today I accept without real comprehension the phenomenon of instant communication oral and visual via satellites orbiting through space.

Wendy came off the operating table, her life hanging by a thread. Acute inflammation of the peritoneum and gangrene were what the surgeon had encountered. In her struggle for recovery, cables flew to Paris and telegrams to Missouri. Her eventual deliverance came, possibly flowing from both directions, and helped by my own frantic prayers. The surgeon called the recovery a "miracle," enunciating the unprofessional word in a low tone as if ashamed to be saying it.

We hardly ever spoke of the Work during her long convalescence. On advice from Paris, Wendy had been taken off the strenuous exercises and at first her avoidance of the subject seemed natural. I redoubled my own inner efforts as if to make up, in some indefinable way, for the inactive member on my end of the Rope. I could observe clinically what the Thin One's illness had taken away from her, but her subjective state could not even be guessed. I suffered in silence waiting for her to come back to our common aim, refusing to admit the gathering evidence that she had lost her desire to go on.

I knew intuitively what would happen if she abandoned the Work which had already left its deposit. She would drift back into outer-world life, famished to the end of her days, with her memories of the master's table. The anguish of my fear for her was a strange pain that taught me something about the deeper meaning of "brotherly love," of caring for the soul of another as Gurdjieff had foretold. These thoughts wrung my heart as I hurried through my anxious days of thorns.

In contrast, my outer-world prospered, proving another of Gurdjieff's statements — that with "thorns" in the inner world there would always be "roses" in the outer world, in "law-able" compensation. My roses were a raise in pay and promotion to advertising director. I began traveling for the company, visiting for promotional purposes their information offices scattered from coast to coast. Then, in December,

my literary agent telephoned that my book had been accepted
by Knopf, with an advance royalty payable on publication
sometime in early summer of 1938.

I was trembling when I hung up the receiver. My secretary
asked me if I had had bad news. "No," I said, "it's my
book . . . accepted . . ." I knew then what a flood of
feeling, unobserved by me, must have been involved with
that manuscript. I had played my role of indifference to
writing success so successfully that I had even convinced
myself I had no heartstrings attached to it.

Know thyself . . . Despite all the years of effort, I still
had unplumbed places, alien selves. This was as fascinating
to ponder as was the fact, signed and sealed by a publication
contract, that I could call myself a writer once again. I cabled
to Canary that my "exercise in unrolling the reels" had sold
as a book, and went home to Wendy with a bottle of
champagne under my arm.

I told her where that royalty check would be taking us —
straight back to Paris, back to our source, for badly needed
nourishment at the master's table. I was too wildly happy at
the prospect to see anything but a reflection of my own
delight in the strange smile she gave me. Only afterwards,
did I remember . . .

Wendy never came back on the Rope as she had been.
Throughout the spring, I tried to believe that her indifference
to the great ideas which had been our common center of
gravity was a passing phase. The phase had its time in it;
when that time ran out, she would start to remember herself
— *re*member, put together the pieces of her scattered selves

and unite them into one again. So I told myself in optimism
. . . until July of '38 when I found I was sailing alone for
Paris.

I never knew the cause of the inner change that made
Wendy refuse to go with me to Paris for what might possibly
be (until after the approaching war) the last reunion with
Gurdjieff and our Rope companions. I had felt a struggle
going on in her, affirming and denying — a longing to go, a
wariness holding her back. Had she come to the point where
she felt she had not the needed strength? Had she ever
really, with the whole of her believing being, accepted what
he represented, as I had? Or had she simply followed me,
having no place else to go? She was so completely restored
from her illness that I cancelled out that easier explanation.
Whatever the reason she wanted no more. I was like a
shepherd grieving over a lost sheep all the way across the
Atlantic.

The first days at Gurdjieff's table were a mixed experience.
He received me as if I had left him only the day before,
commented on my physical state — "All your dirty [psycho-
logical] fat is burned off" — and did not mention the Thin
One until the third painful day. He took me aside after lunch
and spoke of his disappointment in her failure to appear, if
only to show her good wishing for him and his Work.

"She did not know what work I made for her," he said in a
sorrowing tone. "Every night, for her, I made special séance.
Now, no longer can I make this. *I have not the right.*" He
shook his head, added, "And about her, now we no longer
speak." And he did not for the rest of my stay.

My three weeks in Paris were divided between business (I

had persuaded my boss to send me abroad to scout possible extensions of his travel service into the European field) and Gurdjieff. Each morning in the Café de la Paix, I sat for a while with the master, re-membering myself, drawing into myself the regenerating force that emanated from him; then I went forth to my rendezvous with directors in the French travel world, briefcase under my arm and not a doubt in my mind about the outcome of my promotional mission. I was never able to formulate for Gurdjieff just what that work was which had earned my way back to him, but he accepted without comment my erratic goings and comings. I saw my future then as a succession of jobs which I would use, like magic carpets, to carry me to him as long as his Crocodile was *persona grata.*

Persona grata . . . as long as I made effort in his Work, as long perhaps as he could see on my face what he had once amusingly called "a lively look for trying." I must have had that look during the whole of that poignant reunion in Paris.

My inner struggles centered on just one warning injunction Gurdjieff had given me the year before. He had made scores of illuminating comments on the pitfalls my all-or-nothing nature could lead me into, but this one stood out above all, printed in my memory like a war-scare headline: "Never let the emotions lead you into self-forgetting . . . never lose Self with the mind." The Thin One's absence from the Rope tore at my emotions everywhere I turned, most often in Gurdjieff's apartment where I often caught myself waiting for her to turn up late after having dallied too long before the Champs Elysées show windows. Then I remorsefully began work on the self again, growing a little stronger after each slip into self-forgetting.

I became aware of a major inner change toward the end of my visit. Like many who came under Gurdjieff's dynamic influence, I had a certain obsessive idea about the Work — that proximity to him was one of the conditions for its fullest expression. This misconception vanished one night when I was working hard against all my Crocodile nature which was threatening to manifest itself indecently (emotionally) at his table. Suddenly the realization struck me that the efforts I was making under his eyes were no different from the efforts I had made — for other reasons but with similar intensity — during the year and a half of absence, far out of reach of his reminding shocks and prods.

It was a liberating discovery. The implications of it seemed perfectly clear — this must be, in this Work, a factor of self-initiation that could appear after a certain period of apprenticeship. *You initiate yourself! Why,* I asked myself excitedly, had Gurdjieff *never told this?* The answer was there in the next breath: Because he wanted you to discover it for yourself.

My heart overflowed with love for him as I looked toward the head of the table saying inwardly, "You old Sorcerer . . . you . . ." I knew then that I was ready to go back to the rat-wheel of New York life with no more regret that I could not stay forever at his table. I would never again say, How little we have, standing alone.

I made sentimental journeys around Paris saying goodbye to Notre Dame with all its saints and gargoyles, to St.-Germain-des-Prés and the beloved neighborhood cafés, to the wonder of the Concorde fountains, to the palace of the Louvre and every pansy bed in the Tuileries. I let my emotions fly out, heartbroken with the certainty that I was seeing Paris for the last time before Hitler reached for it as he was then reaching for the Czech's Sudetenland. I even welcomed my emotional binge, in compensation for the costly calm achieved at Gurdjieff's table. The last day was nearly unbearable — one of those windless August days like a trance over the city, making it seem to be waiting for something . . .

As Canary drove me to my ship at Le Havre, I wanted to weep for every haycock studding the Normandy fields like little yellow tents. This was the last harvest before the storm, and I knew it in the depths of my francophile heart. I could scarcely bear to look at those conical hay tents tied at their tips with tidy bunches of straw.

Aboard ship, after the last promontory of France had faded from sight, it was time to get my Crocodile in hand. It had had its day with me. Now I would have my day with it, not only now, but from *now on out,* I told it firmly, and put it to work for and with me, trying out a new instruction the master had given. Later, I gave it a long walk on the deck for good behavior. "Keep friends with your animal, so that he will help . . . not hinder."

You could work endlessly on any one of Gurdjieff's "inner animal" teachings, working against your nature in order to get it to work with you. A ceaseless beginning over again, with now and then a start just a little bit farther up from the bottom, just a little bit stronger on each new try. I thanked God for my inner animal, for its all-or-nothing nature, its appalling appetites and strength. I thanked Gurdjieff for identifying and naming the creature I was caged with for life, that animal nature which I used to call by St. Paul's more unadventurous term "the old man" or "old Adam within," on whose aged neck I had once believed I could put my foot down any time I wanted!

Engrossed in the summings-up which always preoccupied my mind after taking leave of Gurdjieff, I was strangely happy. Though he had spoken so little that I had scarcely made a note during my visit, I felt nevertheless that he had given me much more than words could convey. During the first difficult days at his table I had felt understanding flowing from him and a kind of mercy in the way he had let me alone to work my own way out of an impossibly confused inner state. And there was that curious sense of freedom from the clinging-vine attitude of the usual impassioned disciple, which had come with the realization of a change in my being.

I walked much of my way back to New York, pacing the decks and remembering. He would be coming in the spring, Canary had said, if war did not break out before then. And if it did, I knew that sooner or later I would get back to him somehow. I had done it this time on my own and I could do it again. I had only to be, as our master advised, "resourceful in life . . . not live from day to day without plan, like a donkey!"

The Normandy I had grieved over in August expanded in September of '38 and became whole countries, even European civilization itself, after Chamberlain flew to Berchtesgaden and gave Hitler everything he asked for including the dismemberment of Czechoslovakia under the infamous Munich Pact. Through the autumn and winter, while news headlines proclaimed the inevitability of war, I watched transatlantic liners docking below my office window, crammed with American expatriates returning to safety. I watched the stock market soar on anticipation of armament profits, listened to our salesmen's happy talk of the boost all this would give to domestic touring. After a while I shut the door quietly on my inner world to keep it safe. For the duration, I told myself.

But I opened it wide, once, in the early spring of '39 when Gurdjieff at last arrived in New York. He sailed in on the S.S. *Paris* with Canary, his worn-out secretary; remained for about two and a half months, then sailed back to France to vanish from our sight and communication until after the war.

From the first view of him at the head of the gang-plank — brown face beaming, moustaches twisted up horn-sharp and a too-small beret perched on his great shaved head — I was seeing in vivid live enactment a wondrous addendum to the chapter "Beelzebub in America" of his First Series.

Wendy, Louise Davidson and I stood apart from the group of his former American disciples gathered to greet him, giving them first chance to salute the master they had not seen in more than five years. He called each by name and promptly handed out tasks — the men to look for his seven pieces of luggage, the women commissioned to telephone around for hotel accommodations that would "correspond" to his needs . . . (They had confided to us that it would have to be some other than his previous 57th Street hotel where, because of "carpet and furniture disasters," they doubted he would be accepted for a second visit) . . . then he called us to him by the names we had not heard for so long — "Theen One . . . Sardine . . . Kroko-*deel!*" — startling to a standstill all the debarking passengers within earshot.

Beelzebub in America — an interlude that turned upside down every established custom of New York living, transformed a Wellington Hotel suite into a working-cooking replica of the shuttered Paris flat, and overlaid on the joyless face of the city so many laughing memories that I never saw it quite the same, ever again.

Gurdjieff received his people for the first three days in Child's; then announced that he would henceforth receive in his hotel — from noon until 3 P.M. and from 6 until 8 P.M. daily.

Within a day or two his suite, comprising bedroom, bath and living room, turned into a Near East restaurant. Woolworth paper cups and plates, pyralin soup bowls, gallon cooking pots, knives, forks, and spoons were procured and stacked on bookshelves; on the tile floor of the bathroom stood a shiny new electric stove and a coffee-making Sterno. As our master found his way to the Greek and Armenian shops of the Eastside, watermelons, sacks of goat cheese, all his favorite fresh tarragon, mint and young cucumbers, crocks of dill pickles and cleavered carcasses of baby lamb crowded the living-room "cooler" — the fire escape outside the window. In bureau drawers he kept *lavash* — unleavened Turkish bread sprinkled with sesame seeds and kneaded so thin it could be rolled up neatly — and tins of Beluga caviar. The only traditional adjunct to the Gurdjieff meals which none of us could find for him anywhere in the city was his esteemed Château de Larresingle Armagnac. He compromised for one day, poured bourbon whiskey for the toasts; then decided that he could do better with his own home brew, which we all helped him make from triple-distilled alcohol shaken up with lichee nuts and small pieces of toasted lemon skin. It was a frightful drink, so strong it ate the varnish off the table, but we swallowed it loyally and eased the throats immediately with tarragon and goat cheese wrapped in *lavash*. Shortly after, we found an Armagnac acceptable to him.

Chicken and apricot soups thick and spicy, the famous curry salads of chopped greens, tomatoes, garbanza beans and radishes, mounds of steamed *kasha* with small spiced meatballs . . . all the familiar dishes of the master's Paris cuisine appeared in turn on his New York table, their aromas drifting through the hallways on his floor and even into the elevator shafts so that you could sniff the menu riding up.

We on the Rope, having had more domestic experience with Gurdjieff than the older American disciples, developed a technique for garbage disposal. After the dinners, we emptied wastebaskets into boxes and bags, wrapped and tied neatly with string, and walked to the elevator each with her parcel of garbage. The first night we did this without informing the master, feeling only that the hotel people must not see all those bones and melon rinds. But Gurdjieff caught us going out the door with bundles, asked what was in them and we told him: "We will place these in the middle of Times Square, Mr. Gurdjieff." He nodded with delight: "Of *course!* Put in most important place . . ." and gave us his smile. Sometimes we would drop our parcels in the refuse bin on the corner of Fifty-fifth and Seventh, but when the doorman was looking, we walked proudly to our car with them as if carrying gifts from a generous host. Once we had to drive many blocks before finding a refuse bin close to the curb and by that time the air in the car was unbreathable.

Why the hotel management (which had posted "No Cooking" signs in all rooms) did not throw Gurdjieff out after the first days of his aromatic illegal cooking was a mystery until one afternoon when he confided to us that, the night before, the hotel housekeeper had invited him out to a motion-picture theatre, and after the show he had escorted her to the Brass Rail for a midnight snack. "So now," he said twirling his moustache, "I have relations with the hotel staff!" We knew what that meant — he had turned on the magic of his irresistible personality, made a housekeeper feel like a queen for a night and his willing accomplice for the remainder of his stay.

In the New York group there were more men than women, especially on Saturdays when the males accompanied Gurdjieff to a Turkish bath, returning to the hotel for a late night dinner to which the women were invited only after the masculine company had finished dining. In the predominantly male atmosphere, Gurdjieff accented his Rabelaisian side, told all his scandalous old jokes, encouraged the men to reciprocate and rocked with laughter at their feeble efforts to top him. It was fascinating to see American businessmen looking at the master with eyes of love, to hear them argue heatedly over meanings of words he used, each believing he understood more than another and to watch Gurdjieff benevolently biding his time to put them all in their places.

I remember a "bath night" when one of Gurdjieff's most pertinent life teachings came out of just such a word squabble. His old Russian friend, Dr. S., was present and did not take lightly the attempt of an American to clarify something Gurdjieff had just said to him. "Only *he* can say such things to me," Dr. S. cried, gesturing toward Gurdjieff. "Not you. You are small man. But he . . . he can say *anything* to me and I can take it. You know why? *Because I love him* . . ." The American (named D.) saw he had unwittingly given offense and apologized good-naturedly. Gurdjieff waited until all was said, then turned to D., whom he cherished like a son, and began speaking in a low gentle voice:

"In truth, D., one fault you have. Though you are known as a kind man, a good nature, and though everyone knows you do not wish to give offense, you do this unconsciously sometimes. It is a fault that spoils all life for you. *You do not have considerateness for state of your surroundings.* It is necessary always to know what is around you, the state of *man* around you. With a cow, you can spit in its face and it does not take offense; it licks, shakes its head. Not understanding, it does not take offense. But man around you is already more high — he has *states*. You must know what is the state of every man around you in the room. Man of course is most of the time asleep, but this makes it even *more* important that you be sensitive . . . because when he awakes, even if only for one moment, he is already in a state — for this one moment he is delicate, sensitive. Perhaps it is the *only* moment in his life when he can be enlightened. So you must consciously try to understand, to be sensitive for him. *I* know what is the state of each man around me because I have this knowledge. You must try *always* to have considerateness for state of surroundings if you wish to be objectively *bon ton!*"

My memory recorded the slowly spoken words, then connected them in quick association with another earlier dictum on man in relation to surroundings . . . (Was it two, three or four years ago that he had exclaimed, "The *terribleness* of it is that man, *real* Man, must remember if not himself, then what he does in relation to his surroundings. Man must *always prepare* for what he does, necessary at all times that he *thinks* what he does . . ."?) and I had no sense of time lapse in the continuity of the teaching.

That timeless continuity would always be, I thought, whether you were privileged to see the master daily, as had the Rope, or periodically over intervals of years as his New York followers saw him. Once you had worked under his personal guidance, once that "unchangeable source" with its single aim had been set up within, you would never come to him as a stranger no matter how many years or crucial life events separated you from the previous encounter. The reflection brought a curious consolation as I sat with his larger, totally different American group — an outsider to their experiencing of the master, yet one who by the mere fact of being invited by Gurdjieff to participate was given to understand that she belonged in the chosen tribe he called "my people."

During the entire magical interlude of his New York visit, I was keenly aware that we were having our last communion with him until after the war — about which he never spoke, thus making it seem like something preparing to explode on another planet. It is fantastic now to recall the headlines that screamed crimson each day from the Rockefeller Center newsstands — NAZIS OCCUPY BOHEMIA AND MORAVIA; ITALY SEIZES ALBANIA; ENGLAND AND

FRANCE ABANDON APPEASEMENT — and to remember Gurdjieff sitting in his always crowded hotel room with his American men, his small feet out at right angles with heels together in ballet position, hands on spread knees, leaning forward and telling his hoary old Scotch and Irish jokes with disarming bonhomie, then by cunning quick transition switching to serious talk when no one was prepared for it . . .

"Man must at all times *mathematically* hear, *mathematically* understand, *mathematically* answer. Only *this* is life. Always he must be *with his 'I'* . . . only then is he not man in quotation marks. No matter what he has in his surroundings — people, noise, alcohol — always he must mathematically understand. Never lose the Self, even when drunk. He can be drunk, but *never* can his 'I' be drunk . . ."

Night after night, the same theme — *his* headlines for the inner world of man, the only world that counted, the only one toward which his talk was directed . . . and always in continuity, always in reiteration, always like a message from outer space coded to a single note, a single letter, the timeless I of man.

Beelzebub in America . . .

From my office window on May nineteenth, I watched the S.S. *Normandie* back out into the Hudson stream. Gurdjieff was aboard with the faithful Canary who would remain in France until the State Department would order all Americans home. I had no wild regrets that I could not be on the pier to wave him off. I had said my farewell thanks after my last dinner in his company; repetition could not have improved them.

I had delivered my farewell over the heads of his Americans sitting in close circles around his sofa, cross-legged on the floor. The quick passage of words between us came back with echoes of mirth as I watched the flag-dressed liner pause midstream and begin to kick back foam: "Thank you, Mr. Gurdjieff!" "For *what?*" his jocular exclamation seeming to deride my farewell effort. "For *all!*" He had winked then at his men and said, "*Listen* how she tells all! Only *one small part* is . . ." goading me to have the last words, to say something I had always wished to say but until then had never found the opportunity. In his idiom, I fired back: "One small *your* part, Mr. Gurdjieff, *seems* all . . . *even* to a Crocodile!" and had made my exit on the sound of his chuckle.

"One small *your* part . . ." I said to the white liner steaming down stream. Then I shut away, in my inner world, that one small part of him which I ventured to think of as mine.

For the duration . . . *Do-sveedanya* . . . till we meet again.

CHAPTER ELEVEN

THE KAISER shipyards at the northern end of San Francisco Bay were moving toward peak production when I entered them in the spring of '43 to become a welder. They were pneumatic thunder, electric-arc lightning, smoke and sweat and a massed human effort geared to a single aim — to build a Liberty hull straight up from keel to top deck in seven to nine days' time. They gave me my intensest experiencing of humanity at its roughest, toughest and noblest and supplied the chapter in my work life of which I am proudest — if only for having survived it.

After Pearl Harbor, shipyards ringed the American coasts from Pacific to Atlantic. The Kaiser yards in my hometown bay were, if not the biggest, certainly the most spectacular. They called people from every walk of life — shopkeepers, businessmen, salesgirls, housewives, college instructors, farmers, factory hands (from "nonessential" industry) and writers like myself (sick unto death of writing idiotic ad copy for a living while half the world bled to death) — Negro and white, Red Indian and Mexican, Chinese (from San Francisco's Chinatown) and dust bowl refugees from the prairie states who had emigrated to California in *Grapes of Wrath* jalopies after the great drought winds of '36 and '37

had blown their farms away . . . "Okies" and "Arkies," the
only Americans I ever met who were completely independent
of rubber-stamp conformity to any society, including their
own.

I had sat like a "Sister Anne what dost thou see coming" at
my Rockefeller Center office window for the first year of the
war, watching with a pang the great ocean queens down at
the French and Cunard Line docks take on their coats of
battle-gray paint, turning almost overnight into anonymous
troopships with only the racy slant of funnel left to betray
their pleasurable pasts. News of our master had ceased with
Canary's return to the States and Elizabeth Gordon's intern-
ment (after France fell) in a Nazi camp for British nationals. There was now nothing left to look for out of that
Atlantic-facing window. I tried to get into the Waves, passed
the exhaustive Navy physical tests, but was finally turned
down because the complement of Lt. j.g. commissions which
my age and background called for had been filled. Then the
shipyards began to run ads in the New York papers — "We
teach *anyone* welding in two weeks — *with pay!*" — with
photos of young housewives becomingly bonneted in the
welder's black hood. I saw the Crocodile in such a hood and
chose the shipyard nearest to my mother's home in San
Francisco.

In Richmond's Yard #2, I was number 053566, a figure
without sex, identical to the thousands of other women who
welded their way through the war shoulder to shoulder with
the men and (save for size) were indistinguishable from
them in the Martian welding regalia: nineteen pounds of
brown horsehide overalls and jacket, blunt steel-toed safety

boots and deep-cuffed welding gloves cooked stiff and black with heat. I loved the yards from the day I entered them, though I never knew from shift to shift if I would emerge alive. I chose the swing shift, from 3:30 P.M. to 11:30 P.M., so I could see the yards by day and by night.

My Crocodile got me through the first two weeks in the training sheds — a most extraordinary contest of will against flesh. I lived exclusively in the physical center throughout that killing initiation into the mysteries of electric-arc welding which could only be described as a passage through hell. Every known threshold of sensation was reached, passed over. At the end of the eight-hour shifts, I emerged from the smoky sheds bent, burned and broken, incapable of thinking of another day of it — until I looked off to the shipways, to the row of twelve cradles with Liberty ships rising up within their basketlike scaffoldings, a blazing stage of terror and fascination, arc-lighted under the night sky. Then I knew I would be back. I could never quit until I had played my part on that iron stage.

Henry Kaiser's experts made spot-welders of us in two weeks, as advertised. This meant that we could "tack" (spot-weld) in the flat, vertical or overhead position the iron "dogs" against which bulkheads, brackets and so forth were lined up to chalk lines the shipwrights snapped with a string. Many in my graduating group elected to work in the Prefab — a vast roofed-over enclosure where ton-weight sections of the ship were made on assembly floors; I spoke for work on the ways and was sent aboard my first Liberty as "tacker" on a welding team that had just lost a member. From that first wild day in bedlam, I knew I was ruined forever for ladylike work in business offices, that however I earned my living afterwards, it would have to be in something as thunderous with purpose as that shipway where death hung over our head every moment and every ounce of agility was called into play to avert it.

We continued learning to weld on the ships, pushed by the team leaderman into bigger jobs as soon as he saw we could handle them. The welding teams had twelve members, all in various stages of proficiency, with a few professional welders too old for army duty scattered through them. The old-timers taught the greenhorns, showed them the tricks of the trade and planted in their breasts the pride of the profession and the longing to "draw a bead" as shiningly perfect as theirs. There was a gaunt six-footer named Tom on my team who took me under his leathery wing and got me into production welding by the end of my second month on the ways. Then I was really In, a contributor of measurable welded footage to the team's total, posted at the end of shift, the goad that drove the many teams working aboard to do their utmost to be first in footage. The teams had a tribal spirit, loyal, boasting and proud, each believing itself to be the best (most productive) in the yards and its leaderman the noblest savage of them all.

My team may have been only average in makeup and background, typical of the hundreds that worked in the yards, but I thought it the most extraordinary collection of humans ever bagged together in the dozen lot. There were five women and seven men on it, including a Negro couple from the Carolina bayous who spoke Gullah together. Of the seven men, four were Okies working off the multiple mortgages on their Oklahoma farms with shipyard wages; two including Tom were master welders, and our coal-black brawny Gullah man. The five women included a Mexican salesgirl delicate and lovely as a Spanish doll, a big Finn from Minnesota, an Irish waitress from the Berkeley campus, the Gullah wife and myself. Our leaderman, Johnny, was from "back East" — a small quick man with a slight limp who got up and down the ship's ladders so fast his feet never seemed to touch the rungs, and actually never did when one of us was in trouble.

As swing-shifters, we ate lunch around seven in the evening, always in the same place — at the foot of the starboard gangway, slightly back under the curve of hull toward the bowsprit end of the ship. Each team had its special lunch spot and always ate together, grouped around its leaderman. When a member was late in coming, Johnny became anxious, often climbed aboard the hull to hunt his missing sheep, perhaps working solitary in some dark hole where the blast of the midshift siren had not reached. We looked like troglodytes in our horsehide "leathers," squatting back in the shelter of our iron cave, eating ravenously from black tin lunch boxes, speaking only in grunts until the food was gone, the Thermos bottles emptied — all within the first few minutes of the half-hour break. Then we lay back on beds of scrap iron, lit cigarettes and waited for Johnny to start the ball rolling with the latest news of the yards, which Big Shot from Washington might be making a tour of inspection next, how far ahead of, or behind, schedule our ship was, where he reckoned our team might be working next day . . . and presently the sound of a human voice talking naturally without grimace or strain (as in the clangorous hulls) started up others and you heard the Okies bragging about "one of the purtiest passels of black bottomland you-all ever seen" or

"Ah got me a pair of mules that cain't be beat nowheres in the whole goddam state" . . . and planning their next leaves of absence (always permitted) from the yards to "git one more crop in this-here year." Background music floated down from the yards' loudspeakers, dance tunes that set the girls to reminiscing of dancing parties long long ago, back in that almost unimaginable time of normal nightly activities, before swing shift took them over, used them up and returned them to their homes each midnight dead-beat. When someone occasionally asked me what I did before coming to "this here madhouse," I had to stop and think before answering. I felt as if I had been born in the yards, had no other past but this communal team activity, no other home but this curved niche beneath some ten thousand dead-weight tons of an iron ship hull.

I had made a habit during my time with Gurdjieff of jotting down anything I heard or read which echoed or suggested any aspect of his teaching as I had understood it. I had in my notebook, for instance, a variant of the master's "going whole hog" when on a spree — from Amiel's *Journal Intime,* published in France in the late nineteenth century: "In order to truly understand an experience, one must first go completely into it and then come entirely out of it." This was what I did in the shipyards. I went so completely into them that all awareness of other ways of being vanished from memory. The body acquired new reflexes, the muscles established new thresholds of endurance. The molten pool at the tip of my welding rod was the central sun of my existence.

I looked into it through the small window of protective dark glass set into the front of the welder's hood. I manipulated that 9000-degree Fahrenheit pool with the tip of the rod a fractional space above it, the "gap" that created the arc, weaving its fire upward (for vertical welds) into columns of flattened beads, horizontally (on the overhead) into beaded overlaps that knit undersides of decks to bulkheads, pulling the pool onward with the crackly frying sound that denoted the good arc — coaxing, guiding, never taking eyes from that small bright sun for an instant, until the rod burned down to its butt. Then I tipped back my hood, put a new rod in my "stinger" (electrode holder), dropped the hood with a head nod and went back to live for another eight or ten inches in the heart of the fiery sun which owned me body and soul.

The obsession to produce a perfect weld dominated all thought for months, until I was able to do it — but only now and then. I understood why the professional welders like Tom were such a temperamental lot. I saw welding as an art, its practitioners fire artists who rejoiced on days when everything went well, who cursed and brooded on days when, as they exclaimed, they were unable to "run a single goddamned pass." It might be their generator that was "acting up," or the coating of the rods they declared to be inferior, or simply something within themselves which refused to co-operate in the exquisite control of body that welding required, especially when done from crouched, kneeling or belly-flat positions. A good weld, after its slag was wire-brushed off it, was like a string of silver overlapping beads glowing against the dark iron of beam, bracket or bulkhead. When a welder was in one of his good days and had "poured it on" in beauty, he trotted over scaffoldings to his nearest teammate, summoned him or her to come and have a look. During waiting periods when welders were tapped to stand out from under while the gantry cranes brought aboard some ton-heavy section, you saw these mutual admiration meetings going on in all sorts of corners where the leather-clad workers gathered.

Out from under . . . In the deafening din down inside the hull, speech became touch. A tap on the shoulder from the leaderman was the signal to scurry to a safe place when gantries appeared overhead. The gantries worked in pairs, one on each side of the ship, like gigantic iron insects seventy-five feet tall with steel arms that looked like sensitive antennae moving always in unison against the sky. Both gantries were commanded by a single signalman standing alone amidships on a top deck beam or on an edge of overhang if some top deck plates were already in. He used the whole of his body to tell the gantry operators what to do after their load dropped from sight. The load might be an eleven-ton stern frame, or a preassembled bulkhead that blocked out the sun. Slung from steel cables it swung forward or aft, to port or to starboard, in obedience to the signalman's swift incisive movements of arms, hands or even fingers, or quick strange torso bends to left or right — each gantry operator reading only *his* side of that communicating body. To us gazing up from below, it was a death-defying man dancing a great hunk of iron into position.

Occasionally only one gantry cable dropped into a hold with a yellow metal basket on its hook. The shallow basket was curved and shaped precisely to hold the body of a man. The injured worker was lifted into it, the hand signal given, and you saw it fly up out of the hold, swing high over the ship, very frail-looking against the sky, the body a diminutive shadow in the brightness; then it dropped swiftly from view to deposit its load beside the waiting ambulance.

So-and-so "went off in the basket today" . . . tersely the word was passed. The injury was never named, the cause of it only if someone happened to have witnessed. A stack of iron "dogs" falling from a scaffolding, a barrel of rivets, a shipfitter's sledgehammer. With scores of bodies on the stagings, working one above the other, and always a crew crawling about the chaotic bottom of the hold, anything could happen any minute to anybody. Now and again, but rarely, when the basket dropped aboard, there was nothing but a splatter to pick up. *"That* one, they had to *sweep* up with a dustpan" was how news of these fatalities was passed on. Fortunately, I never saw a worker caught under the load of a crane cable that had given way, but one of our Okies did and he vomited his guts out for an hour after.

Except for brief periods of rod-changing, we welders lived mainly in the dark of our hoods watching only that single pool at the tip of our rods, talking to it, sometimes babying it along with mournful song, while all around us the ship grew and took shape in a seemingly mindless bedlam which increased in sound and fury as it neared top-deck height. It always seemed like the same ship, though we transferred to different ways every five or six days to begin again in the double bottoms of a new one. Since every Liberty ship was exactly identical to every other, it was the same ship over and over, the same type of welds poured into the same angles, corners and beveled butts, and every finished hull that went down the greased slipways from any one of the twelve cradles of yard #2, stern-to into the bay, was "ours." We knew every inch of her 441-foot length and 57-foot breadth abeam, every corner of her five cargo holds, every curve of her propeller shaft tunnel from engine room to fantail, every crouch hole in her deep tanks and chainlockers. When the loudspeakers struck up the heart-catching "Anchors Aweigh!" music, we knew one of ours was sliding down to the sea. If we were not working too deep in a hold, if we were not too tired to hoist our nineteen pounds of leathers up the ladders, we climbed to a top deck perch to watch her go. A stirring sight always — that black iron hull scabby with rust, her single smokestack sticking straight up like an old chimney, no racy sheer to her decks cluttered with hatches, cargo masts and windlasses, no real ship's beauty to her anywhere, but a sea queen the way we saw her with our workers' eyes, rocking about with a kind of wallowing motion as she got her first taste of salt water. Someone always cried out, "By God, she floats!"

Often they went down to sea with welders' initials beaded in hidden corners of beams or brackets where inspectors would not spy them, or hearts with paired initials pierced through with neat arrows. We signed our work occasionally, like artists. I always burned my sign up under a hatch end beam, my favorite welding job. I would not venture to say today how many Liberty ships went off to the war with a small Crocodile etched beneath their hatches.

The big thrill came when we worked top deck of a ship to be launched during our shift. This happened only now and then, but when the timing put us aboard such a ship, the team experienced its apotheosis. Welders were the last to leave a readied ship, in its last moments the only workers aboard it. We were gods in leathers then, lifted up for final ministrations to an iron queen whose launchers were already gathered on a platform down beneath the land-pointing bow. Sitting shoulder to shoulder before the last open deck butts, we poured the metal into them from the huge black-coated rods that flared ultraviolet lightning to the skies. Johnny pulled us wildly from job to job — an unfinished patch on a hatch coaming, another discovered along the port bulwarks, finishing touches here and there in the deckhouse. Get onto it *quick!* Hurry . . . hurry . . . thirty minutes to go!

Decks were snake nests of welding cable. From far beneath the hull you heard the dull thump of sledgehammers of the gang knocking out the blocks. Port and starboard gangways had long since been pulled away from the ship, only a skeletal ladder left on the starboard side. Between last-minute jobs we stood with lines over our shoulders and rods ready in our stingers, waiting to jump where Johnny pointed. The band music floating up from the launching platform was not for the Navy or company wife who would break the champagne bottle against our bow, but for us who had stitched this ship together with fire and would stay aboard her until not an inch of crack was left unwelded.

Then she was done, ready for the outfitter's dock across the water. *"Lines overboard!"* was the last command. Over the bulwarks we paid out our hundreds of feet of welding cable, the first welder through with his helped the next, whole coils were picked up and flung writhing through the air to fall in a tangle on the ways below. Then over the side we went, one by one, rodpots in one hand, stingers over our shoulders, descending the last single-laddered gangway as the first bars of "Anchors Aweigh!" blared from the loudspeakers. We barely touched boots to the ground before the ship started to move. Groaning at first, then gathering momentum, she slid past our bloodshot eyes every foot of her a piece of us, from stern to flag-draped bow. After the flag slipped past we stood on the way, staring at the bottom of an empty ship's cradle into which another flat keel would be set that same night by the graveyard shift. On the raised launching platform well-dressed people were shaking hands, congratulating each other for one more ship *they* had sent on her way — ladies in fur coats with orchids pinned to them, naval officers and company VIP's in formal attire. We welders grinned at each other as we walked past their fashionable stage in our filthy heat-shrunk leathers, following our leaderman to another way, to finish off the shift on another ship, the same ship always, "ours."

I lost track of the number of Liberty ships I worked on. I lost track of time. Then one day an old college friend whom I seldom saw except on occasional days off when I rejoined daylight society severely pointed out that after a year of that man-killer labor, I ought to be thinking of a less strenuous job. There was a new international relief outfit, called UNRRA, which was shaping up and an office in San Francisco was interviewing applicants. "Specialists to build up shattered countries after the war," she said. "People with foreign languages and background — the kind of thing you've got."

The application handed to me after an exhaustive interrogation by a multilingual Swiss lady, had exactly one query that fitted me: *Are you flexible?* I wrote a thumbnail sketch of my Jack-of-all-trades life, laughing inwardly and proudly as I wound it up in the shipyards where flexibility began in the bones. I underscored the fact that I had already welded for over a year whereas statistics showed that six months was the average work life of the nonprofessional welder. I was

informed that the FBI would check into my past as presented
on the application and that in due time, if all went well, I
might hear from Washington. I told my teammates next day
that if any of them saw an old gumshoe sleuthing around in
the holds, he was looking for me, not them. Johnny said
sweetly, "I hope you make it, Kate." I, of course, went on
welding while waiting although I did not believe that I had a
chance of making the grade for overseas service with an
organization that was then seeking trained agronomists capable of rehabilitating a devastated country, or engineers
who could set up a national industry that had been bombed
flat. Even sewage experts had been called for on the application. I had merely shot an arrow into the air, I told myself.
But sometimes in the dark of my hood alone with my
thoughts, I saw what that arrow could bag for me if it fell in
the right place. A return to Europe, possibly to France. My
heart always stood still when I thought of Paris. The flat on
Rue Colonels-Renard — was it still there? Was Gurdjieff still
in it?

I could not imagine him dead, or even defeated. He would
ride out that long Nazi occupation of France, somehow. I
remembered something he had said back in June of '35 when
Paris had gone on total strike — nothing moving in the
streets, no telephones or newspapers, people queued up
before empty food stores. He had prepared for the Rope on
one of those strike-bound days the most extravagant dinner
ever served at his table. He had enjoyed our mute astonishment, then explained: "I am *accustomed* to revolution . . .
all my life I have had it!" And he had advised us like an old-
timer how to prepare for continuance of the revolutionary
upheaval which had stopped the city dead in its tracks: "Buy

candles, buy a big piece of bread, water you can find — then you have all that is necessary. For me it is simple thing . . . all my life I have had . . ."

I thought of the master with increasing ardor after filing my application with UNRRA. The mere fact of having made the move toward overseas service seemed to have brought him a little closer. Though acceptance seemed highly improbable considering my nonqualifications as agronomist, engineer or sewage expert, one part of me — the guileless Crocodile — believed that it just might come about. Even my mind occasionally corroborated the hopeful attitude of that Crocodile. It reminded me that I generally got what I wanted out of life, *when* I wanted it hard enough. Even in such a wild deviation as this welding experience I had got what I wanted. By working like the devil possessed, by practicing every spare minute on old pieces of iron found about the ships, by *desiring* it, above all, as passionately as I had ever desired anything in my outer world, I had got the small plastic ABS (American Bureau of Shipping) card certifying that I had qualified as an ABS welder "in three positions — flat, vertical and overhead." I had passed the stringent ABS welding tests because I wanted to prove to myself that I could come out on top of the heap, a member of the welding elite. When Johnny had handed me that hard-earned testimonial he had said, "With this card, Kate, you'll never want for a job for the rest of your life!"

Now, in the spring of '44, I was wanting with the same intensity another kind of work which was as unimaginable in its duty performance as welding had been when I had first gazed longingly at a picture in a New York paper of a woman in a welding hood. Now it was overseas service.

We'll get it, said the Crocodile, we *always* get what we want . . .

Still waiting, I welded through my second summer in the yards while the Normandy campaign was in progress. Every place name mentioned in the war communiqués tore at my memory — St. Lô, Caen, Bayeux, Cherbourg. During lunch periods under the hull, I told my fellow welders everything I read about that incredible Operation Overlord which had joined us with our Allies at last, back to the continent from England, by an almost continuous bridge of ships across the Channel. Warships, troopships, all kinds, maybe some of ours, I said. Years later when naval memoirs began appearing, I learned that five hundred seventy Liberty ships had served in the beachhead landings during June of '44.

The two or three on my team who signed their paychecks with an X, listened to my reports with open mouths. Flashes of shy pride showed on their farmer faces as they realized that maybe they had given something to all this; maybe they were working for something more than another pair of mules for a piece of black bottomland back in Oklahoma or Arkansas.

I remember a day in late June when we had worked our way once again to the top deck, a day or so before launching. Johnny had sat five of us along a clean-chiseled deck butt, each with about ten feet of it to weld. I was beginning to look at everything with what I call my "going-away eyes," that sharpened vision coupled to the emotions which frames in permanence a beloved face or scene. I had come to the realization (after passing a birthday in the yards, "pushing into the forties" as I had described it to my teammates) that I could not last out another winter of welding, and must quit before the rains came, whether UNRRA called me or not. If not, I would try to do a book on the shipyards, something about how America looked with sleeves rolled up, getting into a fight far removed from the battlefronts.

From the top deck I looked at the eleven other shipways to right and left — thickets of scaffoldings with iron shapes growing inside them, waterfalls of sparks showing where welders were working. Aft of the shipways the waters of San Pablo Bay reflected the afterglow of a late summer sunset and far across that red expanse the city of San Francisco was beginning to twinkle with its first evening lights, a fairy town set up on its many hills. *Remember all this,* I said to my Crocodile. Remember, too, these summer moths drawn with suicidal frenzy into our ultraviolet flares, frying to death on the instant, welded into these deck butts from which we cannot lift our rods to brush them to safety. Remember their huge faceted eyes and furry wings, visible for the split second when they fly into our flares to vanish in the holocaust we make. Remember the drifts of their pale bodies all over the decks, visible when we throw back our hoods to change rods. Remember, remember . . .

"Them critters, they gimme the willies . . ." Remember that farmer voice next to you, and Tom's exclamation from farther down the line, "What are we doin' for Crissakes, weldin' this tub together with *moths?*" Remember, too, how we suffer doing close work with the big rods, the "flashes" we sometimes get when a neighbor strikes his arc just as we throw back the hood. The searing pain of those "flashes" — blisters on the eyeball that make big men cry, that can be eased with a drop of castor oil on the eyeball but only partially — the long agonizing wait of eight to ten hours until the pain passes, leaving no damage to the eyes, *so they say,* but who could ever believe that?

Remember how many of us who sweat out two pounds of body liquids on every shift — our Levis beneath the leathers stained wet from belt line to knees — are regular donors to the Red Cross blood bank over yonder in the Kaiser infirmary, how many of us — like myself — have won the little gold "K" (for Kaiser) pin attesting to the first gallon of blood donated, and are working now toward giving the second gallon, a pint at a time spaced out over three- or four-week intervals (depending how the red-cell count holds up), absenting ourselves for an hour or so during shift, then returning to our scaffolds to go on with the job.

They were flying whole blood to the Pacific front during the summer of '44 as our Marines worked up through the Solomons toward Guadalcanal. The yard's loudspeakers called for blood and more blood and everyone bravely gave, but seldom spoke about it, as if that brief absence from the decks had a shameful aspect of some sort. Ordinary idiots, I used to think as I watched my teammates go and come secretively. *A la santé de tous les idiots ordinaires* — the highest category in the master's scale, the least "spoiled" by life, the most responsive to a call from humanity bleeding to death on South Pacific islands whose names few had ever heard and most could not even pronounce.

Though I lived with a college friend in Berkeley during my time in the shipyards, I was seeing my mother in San Francisco on days off, renewing the wonderful bond I had always had with her, making up as it were for lost time during my years abroad and in New York. Since her retirement I had always sent her an income, keeping her (as we joked) in the style to which she was accustomed, in a small bachelor's flat on Powell Street near the corner of Bush where she could look out on the cable cars which she regarded as personal possessions, like all old San Franciscans. My shipyard work frightened her, but she was proud of me for being able to do such unimaginable things and bragged about it to the booksellers as she combed their discount tables for any old copies of my three books. She always bought them promptly, as if each were a member of her family offered to the public at reduced rates.

After I told her of my application for UNRRA, she began reading back files of newspapers in the public library, beginning with 1941 when Roosevelt had coined the term United Nations to describe the countries fighting the Nazi-Fascist Axis. She soon knew more about the new organization than I did, and began rooting for my chances to join it — which meant that she sat quietly with hands folded in her lap, "holding the thought." One day when I visited her she told me with great excitement that a mousy little man who had flipped a badge too fast for her to read without glasses had called on her a few days before, mainly to ascertain, so it seemed, that I actually did have a mother. "As if," she laughed, "you had come out of the Everywhere into the Here like that old nursery song I used to sing! But you're going to *get that appointment,* you just wait and see. I've been holding the thought!" That night, acting like a well-heeled shipyard worker on a spree with an old girl friend, I escorted her to the Hotel St. Francis for a champagne supper and paid court to her over the candlelit table, telling her she outshone every other dowager in the restaurant even if she didn't wear diamonds. "You're a fine figger of a woman, Julia," I said gruffly, imitating her old sea-captain father whom I knew only as a salty legend. "A *damned* fine figger of a woman . . ."

And I began looking at her with "going-away" eyes, thinking of something Gurdjieff had once said about mothers. I could not recall his exact words, only the feeling that they had conveyed — that as long as one's mother was alive, man never achieved his full stature as a being alone on the planet. Death of the father never gave this awareness, only death of the mother — the great central life source of every human. Only when she was gone would one know the essential loneliness of life . . . As I gazed at her aristocratic little face that lighted so quickly to merriment around her (life having given her so little to be merry about, she was doubly vulnerable to it), it struck me that I had not only always taken her for granted, but could never conceive her *not* being on the same planet with me — the understanding heart, the receptive mind, to which I had brought every dream and hope, from which I had drawn the constant nourishment of absolute faith in me to achieve whatever I set my hand to.

We sat for a while in Union Square after dinner. She had her special bench there where I sometimes found her taking the sun when I got over to the city early. She knew the life stories of all the oldsters who sunned themselves on adjacent benches, fed the pigeons and watched the world go by. This night we sat in the light-spangled square holding hands like lovers.

"And if I *do* get that appointment, my dearest, and *do* get sent overseas . . . will you wait for me?"

Will you wait, the Crocodile carried on mutely, until it's all over and I can come back and start writing again, writing the books *you* always wanted to write and never found time to because you had to raise us three alone . . . writing with the kind of book love you bequeathed to me, and you editing with your fine literary mind, but being much more toughly impartial toward my pages than you are now . . .

"I'll wait for you," she promised. "I'll be right here . . . or just up the Powell Street hill where you keep me in such undeserved comfort."

A letter from Washington arrived a month or so later, saying noncommittally that if I were still interested, it would be advisable to appear in New York in early fall. Someone from the London Mission of the UNRRA would be there to interview applicants. I told Johnny I planned to quit on August 15, the midmonth payday that would round off my year and a half in the yards. "And I might very well be back in the spring," I said. "You can't count positively on being rid of me yet."

August fifteenth was a day like any other in the yards, except that it was my last day and I knew this with every fiber of my weary body. Johnny acknowledged my departure by giving me the prize job available to that day's swing shift, one he knew I always coveted, which he generally assigned to a man because it was tough. He disposed of all the team first, sending them off with their lines to various places in the hold #4, then turned to me with a grin and said, "Kate, you take the overhead on bulkhead number one hundred sixty-four."

This was the single pass that welded the top of the

bulkhead to the underside of the deck, a glorious challenge for my last job — some fifty-seven feet of overhead, all mine, all to be finished in that shift if possible. I scurried with fast-beating heart to inspect my work place, to see if I had enough line to get to it, to get the feel of the aerial scaffolding — a two-plank runway with sketchy backrail, suspended under the deck, just about a man's height from the top of the bulkhead. Beneath the slung planks yawned the vast space of the hold. If I did not spend too much time gazing down into that fascinating iron abyss, I could make it.

I paid out my line the length of the scaffolding, hooked rod pot securely to the railing, grinned at my comrades down below as I buttoned the collar of my leather jacket tight at the neck to prevent sparks from falling onto my skin (to give "slag burns" that festered for days) threw a loop of cable over my shoulder and walked with it to the port corner of the bulkhead. I said, "Here we go, Crocodile!" as I dropped my hood and stuck my arc to begin my fiery stitching across the long footage of clean neat crack.

I hummed the weld along with Beethoven's Emperor Concerto, played that noon over breakfast in the Berkeley apartment on my friend's superb phonograph, its heroic passages still ringing in my ears. The humming filled the inside of my hood; outside it the frying sound of the good arc crackled an obligato. After the first hour when my Crocodile began groaning at its arms' constant upreach, I paused long enough to give it a cigarette, leaning on the two-by-four rail as I smoked, looking down into the hold — a Dante's Inferno of flare and fury where humans crawling about their jobs looked pathetically shrunken and foreshortened as if already half consumed. *Remember all this . . .*

My upheld arms were nearly senseless by lunchtime, but I was halfway across the bulkhead when the whistle blew. Down under the hull in our customary eating place, Johnny asked if I'd like to have a teammate up there with me for the second half of the shift. I declined his offer and almost added, "My Crocodile will see me through . . ." The loud-speakers gave some spot news from the western front, something about a second Allied landing in southern France east of the Rhone, a thousand ships, possibility of a drive north toward Paris. I could not hear it clearly after the name Paris dropped into our dusky cave.

(Much later, I learned that what I had heard that night of August fifteenth was the opening of a door for me as a refugee worker overseas. As the Allies advanced through France toward the Rhine, they were to discover the hordes of Hitler's "slave laborers," the populations of Poles, Balts, Ukrainians he had driven from their homelands to work in the Nazi munition plants and factories then under Allied bombardment, places too dangerous to risk Germans in — his master race of Herrenvolk.)

Before the second-half siren blew, I said goodbye to my teammates, knowing how at the end of a shift we all streaked for home, a flight of brown bats out of hell. But some, when they had finished with one job and were waiting for Johnny to find them another, sometimes came to visit me on my narrow scaffold. In the dark of my hood I felt the scaffolding jounce as they walked over its loose boards and I knew they were watching me over my shoulder from behind their dropped hoods, until I finished a rod. Then we exchanged smiles, maybe had a cigarette together sitting on the planks with our leather-clad legs hanging over into space, not attempting speech in the din except by nods and grins. Occasionally one of them would take my stinger and run a rod for me — not so much to give me a moment's respite from the ache of continuous overhead reaching but rather to present me with the only kind of going-away present they had to offer — some eight or ten inches of silver beading, exactly matching my own, thrown up there for a present in the diminishing length of my still unwelded crack — their signing-off with me, their bon voyage written in beauty, especially by the boys who signed their paychecks with an X.

I finished my bulkhead just before whistle time and coiled my line neatly at the far end of the scaffold before climbing off the ship. I turned in my identity card as I passed out the gates of yard #2 that night, in a flow of fellow workers going off shift, breasting the flow of graveyard workers coming on. I could not believe that I would not be returning to the yards next day as usual promptly at three-thirty in the afternoon.

CHAPTER TWELVE

THE UNRRA base camp at Jullouville on the west side of the Cotentin peninsula was perhaps the first international town ever set up on earth. When I checked into it in late June of '45, it contained some three thousand Allied relief workers — a Babel as wild as the shipyards and speaking even more tongues. Europeans from the liberated countries of France, Belgium, Holland, Denmark and Norway predominated in the camp's population, while the British were in the majority among the English-speaking, which included Americans, Canadians, and some Australians and New Zealanders. All were recruits to the huge relief organization that came into being after the Allied armies had broken through the Siegfried Line and discovered, inside Germany, an estimated nine million uprooted human beings — for whom the strange title of Displaced Persons had been invented.

Ever since the beginning of the year I had been in the processing mill, waiting for calls to go here, go there, filling out questionnaires, writing my life story over and over, embellishing the flexibility theme after I discovered in Washington that not only had three other female recruits come out of the shipyards, but one had actually worked in Richmond's

Yard #2, on the graveyard shift that followed mine, a social worker turned welder pro tem who had doubtless picked up the same welds I had left unfinished at whistle time. We laughed together like conspirators, sitting around an impressive table in Washington, writing out our testimony for UNRRA's key question — Are you flexible?

From Washington I had been sent to the University of Maryland for a two-month course on field planning and operation, to listen to lectures about displaced persons given by people who had never seen one; and had finally wound up in London for another month of the same, while every nerve in my body strained toward the day when I would put my foot down once again on the soil of France.

When that day came at last, I had not been able to see France. Tears had blinded me when the little Channel steamer began poking its way through the awful wreckage of Le Havre port. Then fury had blinded me, looking out from the back of an army truck at what man's mad passion for war had made of Lisieux, Caen, the hedgerows and apple orchards of the lyrical Calvados countryside. The men who had died beating their way through such devastation were impossible to think about as individuals, only as some kind of mass madness that had happened to humanity, had been done in it and to it by forces of devastation beyond conjecture. The blasted beach fronting Jullouville had coils of barbed wire sticking out from its sands, its breakwater a scattering of cement blocks like gigantic dominos scrambled for the beginning of a new game. Only the assurance from the UNRRA driver that Mont St. Michel across the Gulf had not been bombed gave me courage to climb out of the truck.

And I stood then, not on any recognizable soil of France,

but on some kind of new earth — a battered beachhead for the first grassroots experiment in international cooperation on the grand scale.

UNRRA had taken over the little town for its base camp and collection center, possibly because it still had a few school buildings and dormitories left standing — the barracks housing for its hastily assembled thousands of Allied civilians. An UNRRA personnel officer who spoke English like a Norwegian told us to shoulder our duffel bags and follow him to the registration office.

I was a torch carrier for the international idea from the beginnings of my days in the base camp, though all I saw at first was nationalism vociferously, sometimes vengefully expressed. The French clung together in their groups, the Netherlanders, Norwegians and Danes in theirs, while the British looked down their noses at their American and Canadian cousins who had never suffered bombardment and were therefore presumed to have no idea of the real terror of war. All, except the North Americans, talked only about getting inside Germany to "take back" from the defeated Nazis everything they had stolen — linens, jewels, silverware, paintings, rugs, farm equipment, automobiles — an interminable inventory of domestic goods plundered from their homes during the Occupation. At the immense mess tables the Europeans were like starvelings, gobbling up the U.S. Army white bread, jams and butter not tasted in five years, tearing into their meat like wolves, cornering platters and refusing to pass them on the pretext of not understanding the applicant's language — a mass national hunger that had to be appeased before any such lofty concept as international humanitarianism could be entertained. If the torch I carried wobbled a bit in the first days, it was only from astonishment.

The small group of American women with whom I had traveled swiftly departed the scene and took up residence in the nearby village of Granville, formerly a stylish beach resort with dike promenade and casino. They called the Jullouville dormitory a den of thieves, predicted I would have every nylon stocking and flannel shirt stolen from my duffel bag and laughed pityingly when I sang them my torch song: How can you acquire the international spirit if you don't sleep and eat with your fellow Allies?

My army cot was set up in a corner of a cement-floored room housing some fifty women. Cot space was rigidly rationed; adjacent sleepers could touch hands across the narrow footways between camp beds and sometimes did, by accident, when a fellow sleeper had nightmares and flung herself about, groaning as if back in the homeland air-raid shelters. Sometimes in the night I sat up and listened to the moaning of my European sisters remembering the war in their dreams. A Canadian nurse three cots removed from me sometimes did the same. We would look toward each other, two heads faceless in the dark, our compassion inexpressible save by pointing a finger toward the cot whence came the strangled crying. If it went on, the nurse got up and laid her hands on the tossing form until it quieted down.

There was only one body in the dormitory that never seemed to move, even after the clang of the breakfast bell swept through the school halls and sent us pell-mell down the cement stairs to get to mess tables before the hungry Europeans had emptied all the pitchers of milk and bowls of sugar into their coffee mugs. The quiet sleeper was a young

woman who lay flat on her back on a low English army cot
nearest to the dormitory exit, almost blocking it — the very
worst place to drop one's duffle in, like in the middle of
Times Square at the rush hour.

Each time I stepped over her, I wondered how she could
sleep through the racket of bells, boots and morning halloos
in a half-dozen languages, her khaki blanket drawn up close
under her chin, her bird-beak nose pointing straight up, a
pale refined mask under rough-cut brown hair. Against the
foot of her low cot her duffle bag lay like a buffer with its
stenciled side to the floor so no one could read her name or
country of origin.

Because I never saw her in any of the orientation classes
that went on all day — lectures about DP's by people who
had actually seen a few for a change — or in any of the
queues for UNRRA shoulder patches, additional field equipment and so forth, and never that I could recall in the
mass stampede to the Post Exchange for the weekly ration of
Hershey chocolate bars and Chesterfield cigarettes, my curiosity about her increased. Had anyone ever seen her awake? I
asked. A French nurse told me she had seen her once or twice
in medical lectures, looking faintly amused at blackboard
diagrams of the correct setup for field hospitals, as if all that
was *vieux jeu* to her. She was a Belgian, seemed rather
uncommunicative and standoffish. *"Une originale, san doute
— comme tous les Belges!"*

Une originale . . . an odd one indeed. I expressed the
hope that she would never get on *my* team as nurse. "I doubt
she'd last a day in the field. She's already done for!" Moreover, said I, she was totally immune to the daily indoctrina-
tion in "team spirit," the intangible asset preached constantly

to us in general lectures, mandatory for all, prior to being "teamed up." I knew about team spirit from the shipyards, but only on a national scale. To create the same all-for-one one-for-all spirit on the international scale was a mighty problem. Over and over we were being told, "You are no longer French, English, Dutch . . . you are *internationals* now, you've got to learn to think as such. We have no place in this organization for national individualism."

Appointed in Washington as an assistant director, I knew that one of my responsibilities in the field would be the maintaining of team morale, especially among the women officers — nurses, welfare workers, cooks, secretaries and administrative assistants. Rumors filtering back to the base camp hinted of dissents and disagreements, sometimes outright feuds developing among the UNRRA officers. I had nothing to do with the makeup of the team I would go forth with but this did not prevent me from visualizing the kind of people I wanted on it — hardy, open-minded, flexible. No "Sleeping Beauties" like that Belgian nurse I stepped over lightly each morning.

The teaming up was like a gigantic grab-bag operation, carried on in a sandstone villa in the center of our international town where the high brass of the base camp sat over thousands of personnel files, matching up likely correlatives and creating the teams on paper. The team makeup was then posted on the huge camp bulletin board — a kind of wailing wall to which we all flocked each morning hoping and praying to find our names on some one of those listings of the lucky who would soon be on their way.

The only thing I knew about my eventual team was that I would go out with a French director. I had been called once

to the villa and asked if I had any preference as to nationality
of the director under whom I would be second in command. I
had plugged ardently to be teamed with a Frenchman, despite the fact (pointed out discreetly by the British military
personage who interviewed me) that French directors were
just then in rather dubious repute, not a few already ordered
back to base for reassignment to the French Zone after
having failed to get along with the American Military Government officers in the U.S. Zone. I had jolted my British
adviser into granting my request by telling him that I "understood the psyche of the French." It was the word psyche
that did it, I thought. No one — his startled expression
implied — ever used such a word in ordinary speech. (No
one, dear Colonel, except so-called Gurdjieffians . . .) I
smiled my thanks as he wrote *Fr. preferred* on my file and
passed it along to be matched to a French director in search
of an American assistant.

Having singled out from among Jullouville's thousands of
potential co-workers the only one whom I did not wish to see
on my team, whom I had summarily dismissed in my mind as
a "weak element," incapable of standing up to the rigors of
the field, it was inevitable that the dormant Belgian nurse
would be on it. I say inevitable because it had to be nothing
less than Fate that put her there, Fate that had plucked her
file out of hundreds of unmatched nurses' files and melded it
into my team with what I took to be an ironical flip of the
wrist.

When I discovered her in the lineup of team officers whom
Pierre, the French director, had called together to meet me, I
could hardly believe my eyes. Or hers either, for that matter,

seen for the first time wide open. They were deep blue, spaced far apart and extremely intelligent. Her handshake was Belgian in brevity, and as firm in grasp as that of Jean, her male compatriot on the team, the Belgian messing officer who obviously doted on her and called her "Chouka" in the Flemish diminutive.

Chouka . . . Jean . . . Pierre. Under such names my teammates have already been introduced in the book I wrote about displaced persons after my great adventure in "humanity-ness" had ended. I continue with those names now as I fill in the unwritten stories of some of those fellow workers treated with short shrift in the earlier book to save space for the vaster, and then more timely, picture of the refugees. For the same reason I also omitted many of my own personal events, presenting myself in *The Wild Place* as a kind of Seeing Eye witnessing the humanly unbelievable.

Now with the long view I see clearly the machinations of that force I call Fate operating benevolently on my behalf from the moment, on a July morning of '45, when I jumped off into the unknown with a dozen total strangers, heading eastward into the wilderness of World War II's destruction, toward an unmapped country called DP-land, on the other side of the River Rhine. Possibly for the first time in my life I was rightly cast for a role I was given to play.

I was, for one thing, where I had always wanted to be — in on the ground floor of something new and untried. I saw our relief team as a United Nations in microcosm, not sitting in easy style around some diplomatic round table, but bundled into two army trucks that jolted expletives from us in five different languages with every neck-twisting pothole they rolled into. We looked like gypsies in cast-off army clothes when we clambered out of the trucks for a midmorning "sanitation halt." Already the first taste of roughing it had brought us a little closer to one another, especially to the members in the second truck who had to swallow the dust of the leader. Chouka was among these, her face powdery with dust, but smiling. I began to revise my estimate of the one I had prejudged a "weak element."

We made Nonancourt, the UNRRA way station and billets, by late afternoon of our first day on the road. The billets were in a lovely château whose interior the GI's on their way through from the Normandy beaches had completely wrecked, doubtless in exuberance of finding themselves beneath a solid mansard roof for a change. The château was crowded with other teams en route to the field but two rooms without furniture except for straw pallets on the floor had been reserved for our men and women. Pierre took one look at the sleeping arrangements, borrowed some of my hoarded dollars and went off to the town inn to reserve rooms for himself and me; also to order a dinner for the whole team to which he invited them like a *grand seigneur*.

That night, for the first time since leaving Gurdjieff's Paris table six years before, I drank Calvados. The fiery apple brandy awakened all the precious associations of my prewar years in Paris and every step of my tortuous pilgrim's progress toward return to Europe which had been spurred by the desire to see him once again. I knew he was alive, and still occupying the same flat. Janet Flanner, shortly after the Liberation, had returned to Paris to her former post as correspondent for the *New Yorker* magazine. Though no follower of Gurdjieff, she had promised us she would look him up and take him our packages. She found him well and sent us the news of a visit she had had with him, telling us she had had to recall us to him by our animal names before he had remembered us.

Paris was now just ninety-seven kilometers from the Nonancourt transit base. Tomorrow, I thought, maybe tomorrow . . . Although our orders read: "Team will follow without deviation the routing Nonancourt Château Thierry to Metz to destination Heidelberg," I knew we would have to pass through Paris. Pierre, who had already broken the first rule that UNRRA personnel sleep and eat only in UNRRA billets, could be counted on to stop over long enough in Paris for the five French on the team to visit their families. *Tomorrow* . . .

"Tomorrow, *mes enfants*," said Pierre, "we collect our SHAEF cards and we are off." He filled the glasses for another round of Calvados and proposed a toast to the two most important on the team at that point of our *"voyage vers l'inconnu"* — the drivers. *"Nos deux singes,"* our two monkeys, he called them lovingly.

SHAEF meant Supreme Headquarters American Expeditionary Forces. All the team's cards but one were handed out early next morning. One of the French drivers' cards was missing. Pierre ranted like a mad man to the UNRRA official who said it was SHAEF's error, that it would take probably a week to get the card, through channels, from General Eisenhower's headquarters in Paris. Since no one without a SHAEF permit could put a toe inside the U.S. Zone of Germany, we were stuck in Nonancourt for a week which Pierre sourly predicted would stretch out to two, the way things were run in this "crapulous" organization.

I decided to make the best of it by cultivating the other five women on my team and paid a visit to the château billets that night. The French welfare officer asked me to have a look at Chouka, down with a heavy cold. From her straw pallet on the draughty stone floor, the Belgian nurse looked up at me apologetically, told me not to derange myself, she would be all right in the morning.

"You're coming back to the hotel with me," I said. "One more night on this cold stone floor and you'll be down with pneumonia, *mon amie.*" I asked Nanette, the French welfare worker, to help me with the nurse's duffel, told her I had a brass bed big enough for the three of us if she too wished to transfer to better lodgings and live illegally on the French economy for the duration of the *détente* in Nonancourt. Nanette declined my offer; my taking even one of them in was *quite* enough, Madame, she said with a mischievous smile. (Later, through the grapevine, I learned that my impulsive decision to share a decent bed with a team sister had definitely scotched the rumor that I was sleeping with the French director!) I walked off with the reluctant Chouka who refused to permit me to carry her knapsack. Rank was rank, she insisted hoarsely.

She slept through the entire night and much of the next day exactly as she had slept in Jullouville — flat on her back, motionless, soundless, like a sculpture on a tomb. Occasionally during the day when I looked in on her, I studied her face. Though she appeared to be somewhere near my own age, she had not a wrinkle, not even a small smile crease in the corners of her eyes. Life had left no marks on the marble-smooth countenance. When at last she arose from her prolonged sleep, she was completely recuperated. I insisted that she stay on in the inn for the sake of prudence, and also, I said, because her quiet company provided such pleasant release from the voluble Pierre. When she saw she could be useful to me, she consented to stay.

On the third day of desolate inactivity, Pierre called me aside to ask if it would bore me to chaperone that Nanette, who had been pestering him like a mosquito, for a one-day trip to Paris, to visit her family. *"Si cela t'ennuie, Kate . . ."* he was actually begging me to go! And using the intimate thee-thou form of address to weaken the resistance he anticipated. Unable to speak, I nodded assent. Only if I went along would he trust that wild little Parisian to return that same night. Also, he said, there just might be military inquiries en route and since he was taking it upon himself to write the illegal permit for an unauthorized trip — "for compassionate reasons" — he knew he could count on me to get him out of any trouble with the American MP's. I suggested that he write a permit also for Chouka who, in one of her rare confidences, had told me she had a sister in Paris not seen since '39. I knew that my roommate would jump at the chance.

Early next morning the three of us boarded the local narrow-gauge milk train, with Pierre on hand giving final fervent warnings about what would happen if we did not return on that same train that same evening. The nurse and the welfare worker were to keep their mouths shut if any MP's were encountered; they were to obey me to the letter and were to turn up in the Gare Montparnasse at least one-half hour before train time which was four-thirty that same afternoon. *Entendu?*

We had a third-class compartment to ourselves. Chouka

and Nanette sat opposite me, looking very formal in dress uniforms, neckties knotted neatly, brass buttons shining, headgear set at the correct angle — the French girl in a khaki beret, the Belgian in the visored cap of the British first-aid auxiliary in which she had served, Belgium having had no women's outfits in the war. They told me that I was really too kind to accompany them since I had no family ties in Paris and what would I do during all those waiting hours? I had to throttle the Crocodile to prevent it from babbling out my own truth about the journey — the realization of years of longings, plans and prayers. Chouka, when she caught my eyes, seemed to be examining them clinically, as if aware of the inner emotions perhaps reflected in the pupils. Was she one of those rare beings who knew the states of people around her?

The little train pulled into Gare Montparnasse around eleven that morning. I felt as if I was walking in a dream — out of the station to the corner of Boulevard du Montparnasse and Rue de Rennes, to a familiar old café, still there, same red awnings, same sidewalk tables and spindly chairs; everything the same except the shocking sight of the streets in which no motorized vehicles moved — no taxis, no lumbering green buses, not a thing on wheels except an occasional horse-drawn farm wagon or pushcart. The thundering vehicular blood of Paris had drained away for lack of gasoline. The dead look of the long boulevards struck me speechless; I sat down abruptly at one of the tables. When I got my voice back, it sounded angry, authoritative, uncompromising — no tones my friends had ever heard from me: *"This* is where we rendezvous at exactly four o'clock this afternoon. Right here, at this table . . ."* I rapped it with my knuckles. *"Sans faute. Entendu?"*

They nodded mutely and hurried off to the iron-arched stairway leading down to the Metro. At least the subways were running. I ordered a coffee (an ersatz brew of roasted barley) so I could continue sitting until I could "make all quiet inside," get myself into some sort of state that might hopefully resemble, in Gurdjieff's eyes, the kind of disciplined person I used to be in his presence. When at last I descended the subway stairs I discovered that my legs had unaccountably turned into wobbly cotton-stuffed appendages. Dear God, let him not say, *You have lost too much,* and close the door quietly in my face.

At the Concorde stop I got out, found the stairs leading up nearest to Avenue Hoche, remembering every foot of the way down that avenue to Rue Colonels-Renard, the left turn — and there was Number 6 exactly as it had always stood, a sooty façade undistinguished save for house number from the row of similar apartments that walled in the narrow cobbled street. I stood for a while, looking up, counting my heart beats. Then I pushed open the front door.

In the dim foyer one low-voltage electric bulb gave just enough light to see the old familiar out-of-order sign hanging on the elevator door. I passed the concierge's loge without ringing, and started up the worn carpeted stairs, counting them as we used to, though nobody was behind me now to hear the count and so many more to go. The door to the master's flat was not on open-latch. It took all the courage I owned to ring the bell. I heard it echoing down the inside hall, a clanging intrusion in the silence and I could feel Gurdjieff's presence in the flat. Minutes passed and I rang again. Another long wait, then I heard steps, slow, heavy, shuffling, behind the tall door. A safety chain clinked, the door opened part way and there stood Gurdjieff looking

out with a slight scowl at the unknown figure on the landing.
I had forgotten that my uniform, would be a regalia strange
to his eyes.

"It's Crocodile, Mr. Gurdjieff . . ."

"Kroko-*deel!*" The door swung wide. I rushed into his
arms and began to cry. He also seemed moved, saying over
and over, "Not expect . . . not expect!" in a hoarse voice.
Then he stood me off and looked at me with a slightly dazed
expression.

"So long a time, Mr. Gurdjieff . . ."

He looked older, more tired, darker-skinned than I had
remembered. He led me by the hand to his sanctum of
sanctums, the large "spice pantry" where he stored his special foods. I saw with relief that the shelves were well
stocked with tinned goods, bottles and packages of dried
fruits. He motioned me to sit opposite him at a small table on
which stood a Thermos and two small cups. I watched his
beautiful hands carefully pour a thick black coffee into the
cups. "*Vrai café!*" he said in French, "only place in Paris you
can have such!" He looked up, a glint of his old boasting
humor shining in his splendid eyes. "*Also* cigarettes! . . ."
he passed me one, a Turkish brand. After cigarettes were
lighted, he asked me for an account of myself — how I had
come into Europe so soon after the war's end, what I was
doing "in such dress — like soldier!"

I had a difficult time explaining the United Nations to
him, the slave laborers inside Germany we had come to help,
the people Hitler had conquered and trucked off like cattle
from their homelands. The phrase "displaced persons"
meant nothing to him, nor did "refugee relief," until I
thought to cap the whole operation under the term "hu-

manity-ness," his own expression. Then he nodded and after a long silence said "Bravo, Krokodeel!" — not, I felt, for what I was setting out to do but rather for having got across to him with great effort and, no doubt, a "lively look for trying," the meaning of my presence there in soldier dress. I told him that Canary in New York, also the Thin One, were in such military dress, of a hospital unit which they hoped would bring them overseas before too long to organize the rebuilding of French hospitals with American funds. The way he listened with head hung forward, watching my face like a lip-reader, gave me the impression that he had not heard much English during the war years, possibly none since Miss Gordon had died.

Whenever I finished with one subject, he nodded for me to continue, seeming content to listen to my news of the outside world which was all I could speak of calmly. My inner world trembled under his steady gaze, although nothing in his expression indicated displeasure (or pleasure either) with what he saw looking at and through me. Was I, in those sorrowful dark eyes, the returned prodigal who had strayed too far and lost too much? Or was it his constant world sorrow I saw reflected there? And his anger too when I told him about the concentration camps that had been uncovered in Germany after the Allies broke through. I described the lantern slides shown to us in UNRRA orientation lectures — the hillocks of emaciated bodies the Nazis had not had time to burn in the crematory ovens before the breakthrough. "*Hasnamuss* things, Mr. Gurdjieff," I said, using his own strange word for forces of evil. He had apparently not heard of those camps and ovens. As he listened, hunched over and motionless, his face darkened and a vein in his forehead swelled and beat. I saw the wrath of God in that clouded countenance, a righteous fury that seemed about to explode, though there was no change of expression, only of coloring. Later, inside Germany, when I would see other things for which there was no name, I was to remember that look of holy wrath for man's repetitive inhumanity to man. The memory would lift my own inner fury from subjective to something resembling objective anger.

I waited for Gurdjieff to speak but he seemed lost in a deep pondering, an isolated being within touch of my hand but beyond reach of my thought. Finally I glanced at my watch and told him I would have to go. He looked up surprised.

"You do not come for dinner tonight, Krokodeel?" He had a group of French pupils, he said, answering my unspoken question about the people, if any, he was seeing now. I explained that I was a chief of sorts, with responsibility of leading two young women back to the "army centrum" that same night, to be ready for possible start into Germany the next morning. He stood up then, looked over his shelves until he found what he sought — a box of *loucoum,* the Turkish Delight he had remembered I doted on. I backed away, begging him to keep that box, telling him that we had a Post Exchange which supplied all necessary sweets.

"Take!" His eyes commanded with a flash of the old simulated anger. Then he smiled and spoke softly: "You go on a journey, Krokodeel. Always when man goes on a journey, he must take *one* special thing. So now . . ." he put the box in my hand and slapped its cover lightly, a garish label depicting a Turkish harem scene. *"Also* for you, this can be . . . *reminding factor!"* His last two words had the impact intended.

"As if I needed such . . . from *you!*" I cried indignantly. He chuckled as he walked me through the hall, one hand resting lightly on my shoulder. As he worked to unhook the chain lock on the front door, stooping slightly to see in the gloom, he said as if in afterthought, "When all is finished there in Gair-*man*ia, Krokodeel, you must come home."

Home to him? . . . to the Work? Home was enough, home to the place where my spirit lived. I was unable to say any words of farewell. I simply looked at him, and tried to convey in that last long look all the love I bore him, all the reverence, all the unspeakable gratitude for having found him well, still teaching and the Crocodile still *persona grata.*

As always when walking away from Gurdjieff, I thought of the opportunities I had let slip by while sitting with him in that saffron-scented pantry — questions about his Fontainebleau family, progress of his books . . . I had promised the Rope in New York that I would find out everything. At least I had the answer to one of our most anxious queries — how had he managed to keep his pantry stocked, without money, during the Nazi occupation. The answer, the tallest and certainly the most touching tale he had ever told, was that he had spread, first all over his neighborhood, then in all the shops downtown, the story of a fabulous windfall due him at the end of the war — "a Texas oil well given me by one rich American," he said with that irresistible smile of his. This crafty clever invention was all that he needed to save his situation and enable him to run up huge charge accounts in his favorite Paris food shops, notably the luxurious Hédiard's in the Place de la Madeleine. When the war had started and his American and British pupils had scattered, they had assured him that if he could hold out somehow, they would all come back and bail him out of his debts. And those promises, which *he* knew would be fulfilled, but which no French shopkeeper could ever be persuaded to believe, were his "Texas oil well" — a symbol of the gusher that had already come in ("I tell how letter from New York brings such good news!") — the profits of which he would be able to touch just as soon as foreign currencies would become unblocked and permitted to circulate once again in France. (It came true, his windfall tale, when the pupils came rushing back to Paris after the Liberation, with money for him packed in suitcases and checks without end, all instantly good for the thousands of francs he then paid out in triumph to cheering shopkeepers.)

I jaywalked across the deserted Concorde and headed toward the Left Bank. I had time to walk all the way to the station, circling through my old *quartier,* the Place St.-Germain-des-Prés. Ghosts of former selves met me at every turn, all of them ten years younger, but no faster on their feet than the uniformed woman the empty show windows reflected striding past, with a box of *loucoum* in her gloved hand.

In the corner café fronting the Gare Montparnasse, the table I had designated as a rendezvous was unoccupied. I was ten minutes early, as I had planned to be, to give myself time to get my thoughts back into uniform. I ordered a coffee and set the box of *loucoum* on the table. The houri on the label lay on her side on a purple divan, her painted eyes looking out invitingly from under long hair twined with roses — an Oriental beauty such as Moslems believed dwelt in paradise for the enjoyment of the faithful. The label had an unanticipated effect. I felt a quick smart of tears as I stared at it. In some unfathomable way it evoked Gurdjieff as I had never known him — in his youth, in the Near East, a vigorous tireless searcher through those houri-haunted hermit-haunted lands for hidden knowledge, miracles and mysteries. How much older he looked, how weary now. I had never believed that *Heropass,* his dread word for Time, could ever catch up with him. But it had . . .

A shadow fell on the box. Chouka stood beside the table looking down on me with a startled expression. *"Mais vous pleurez, Madame!"* No, not crying, I said, just remembering . . . I gestured toward the sad streets, gave her a smile meant to deprecate my apparent grieving over the looks of the city. She was not convinced. She continued to watch me anxiously while I opened the box of *loucoum,* thinking to turn her interest to something new and strange. She told me politely that she had tasted this "Turkish paste" before but did not mention where, nor did she ask me how I had come by such a delicacy in the sugarless city. She had no small talk, nor did I at that moment. We sat quietly like old friends, munching the colored gelatin cubes. With the Crocodile back into uniform, I had an absurd desire, instantly suppressed, to tell my composed companion something about that unpredictable animal I lived with, to make her understand that it, not I, had caused the unseemly display she had seen with consternation. I knew, from discreet comments she had made on the volatile Pierre that she deplored any lack of self-control.

Nanette arrived ten minutes late, flushed with wine and happiness. Chouka told her she looked like a cocotte and made her set her beret at a more respectable angle before walking with "Madame la Directrice" through the station swarming with MP's. No one stopped us to ask for papers, thanks to the way the Belgian nurse marshaled her slightly bibulous comrade straight into the train. I saw that I owed that efficient nurse more than one apology. She was not only one of the strong elements of the team, but also one of its most conscientious.

Beginning in the train and later, during the twelve days of rocking in trucks over the broken roads of Germany to our destination camp in northern Bavaria, I learned enough about Chouka's background to put me forever in my place as an infallible judge of people. It puzzles me now, looking back, that I did not at any time realize that what I heard of her story covered only the previous six or eight months before I began stepping over her in Jullouville, and that her career prior to the winter of '44–'45 was never alluded to in any way. Possibly her recent experiences threw me off the track of chronology, containing as they did enough startling ingredients to fill a half dozen ordinary lives.

As I picked up bits and parts of her story, I of course did not know that I was getting only the tag ends of a much bigger story I was one day to write. The tag ends were too bright with bravery and blood to imagine there could be anything more beyond them.

Since the fall of '44, Chouka had been in active service, first in the Belgian underground, then later with a British field first-aid auxiliary which followed the Battle of the Bulge through the Ardennes, behind the lines, but close enough to the firing to discover a few living wounded, American mainly, buried in the snow side by side with dead bodies the retreating Germans had booby-trapped. She had lost three of her girls in that desperate hunt for the living;

then her female unit was ordered out of the battle area, back to Brussels still under attack from the flying bombs, the German V-1's which Hitler had called his secret weapon. On December 16 — a Saturday she would never forget — her outfit was summoned to Antwerp when a bomb fell on the Rex Theatre just at the start of a film that had packed the house — Gary Cooper in *Buffalo Bill*. There were twelve hundred in the audience; more than half were killed outright, including three hundred military on leave. Chouka and her nurses waded through blood for days, picking up arms and legs and even heads found blocks away. All under the theatre roof who escaped death were hideously wounded and there were many of whom not a trace was ever found. In that final winter of the war more than eight hundred fifty flying bombs fell on Antwerp alone, killing three thousand civilians and wounding some seven thousand. Chouka's outfit was on duty for all of it, until the last bomb fell in March of '45. Then, right after V-E Day, her unit had been dispatched to Germany to bring back Belgian nationals from the concentration camps. In June when I first met her in Jullouville, her British *chef* had assembled all the Belgians in the outfit, told them about the relief organization to which they could transfer directly, if any wished to continue in active field service.

And so, she was *"versée à l'UNRRA"* — poured into UNRRA, without having the remotest idea of what UNRRA was beyond the fact that it assured her a continuance of nursing, the only thing she had ever done in her life, the only thing she wanted to do.

"It was lucky for me that UNRRA was there just when my outfit was disbanded," she said once. Since I knew what a superb nurse she was (I had already seen her in action with

sick team members) and how her services would have been
welcomed anywhere in her homeland, her remark made no
sense to me. But neither, for that matter, did her extraordinary smooth countenance on which life had left no trace of
all the suffering she had seen.

In Wildflecken, one month after our arrival, I was to learn
the reason.

CHAPTER THIRTEEN

IN the UNRRA Heidelberg headquarters we had been told that our assignment was Wildflecken, "somewhere up in the bush beyond Bad Neustadt" in the northeast corner of Bavaria; that it contained about two thousand DP's "probably Polish" and the remnants of an UNRRA spearhead team whose director had vanished some weeks before, taking off for parts unknown in an UNRRA truck. "Just flew the coop" was the way the American regional director put it. When we finally arrived at the camp, we could see why.

The camp contained not two thousand but twenty thousand DP's packed into sixty blockhouses (three hundred fifty to a barrack) spread out over a forested mountain flank that covered some fifteen square miles. A city population the size of Plattsburg, New York, or Modesto, California, was teeming with emaciated Poles, blue-eyed ghosts of a once proud race now reduced by six years of Hitler's slave servitude to mere remnants of men. The American Military Government major in temporary charge of the camp handed it over to us like a hot potato. His hasty briefing flattened Pierre and me under Wildflecken's operational statistics, nearly all given in ton weights which I jotted down unbelievingly as he rattled them off . . .

Nine tons of bread baked daily in the old German bakery off in the woods on the northern end of the camp; 600 tons of rations delivered each month by the Army; 1500 tons of potatoes requisitioned from the Germans, to truck in and store before the first snows fell; 36,000 cubic meters of firewood to be chopped, hauled and stacked before the roads iced over . . . The only statistic my mind could grasp was the camp's birth rate — twenty-five infants added to the population last month (July '45) and double the number expected this month of August, not to mention the babies we would receive on every incoming transport. "They're going to throw them at you fast," said the major. "Army's got the cockeyed idea that every Pole in Germany will fit in up here."

Up here, Wildflecken, a real "wild place" as its name implied, was hidden in the deep forests of the Rhön Mountains, miles from any town. It had been Hitler's top-secret training camp for his savage *Schutz Staffel* (SS) elite, off-limits to German civilians since '39 and never shown on any map. In the drive on Berlin, the Allies had swept through it so fast that everything in it had been left intact — barracks, warehouses, mess kitchens and officers' billets, including (our major had reported with a grin) the commanding general's dress uniform tunic, found hanging in a closet in the SS headquarters building over which the Stars and Stripes and the UNRRA insignia now flew.

Three nurses — two Canadian and one English — a young French girl transport dispatcher and a male Belgian supply officer were all that was left of the spearhead team that had come into this wilderness perhaps a month earlier, none could rightly remember when, all were too weary to try.

Pierre hastily melded them into our full-strength team of a dozen greenhorns who had to become instantly operational while learning the ropes. There were twenty-thousand mouths to feed daily, twenty-thousand bodies to be properly clothed, twenty-thousand human beings to be accurately counted, sorted, catalogued as to sex, age, marital status and country of origin . . . "You pick it up fast, this DP business," the major had told us at parting. "Boy, do you pick it up *fast!*"

And that we did because we had to. "This DP business" was with humans, every one of whom had an urgent need begging immediate attention. They could not wait for us to find them in the fifteen square miles of the camp. They came to us in our headquarters offices; they queued up outside doors placarded in English, German and Polish — WELFARE, SUPPLY, MEDICAL, NURSING, ADMINISTRATION. The long silent lines winding down hallways and central stairs contained the colors of humanity in shades of gray, except for the eyes (nearly all blue), and the concentration-camp brands on so many of the wrists, the violet-colored ink of the Nazi tattoo experts.

As in the shipyards, only my first day in Wildflecken remains clear and consecutive in memory; the first Buchenwald brands seen, first anguished problems heard haltingly related through an interpreter, the first testing of myself in that tide of mortal woe that dragged at my emotional center like a powerful undertow. All the days that followed after — a year and five months of them in Wildflecken, six years in all with the DP's — were a blur of endless repetitions and variations on the single theme: man's inhumanity to man.

Each fellow officer made the same kind of discovery in his

or her special field. In the UNRRA mess late that first night, the team around the table had to be looked at twice to be recognized. Their faces had changed. Their talk, what little there was of it, was also altered — no ribaldry from Pierre, no jesting from the drivers, no coquettish remarks from the French welfare girl, just statistics dropped in brief phrases: "Four deliveries today in Maternity, two stillborn" . . . "Fifteen hundred calories daily per DP, no fresh meat" . . . "Estimated more than a thousand unmarried mothers" . . . "Every other kid TB or pre-TB" . . . "Every other adult VD, I bet" . . . "The bakery — Hell's Kitchen" . . . "Schnapps made from stolen flour" . . . *"Security?* With that hand-picked bunch of ruffians called the Polish Police?"

Though the majority spoke English, the official language of UNRRA, they lapsed into their native tongues, mainly French, to express their shock, surprise and occasional fear for the size of the job that lay ahead, its dimensions only just guessed at. Chouka was the only one at the table who said nothing, calmly cleaning up her plate of GI-ration stew, then gathering all her bread crumbs in a gesture of frugality that had a quaint charm, for it suggested something about her European upbringing, an abhorrence of waste in any form. I was glad I had picked her and the flighty Nanette as roommates. It would be like living with two opposite poles of personalities, I thought, *if* ever any of us has enough left over at the end of a day to be able to get down to personalities.

The *real* days, however, had not yet begun — days that turned us gray with fatigue, blue with rage and red-eyed from lack of sleep, baptized us in blood and mud and brought the team together like a clenched fist — all for one and one for all, and every cursing breath of our all for the DP's. The transports began, even before we had had time to explore completely the reaches of the camp, to learn the characters of the Polish Committeemen who ran it *their* way, not UNRRA's, to meet and weigh for trustworthiness the sixty blockhouse leaders who controlled the vital living space in their buildings like power-possessing landlords.

The transports began on our sixth day in camp, August twelfth — incoming transports from all over Germany, outgoing repatriation transports to Poland. Poles went willingly back to their homeland then, there being as yet no hint of the coming Communist takeover. The unending transports trucked the thrice-uprooted to and from the nearest railhead which was thirty-five miles from Wildflecken's main gate. Every man and woman on the team was shuttling (in small patched-up cars taken from the Germans) somewhere in those thirty-five miles of bombed farmlands and dense pine woods, day and night for the incoming transports — welfare and supply officers carrying blankets and food outbound to the railhead, doctor and nurses inbound with the ill and aged too weak to stand the truck trip to camp, or with women starting labor, or with wailing newborns found in the corners of the boxcars.

There was one night, in the beginning of that time of the transports, when the Army trucking-company captain refused to allow his exhausted, therefore accident-prone, drivers to make one more run, though we still had some three hundred DP's to transfer into camp and the boxcars had already pulled out. Neither Pierre's threats nor my pleadings could move him, nor the sight of our charges standing hopefully in the rain beside their mountains of bedrolls, boxes and cardboard suitcases tied with rope. That night, after a forty-eight-hour day, Pierre, Chouka and I decided to stay with the leftover DP's, to keep them company in those woods, to give them reassurance that they were not forgotten or abandoned. We watched them assemble along the railroad siding in family cliques and clans, build windbreak shelters with their multiformed luggage and bonfires from old railroad ties. They had been shoved around so long they knew just what to do. The sandwiches our messing officer had brought stuck in my throat as I saw those refugees bedding down for the night, mute and uncomplaining, their feet toward the fires, their bodies intertwined four and five deep with the grannies on the inside of each sleeping formation, between the warmer-blooded younger ones. As far as you could see up and down the tracks, there were those strange masses of contorted forms outlined in the ruddy glow of smoldering bonfires. It was, I said to Chouka, the living representation of Michelangelo's Last Judgment in the Sistine, only there was no Christ in the picture looking down with a face of mercy. *"Le Christ est absent,"* I said with a rising anger for what I stared at. She took my arm and paced me down the tracks until we were out of hearing of Pierre. Her face, lit by the glow of a bonfire, showed the first emotion I had seen reflected in that controlled countenance, as if it gave her pain to tell me: "You must never again say such a thing, *jamais, jamais, jamais!* The Christ is *never* absent, especially from dark places. He is here in every one of His poor ones, very near to us, too . . . nearer than I have felt Him to be in a long, long time . . ."

She left me abruptly, before I could explain that I was

talking about a fresco. *Or was I?* I was too tired to think. I watched her from afar keeping vigil over the tangled sleepers. Now and then she leaned down over a somnolent mass as if listening to a labored breathing or a moan too faint to reach my ears.

The time of the transports: between the twelfth and thirty-first of that August, we sent 8562 repatriates home to Poland in five transports, and received from other camps by boxcar or truck transport 7340 new DP's. Even today, with the long cool view of perspective, my notebook statistics have not yet become digits. They are still faces, endless streams of them — teen-age mothers with childlike faces, babies with the faces of old men and old men, brown and bearded, often fur-capped, who reminded me fleetingly of Gurdjieff.

By the second month in that time of the transports (never to end as long as we remained in DP-land) we had become accustomed to inhuman sights and sounds as soldiers on firing lines are said to become innured to the sight of sudden death and the sound of the screaming wounded. This to me was a fearsome development, as if callous pads had grown over the tips of our nerve endings. But the physical breakdowns among our officers — jaundices, unshakable colds, tears quite often among the women — proved that our "accustomedness" was only a seeming insensibility. We had reached a threshold beyond which nothing more could register as humane thought or feeling. Our state reminded me of the frog's leg muscle I had once dissected in college and strung up to a kymograph to record the effect of electric shocks applied to living muscle. The gastrocnemius tissue shortened and bunched up after a certain number of shocks and reacted no more but simply remained in its hard clenched state, unresponsive to increased voltage. That was where we were, I thought. The shocks continued but we no longer responded.

Chouka had served, all this time, when not on nursing duty with the transports, as a warehouse chief assigned by Pierre to inventory the huge SS warehouses at the summit of the camp — a job he had inveigled her into tackling because he could not trust the Polish Committee workers to do it alone and had no UNRRA warehouseman to spare for the supervision. She had accepted what I considered a foolish waste of her nursing talent because, said she, "I can never say no."

In her first weeks exploring the warehouses, unopened since the SS fled them, she had uncovered and inventoried hundreds of bolts of fine white linen cloth, exactly what was needed for our nearly sheetless hospitals. Then she had come upon a warehouse filled with targets cut from plywood in exact man shape and size, with painted faces, helmets and uniforms, an army of wooden soldiers (many plugged through around the heart) with which the SS had perfected their sharpshooting. In an adjacent wing there were hundreds of pairs of wooden skis, practice equipment for the Nazi *Drang nach Osten* into Russia and on to Moscow. After a month of the backbreaking labor with a team of young Poles (whom she spared the hardest work because half of them looked tubercular) her stoical spirit suddenly broke. One evening after she failed to appear at the mess, I found her face down on her bed in the billets, weeping her heart out.

At first I could not get a sensible word from her. In reply

to my anxious queries, she sobbed into the feather quilt that she was "no use to anyone . . . a worthless element on the team unable to do any good anywhere . . . a failure, *même une hypocrite . . ."* Her idiotic litany of self-depreciation had the unexpected effect of angering me.

"*I'm* the judge here, not you," I cried. "*I* know what you're good for . . . *I* know what you've already accomplished up there with those Poles who *really* try to help themselves helping you." I pulled her around so I could look into her eyes. Her face puffy and tear-stained, torn with some inexplicable grief, took all the authoritative wind out of my sails. "Chouka, *mon amie,* listen to me," I begged. "You have already made a great contribution. You're the first officer to have pulled a big group of Poles over to *our* side, created in them a willingness to work. Why do you think I've visited your warehouse every chance I get? Just to look at *one* successful program in this godforsaken place. Your boys . . . what you've done for them. They know it, too, my dear. I've seen how they look up to you. In their eyes you're a saint, a real saint . . ."

Her emotion changed on the word. A shocked look came over her face, as if I had said something blasphemous. "*Saint,*" I said again. "Do you think you Catholics *own* that word? . . . That we Protestants have no right to use it? *I* know what saints are. I know one when I see one . . ."

She put her hand over my mouth. "You must never say that again . . . of me," she said in a low voice. She threw herself back on the bed and covered her face. "You must never even *think* that . . . of me. Promise me," she wept, "never, never again."

You can never know the subjective state of another. You

must not try to understand what causes it. Gurdjieff's words. I stood over her, baffled by the picture of utter despair she presented. Yet, team morale was my job. I had to make one more try to help her. Bargaining seemed the safest approach.

"I'll promise," I said calmly, "never to call you a saint again *if . . .*" I lightly tapped the arm that covered her face, "you will give me just one good reason why I shouldn't. Just one good *reasonable* reason." I lit a cigarette and waited.

Minutes passed. Then she began speaking in a voice muffled by the sleeve of her khaki battle jacket still covering her face. She let me have the gist of her private pain in her first stifled sentence: "I . . . left my convent . . . last August — a nun who failed." It was fortunate that she did not see my face then. Something exploded inside me with that sudden revelation. Amazement, compassion, a real Crocodile upheaval of mixed emotions for a situation so unimaginable that I had no right, actually, to feel anything about it, only to listen to that cry from the heart. "I tried for seventeen years to be a good nun . . . and failed. I promised myself never to tell anyone . . . But you, when you called me a saint . . . you cannot know what it means to have you as friend, the only real one I've made in this new life. I could not leave you under false pretenses. Conscience. *That* part of my past came out of convent with me. Now that I've told you, I've probably lost you as friend. Now you *know* what I am . . ." her voice dwindled to a shamed whisper. "A failure . . ."

I moved the concealing arm away from the woeful face that had not a wrinkle or a smile crease because for seventeen years a stiff white coif had uplifted all its lines.

"You idiot," I said gently. "How could you possibly think

you could lose me as friend because you left a convent? What do you take me for? One of those parochial-minded whom you've already *let put upon you* quite enough?" I answered the startled query in her blue eyes. "Shame for being humanly fallible is what I'm talking about. You *let* people put this on you, you let it be done to you *from the outside.*" I put out my hand. "If you'll sit up now like a human being with a backbone instead of lying out there like a sack of despair, I'll tell you more . . ."

And so began the long talks that were so full of wonder for me. What she related, diffidently at first, then with increasing trust and frankness, were detailed descriptions of a religious training, a discipline, a ceaseless struggle against her nature to attain an inner state that would be "pleasing to God" . . . echoes, it seemed so very often, of my own trials and failures when I was a struggling member of the Gurdjieff Rope. I always knew what questions to ask. It puzzled her at first that I had such a ready understanding of Detachment, of the Inner Life — the striving to achieve and perfect it. The discontinuous dialogue, picked up every time we were alone, was a visible catharsis for her, a revelation and a reminding factor for me. Often I slipped Gurdjieff's formulations into our talks; it did me a world of good to be able to speak in his language to someone once again.

The puzzling aspects of her personality became comprehensible now that I knew her past. Her choosing the most undesirable spot in the Jullouville dormitory to drop her duffle in (denial of creature comfort) ; her inability to say no to any request ("No is the *first* word you drop from your vocabulary in the convent") ; her frugal crumb-consumption at table (a studied avoidance of waste of God's daily-given bread) . . . as time went on, the odd bits and parts of her assembled into the nun's formation as she made me understand it, a formation from which she had never escaped. As I watched the emergence of that impregnable spiritual formation, it seemed to me that the only thing she had left behind her in the convent was the dress of her order.

"In the world . . ." was how Chouka referred to her present situation in contrast to her past. The phrase, unconsciously carried over from the cloister, always gave me a pang although I could not say why. "In the world" I became her self-appointed guardian, pledged to keep her secret. Wildflecken was our world peopled by UNRRA worldlings who had actively lived the events of the past seventeen years, and often talked about them. Chouka could be tripped up on any reference to famous names, events, books, plays and so forth, which at one time or another had dominated the world news since 1927, the year she entered the convent. I hovered always near her when the team was gathered for relaxation, ready to jump to her rescue if need be, but never letting her see that I was. She had a stiff Flemish pride about managing alone.

Because I was so keenly aware of her singular situation, I was doubly astonished that no one else on the team observed anything unusual about the Belgian nurse — especially when the mails came in. She drifted away from the excited huddle around the mail sacks, a fleeting look of longing in her eyes. She never received a letter, never waited about to hear if her name might be called. What friends she had were of course all in the cloister, cut off from communication with the one who had "gone out." I suspected that she had not sent her

APO address to her Belgian relatives (all practicing Catholics), thinking it was a charity to them not to be reminded that she was now "in the world." Privately, she assured me that letters really meant very little to her; after seventeen years of receiving letters which had always been opened and read first by her Superior, all sense of surprise was gone. Her letters had seemed to come to her secondhand *"pour ainsi dire,"* the edge of expectancy had long since dulled. I believed not a word of it. Her face very plainly said otherwise when I translated my mother's letters, sharing with her their homely delights and surprises — the first autumnal maple leaf picked up in Union Square, for example, or a swatch of material of the new dress she was having made.

Knowing that Christmas would be only a half holiday for me if Chouka received no box, I asked my mother to make one up for the little Belgian roommate who had become like a sister to me. "Put plenty of goodies from Chinatown in it, she adores everything you send from there. She needs flannel pajamas (same size I wear) and some 'long-handled' underwear . . ."

We had our first snow in early November. It changed the countryside overnight into a maddening beauty. The pines held great snow pads and the hills showed all the ski slopes which we had not noticed before, although we had often heard those Rhön Mountains called "the poor man's Alps." The younger Poles began skiing on the wooden skis Chouka had uncovered in the SS warehouses and subsequently, through Welfare, distributed to the DP's. Their thin bodies, swathed in ragged wool scarves borrowed from the grannies in their blockhouses, looked like blackbirds flying over the white slopes, uttering little windy cries *"Dobre . . . Dobre!"* (good, good!) for the first tangible good that "old aunty UNRRA" had produced for them, since food, clothing and medical care were now taken for granted.

The snows sealed us into our never-never land of the Displaced, about which the outside world knew almost nothing. Nor could any of us enlighten it. One of the commitments in accepting our UNRRA appointments was that there would be no writing about the work from the field, no stories or articles aimed for publication beyond what the UNRRA HQ saw fit to send forth through its lofty public relations staff that seldom got down to the grassroots. The restriction worked on my nerves, goaded me to silent fury every time I read an official press release based on faceless statistics. So many hundreds of thousands of Poles, Latvians, Lithuanians, Ukrainians, et cetera, still in the camps of the British, French and U.S. Zones, so many Polish repatriations from each of those zones as of such and such a date; the tormenting upheavals presented as a sort of international baseball score with the British Zone leading in repatriations, the U.S. Zone in food calories provided — 2000 per day for the non-workers, 3000 for heavy workers like wood choppers and truck drivers. Nothing in those scoreboard readings that touched the heart and told the story, no bodies behind the numbers.

No bodies of the UNRRA field teams were visible either in those statistical dispatches released from above. The area HQ's in Munich, Wiesbaden, Frankfurt appeared to be running the displaced show. I resented the anonymity of the grassroots workers as I resented the facelessness of the DP's behind the statistics. But only in the beginning months, only until the first blaze of selfless devotion to our common aim had burned itself out and the moral disintegration began in those unable to keep the fire burning. Then I thought it better that we remained unsung.

Our original two French drivers were the first to take off without authorization, without ever having given a sign that they had reached the point where they could not face another day of our forlorn life. They simply loaded up an UNRRA truck (with cases of filched DP rations, sacks of flour and their own greatly expanded personal duffle) and quietly rolled out of Wildflecken's main gate one night, presumably headed for Paris and their wives, with enough black-market goods aboard to assure them a fine head start toward resuming their normal lives again. The abrupt desertion stunned me more than Pierre. He called the drivers cretins for thinking they could get across the frontier without authorization papers, prophesied they would be picked up and thrown in the jug where they properly belonged. I had loved the two men — simple honest mechanics who had never before in their lives stolen anything. I could not imagine how such a despair, impelling them to such a sudden anarchy, could have crept into their hearts without any one of us, myself especially, even remotely aware. Later, I heard they were caught as Pierre had predicted and sent to an Army stockade for six months' detention.

As the winter clamped down with subzero freezes and longer lonelier nights, many of our men relieved their boredom, as well as their natural sex hunger, by taking mistresses. The only aspect of this that shocked me was that their mistresses came out of camp, Polish girls whom Welfare was trying to "rehabilitate." Their favors could be bought for a PX scarf, a box of chocolate bars, or even a good home-cooked meal with meat, such as our messing officer frequently prepared for his *"petite amie"* in the kitchen of his bachelor billets. Pierre laughed at my scruples, reminded me that after work hours each UNRRA officer's private life was strictly his own affair and that those Polish girls, who had already passed through the ranks of their conquerors and liberators — German, Russian, British, American — were probably finding it quite pleasant for a change, to "shack up" with domestic-minded civilians!

Chouka's reaction to our loose-living males revealed a tolerant worldliness that seemed oddly at variance with her cloistered past until she got around to telling me about the Belgian Congo where she had spent seven years of her nun's life as a nurse. *"Là . . . on voit tout!"* she said. Many of the Belgian *colons* took mistresses from among the Congolese natives, even when they had their own white wives with them. The only difference between there and here, she explained, was that any Belgian of official status who sired a mulatto in the bush was forced by public opinion to send his *café-au-lait* offspring home to Belgium to be reared and educated at his expense. *Naturellement,* such a costly penalty for profligacy did not in the least decrease the mulatto populaton in the colony, man being what he is — a phenomenon as familiar to her after those Congo years as were the maladies she had nursed — yaws, sleeping sickness, beri-beri. Wildflecken, apart from its maladies, often reminded her of the Congo. Our vast supine population being cared for paternally, our group of caretakers representing in general only mediocre intelligence, only average decency, exactly like any cross section of society anywhere, *n'est-ce pas?* Exactly like *"là-bas au Congo."*

Her observations about life had a keenness of perception, an unequivocal discernment, which sometimes made me feel

I had been born only yesterday. My old notions of nuns as delicate, shielded little beings pursuing the cloistered path toward saintliness vanished before Chouka's level-eyed views. In some way she seemed to have seen more of life than I, and seen it straighter, without shock or surprise for any of its shabby revelations. It was as if she, not I, had sat at a master's table year after year, to understand undeveloped man as he is — unawakened, uncontrolled and utterly predictable. For all my practical training under Gurdjieff, I could still be knocked off balance when trusted team members went suddenly wild. What *was* there, I wondered, in the shut-in atmosphere of the cloister that gave such deep knowledge about life?

There was a beauty in her former way of being, that much I understood, especially when Chouka recalled her Congo years. Those reminiscences, always fascinating, changed in tone as we approached the Christmas season, became a lovely counterpoint to the thunder of our endless truck arrivals bearing humans, bales of winter clothing, German potatoes or the Army's six hundred tons of monthly rations.

With Nanette long since moved to a gayer billet (where Tank Battalion officers were nightly entertained), Chouka and I had the immense officer's bedroom to ourselves. Talk came easily without listeners. I had only to say "Tell me more . . ." and she would describe the cloister processionals, the long white capes of the choir nuns bearing the doll figure of an Infant Jesus forward to the empty Manger, singing *"Minuit . . . Chrétiens!"* while they laid Him tenderly down.

"Christmas is always the happy time in convent," Chouka said, "a time of such purity of act, word and deed. Nothing you can imagine, nothing 'in the world' even faintly approaches *it*. Every heart lifts up in rejoicing at Midnight Mass when Christ is born again. Every Sister — even the vinegar-faced and there *are* some of those in every community — looks like a heavenly angel and sounds like one, though you never hear an individual voice when they chant, never any vainglorious soprano soaring ahead of her Sisters, just that flowing up of jubilation as from one throat . . . It's probably quite bizarre for someone like *me* to say, but I think I shall always be a bit homesick for the cloister when Christmas comes around . . . just that one time, when I remember what they make together, all those choir nuns, for God . . . *une cérémonie très touchante.* Last Christmas I was too busy with the buzz-bomb disasters to remember. But this year . . . You must keep me very busy then. Give me every extra task you can think of . . ."

Her nostalgia for the convent's "happy time" stirred my own memories of the one Christmas I had spent with Gurdjieff. No detail of that exceptional fête had ever dimmed despite the nine years that now separated me from it. And no Christmas since had ever given the same feeling of simple joy as when the master had turned us into children for a day and talked his "language of the smile" to us all.

I told Chouka that I had once participated in "a very touching ceremony" at Christmas, which had spoiled me for anything less. "I know what you mean by homesickness . . . but from the opposite end of *your* stick," I said. "Same stick, though — same canon, I'm beginning to think. We'll *both* keep busy this Christmas."

That Christmas of '45 was made to induce forgetfulness of any other Christmas anywhere. What we had all overlooked was that this was to be the first *free* Christmas in six years for our Poles, and that they would attempt to compress into it all the missed celebrations of their slave-labor years. Pierre, believing that all would be tranquil in camp, put in for a ten-day furlough in Paris, along with five other European officers whose homelands in Belgium, France and Holland were only a day's train travel from Frankfurt. They left us on Friday, December 21, a skeleton crew composed mainly of Canadians and Americans and a few Continentals like Chouka who for various reasons elected to stay inside Germany. Over that momentous weekend preceding the Tuesday Christmas, the holiday spirit exploded in the camp.

Schnapps stills bubbled illegally in blockhouse basements, frequently blew up in the faces of our ardent moonshiners. The nurses began filling their hospitals with cases of hideous facial burns which later (when the imperfectly distilled schnapps would be drunk) would be augmented by cases of methyl alcohol blindness.

The severest storm of the winter turned our Central Supply into an acre of solid ice on which no truck could move. We had to deliver a three-day ration of food to our DP's over the weekend before their holy trio of holidays began. From December twenty-fourth through the twenty-sixth (Feast of St. Stephen) not a Pole would attend to routine. Truckless, we organized our sixty Blockhouse Leaders into sled brigades to drag the contents of the Red Cross Christmas boxes over the ice and snow to their destinations. Sixty blockhouses were served, a hundred or more volunteers from each house dragged the homemade sleds back and forth, back and forth, and when the sleds broke down the clever Poles put wooden runners on their iron bedsteads and pulled them home with song. The processionals wound through our Siberian woods day and night, thousands of bent bodies linked as in chain gangs to the weird bedstead contraptions they dragged, singing always, singing courage and a second wind even into me as I watched what Poles could accomplish for themselves when they had a three-day celebration in view, their first in six years of anguish.

Most of our skeleton team, like myself, stayed on its feet over that wild weekend — Chouka on guard in her TB hospital from which her contagious open cases were attempting escape down ropes of knotted sheets to rejoin their families in the blockhouses for the holidays, the Canadian nurses on constant call in the Maternity where seven deliveries were pending, the handful of male officers in Transport and Supply working their DP gangs overtime to get enough firewood to the blockhouses to keep our population from freezing to death during the three holy days when all normal camp activity would come to a halt.

At midnight on Sunday the twenty-third our mission was accomplished. I padlocked the double doors of the Red Cross Parcel warehouse and drove slowly down the hill to the billets feeling as if I were coming home from all the wars. Chouka, having finally got locks on the windows of her contagious ward, was deep in her first sleep since the preceding Friday. She had left a night light burning so I would see the Deutschepost telegram propped up against it. It was addressed to me in a kind of German-English gibberish — MISS KAUHULWEEN, DIREKTOR, UNRA, WILDFLECKEN. The message was from the UNRRA Regional Office in Bamberg. Like a zombie I read the unbelievable news in peculiar typescript: 1000 POLS BEEING SCHIPPED FROM PASSAU DEZ 26

FOR WILDFLECKEN. WILL ADVICE ARIEVAL TIME WHEN POS-
SIBLE.

The Signal Corps field phone was far up the hill in
Pierre's office, but I took it to bed with me and battled my
way through its peeping cheeping lines, through Hickory to
Danube, through Danube to Dagwood which was Bamberg,
to tell those big brains at Regional level that not a hand
would be lifted in any Polish camp until after, repeat *after,*
St. Stephen's Day which was December 26, so how in hell do
you expect to load on the holy day? Change departure to
Thursday, December 27, then I can receive. *Do you hear me
Bamberg?*

There were the Christmas parties which we had to attend,
not because of the elaborate invitations the Poles sent to us,
but because we discovered that no party would start until
UNRRA appeared on the scene. Too many camp parties, too
few of us . . . we spaced ourselves out among the dances
and masked balls of hospital and school workers, of the
Police, the Wood Choppers, the Truck Drivers and, most
exhausting of all, the punch-drinking parties of the Organization of Former Concentration Camp Prisoners (Buchenwald and Dachau strictly, jealously apart in their separate
"clubs") where we drank their frightful pink punch laced
hotly with potato schnapps and whirled with their members
in polkas, mazurkas and fast Viennese waltzes until the tops
of our heads threatened to spin off . . . and I remember
telling my exhausted little UNRRA band again and again,
"Never mind, *it will all be over on the twenty-seventh* . . .
all will settle down to normal then!"

At dawn on the twenty-seventh of December, the Third
Army's first great search-and-seizure workout in the U.S.

Zone began — the surprise top-secret raid known as "Tally Ho." Every DP camp in the U.S. Zone was simultaneously surrounded by GI's in fur-lined parkas, and house-to-house searches began for the nameless treasures which the refugees were alleged to have amassed under UNRRA's benevolent protection. Our local tank battalion captain had the decency to rap me awake at five-thirty, to tell me that the raid in our camp would start in thirty minutes.

I gave the invading army a taste of the Crocodile that day. I lashed out at full "chicken" colonels for their stupidity in confiscating from our DP's the special Christmas ration we had so recently doled out to them. I chewed them up in shipyard language when they took me to the kangaroo court set up in the Polish Committee offices, and asked me to identify the "black marketeers" they had found with boxes of Jack Frost Sugar, Sun Maid raisins, tins of salmon and liver paste — the unconsumed delicacies from the Red Cross Parcel distribution which the provident were saving for their New Year parties. Every camp leader we needed for the incoming transport from Passau due that evening was pinned against the wall under martial arrest. When I felt something explosive happening in my brain, I took over from the frenzied Crocodile, changed rage to icy derision as I slowly intoned: "I *gave* that Red Cross stuff to our people over the past weekend, permission from higher echelons. *Authorized. SHAEF*-authorized, *get it?* Chocolate for the women, cigarettes for the men, raisins, biscuits and liver paste for all . . ."

Late that evening with the camp still under martial law and nobody but UNRRA allowed to enter or leave it, we received the transport with one thousand human souls, all alone. And once again, as in the beginning days, I saw our decimated team come together like a fist. The Belgian Supply and Messing officers, the Canadian nurses, Chouka, the Dutch transport man and the British welfare girl . . . a handful of broken reeds lashed together by a common aim — to make everything look natural and reassuring to the arriving DP's, always nervous and frightened when coming to a new camp — this time to a camp occupied by two full divisions of the American Army having a sporty practice workout in the techniques of search-and-seizure . . .

Chouka supplied the "idiot relief" I needed at the midnight end of the dreadful day. She got down to the billets ahead of me and was poking around rapturously in a Christmas box my mother had addressed to her which the maid had delivered to our room. The odd-shaped packages wrapped in goldleaf paper from San Francisco's Chinatown she had set aside to await my arrival for their opening. But she had already eaten her way half through the gay boxes of lichees, coconut curls and the Chinese watermelon candies which she loved. Her pale face flushed with delight when she told me that this was the first box she had ever received that had not been opened for inspection by a Reverend Mother; she was making its surprises last as long as she could hold herself in check.

"I only opened the things I knew about," she said. "All these delicious Chinese edibles . . . but you know, Katecha, there is *one* delicacy here I suppose one has to get used to, to like. I ate quite a bit of it . . . oh, please don't take this as any criticism of your wonderful mother's thought for me . . . but truly I think one has to acquire a taste for such an unusual sweetmeat . . ." And she held up before my eyes a piece of the incense that comes coiled like stiff brown spaghetti in octagonal boxes covered with Chinese script.

I kept my face straight as I told her, yes indeed, the taste for that particular delicacy was hard to come by, even among people of Chinese descent. "Because *that* delicacy, *mon amie*, is Chinese incense made no doubt from street sweepings of donkey dung, pulverized with a pinch of sandalwood and fashioned into that edible-looking spaghetti!"

And we began laughing together, laughing until the tears we had held back all day flowed down our faces.

I explained the term "idiot relief" to her that night, after I got my breath back. I began telling her a few things about Gurdjieff whom I had planned that she should meet one day.

CHAPTER FOURTEEN

M Y desire to have Chouka meet Gurdjieff increased as I tried to explain his teaching. Some aspects of it seemed, in my mind, to parallel her own experiences under the stern discipline of her Order's religious Rule; but I failed to make her see any resemblance whatsoever. I discovered how difficult it was to give any idea, to one who had not met the master, of the power of his transforming presence, the deep spirituality that emanated from him even in his worldly moods. When I went into details of his bounteous table, of his rounds of instructive Idiot toasts, or the self-revealing animal names by which he called some of his disciples — in short, the external *mise-en-scène* of his inner-world teaching — I saw by her face that nothing I was telling even faintly related to the struggle to become "part of God" as she had known its practice, as she still practiced it with an indestructible faith.

She wished, naturally, to understand what obviously meant much to me. Often she asked pointed questions which forced me to formulate, in terms comprehensible to her, the foundation principles of this *"travail sur soi-même"* that Gurdjieff taught — a nearly impossible task when all description of his practical inner-world exercises had, perforce, to be omitted. I

solved this problem by referring to them as "spiritual meditations," a term much too imprecise for the facts, but one
which apparently conveyed some meaning to her.

Often when we argued amiably, she from her end of the
stick and I from mine (but same stick, same canon always, I
insisted) I saw her eyes stray to the photograph I had hung
on the wall. It was an enlarged candid photo of Gurdjieff,
taken in his younger days, possibly somewhere in the Caucasus, showing him seated on the ground against a background of leafless trees, a black-and-white cat arching under
the caress of his left hand while two large dogs lolled
playfully beside him on the right. He wore a tall turban of
black astrakhan and a striped wool coat buttoned to the neck,
a Turkish-looking outfit. But it was the expression on his
face that caught you — benevolent, Nature loving, with a
hint of amusement in the tilt of his eyes as if he were talking
to the dogs, telling them that he understood perfectly their
wish to get at that cat but that he expected from them the
obedience he had taught — simply to lie there and look at it
across his knees. *Just look and long,* his face seemed to say.
He had given a copy of the disarming photograph to each on
the Rope at one of our last group meetings in the Paris
flat.

"He won't look like that when you see him," I told
Chouka. "He is heavier now, older, and that black moustache
is gray . . ."

Through the spring of '46 I kept on the lookout for a
break in the momentum of camp life which would enable
me, with a clear conscience, to put in for Paris leaves for
Chouka and myself. Our team had doubled in number, a

strength now of twenty-four officers with only Pierre, Chouka, the Dutch Supply man and myself left of the original twelve who had come here the summer before. Yet even with the reinforcements the daily tasks never diminished; if anything they multiplied. With nothing but time on their hands, our restless Poles began slipping out of camp to do a little cattle rustling around the remote German villages to the west, the hunger for fresh meat driving them into risky sorties. Often they were shot at by Germans, occasionally killed. Rumors of SS regroupings resulted from these excursions "outside"; the returning Poles swore they had seen Germans in the SS black jackets with stiff-braided military cuffs in the woods. The bogeylore of Wildflecken now had phantom SS men added to the processional of nightmare creatures that haunted Polish dreams, led always by the Russian Bear, the most fearsome of all. When we finally got the SS hysteria calmed down, a voice from the other side of the world shocked our population into a wilder panic.

Churchill made his "Iron Curtain" speech in Fulton, Missouri, warning the world of the expansive tendencies of the USSR and calling for a closer alliance between Britain and the United States. The Poles caught every word of it on the powerful radios they had set up in camp. Even before Stalin's reply lashed back over Radio Moscow, they began packing their bags. Rumors that Wildflecken would be evacuated ran through the camp — all too believable, since the Russian Zone was only twenty miles as the crow flies from the camp's eastern boundary. The Polish leaders besieged us in our headquarters — professors, doctors, priests, schoolteachers, bigwigs of the Polish Committee, all our Warsaw elite who spoke fluent French and had salon manners. They asked, through their stuttering spokesman, for some kind of reassurance to take back to the mass meeting gathered in the camp's main square.

Pierre blustered and bullied, in a louder voice than usual, because he also was afraid. But beyond repeating that the camp was *not* evacuating and that UNRRA *was* staying, he could find nothing more reassuring to say. Then the field phone on his desk rang urgently. Pierre took the message over long distance, said "Yes, yes, I have got it. March twenty-seventh at eleven hours . . ." and hung up. His face told me that the mysterious *deus ex machina* which always operated to save our skins had operated once again in our behalf.

The message was the proof that Army did not consider Wildflecken to be a danger spot, he said, else why would they be sending us one thousand *more* DP's? He began to roar with relief. "One thousand incoming Poles in exactly three days' time! Get yourselves back to your posts. Start the machinery to receive them. *En marche! Vite!*" And the leaders marched back into camp bearing the good news on their faces.

Tension in the camp subsided. Casualties from the panic were two suicides attributed to fear and three miscarriages in women who had shoved too much heavy luggage around. I began planning for an Easter furlough in Paris with Chouka. I thought of Notre Dame Cathedral, what it would mean to her to have her first Easter Mass "in the world" in that place of Gothic splendor and rainbow lights, instead of in the bleak camp church, in a former German workshop with factory-like windows shedding a cold white light on a home-made altar flanked by two paper cutouts of the crowned white eagle of Poland. Notre Dame and then Gurdjieff; I linked the two shrines in my mind.

But over that Easter season I was in a boxcar riding to Poland with the first transport of repatriates to leave the U.S. Zone that year. A latent result of the Churchill broadcast had been a severe drop in the number of voluntary repatriates we expected to sign up for the transport. I had offered myself to the bewildered authorities as a sort of live bait to encourage more signatures on the repatriation rolls. With the promised presence of one of their own UNRRA officers as escort, the repatriates' signatures rose from an initial 89 to 220, a touching sign of trust in a familiar presence which compensated considerably for another postponement of the Paris pilgrimage.

I made some enlightening self-discoveries on that trip. After ten days in a boxcar riding home with my Poles across Czechoslovakia to Dziedzice, Poland (and back again in the empty cars to Germany), I had not only run the gamut of DP emotions but had let them become my own. With DP eyes of fear I had looked out of my boxcar at each border crossing, expecting to see a Russian bogeyman in gray ankle-length greatcoat with stiff epaulets emerge from the customs sheds, bear paw outstretched to confiscate the repatriates' hoard of UNRRA foods, chocolates and cigarettes. I had gazed at the first pale green grain fields of Poland through DP tears of homecoming joy and sung their thanksgiving hymns when at last we pulled safely into our destination town all flag-draped for us and gaily postered with promises believable because I wanted them to be: *Welcome to Poland! We will all work together!*

With DP delight I had discovered that one American

cigarette was worth six zlotys, sixty cents, inside the homeland, and I bartered (with my own PX cigarettes) as lustily
as any repatriate through the small shops for books and art
crafts to take back to Wildflecken (to prove that Poland was
a going concern) and for a bottle of genuine Polish vodka to
take back for Gurdjieff — to prove, I supposed, that the
Crocodile remembered him even in my wildest swing away
from the teaching presumed to be part of me. *Never let the
emotions lead you into Self-forgetting. Never lose Self with
the mind.*

I was as empty as the boxcar which rolled me back to
Germany, a Crocodile coming home from an emotional
spree. The bottle of Polish vodka in my bedroll was the only
evidence that I had had one moment of remembering both
self and source.

Chouka and Johnny, our Norwegian welfare worker, escorted the second transport to Poland carrying only 154
repatriates. Despite my stumping of the camp with hallelujah
accounts of the total absence of any signs of Communism in
their land, our DP's hung back as if they knew there was
another side to the bright coin I presented — as indeed there
was. Chouka brought it back in a report that sounded as if
she had gone to a totally different country than the Poland I
had looked at through rose-colored glasses.

Chouka of course had no crocodile to contend with, no
past that encouraged emotional response to any situation. She
had arrived in Poland the day after the big May Day celebrations had left every town through Czechoslovakia strung
with scarlet hammer-and-sickle banners, and she knew, like
an old Underground hand, what to look for inside Poland —
evidence of partisan activities. Behind the cheering pavilions

of the Polish Repatriation Committee in Dziedzice, she found the "little people" who would not talk above a whisper but would point out for her certain "Polish" workingmen who were Russian agents in disguise. She visited not the false-front book and art shops I had patronized, but the shabby little food shops that told the real story of inside Poland, pricing the sky-high foodstuffs on sale, especially lard. Her nurse's eyes had quickly spotted the excessively dry skins of children and adults which denoted lack of fats in the diet. With lard selling for four hundred zlotys the kilo (twenty dollars the pound) the prevalence of the dry skins was explained.

As I helped her translate her practical observations into English (for UNRRA HQ and the Displaced Persons Officer, 15th Infantry Regiment, Schweinfurt), I wished that my own earlier repatriation report, singing optimism from every line, might be withdrawn. Here was the level-eyed factual account I should have written. One of her paragraphs reporting activities after her DP's had been handed over to the receiving committee told me where I should have been at that same time on my trip (instead of embracing my Poles in tearful farewells): "Later, our train pulled out of Dziedzice station to a spot about two kilometers down the line where boxcars were cleaned. Here all sorts of people gathered, mostly poor barefoot types hoping to pick up some food scraps. A very old woman, one of the yard cleaners, told us in broken German that she lived almost entirely on what she picked up from these transports. Her husband, she said, died in Buchenwald and she received a pension of one hundred zlotys monthly from the government (ten dollars), hardly one day's living expenses."

Even the photographs she had brought back told a clearer

story than mine. Instead of wasting film (as had I) on farewell parties in the Dziedzice station, focusing on ex-DP's waving from windows of railway cars placarded Cracow, Katowice, Warsaw, Chouka had made documentary shots of the look of a Polish city — store fronts, municipal buildings, postboxes on street corners, familiar civic sights to suggest a familiar continuing government. After her film was developed in Wildflecken, we made a great poster display of the prints to encourage signatures for the next transport. One of her admirable shots, a postbox on a pillar, brought the repatriation movement to a standstill with its truth unperceived by us. It was not the familiar postbox our DP's had known, with the crowned eagle of Poland embossed on the face of it. Chouka's postbox showed the eagle all right, but without its customary crown. The Communists had uncrowned the sacred symbol of Old Poland, of the *only* Poland our refugees would return to voluntarily.

Soon after, when the higher echelons of Army and Military Government began "exploratory talks" on forcible repatriation, I put in leave requests for Chouka and me. I would have no part in any forcible repatriation of the people we had fought the war to free. I dared not be around when such a colossal injustice was being discussed. Even the echoes of it filtering down to the field in the Army-jargon directives we called "poop" drove up my blood pressure.

We got away on furlough by the middle of June. The military train out of Frankfurt, reserved exclusively for the uniformed forces, went with priorities straight through to Paris. The desolate DP-land we had left behind became more unbelievable with every mile speeding west. After we crossed the frontier into Lorraine, it ceased to exist — like a bad dream which one escapes by waking up.

I began again to prepare Chouka for Gurdjieff. I tried to make my reflections sound objective, told her the conflicting impressions he often made on newcomers, that she must not be surprised to hear him call me Crocodile, the only name by which he knew me. How, she asked wonderingly, could a woman of my intelligence accept such a denigrating sobriquet? Even appear, *ma foi!*, to enjoy being called that? I launched into an exposition of man's inner nature as the master saw it in each one of his disciples and sometimes named it, but only *sometimes,* to help someone, in Paulist phrasing, struggle with the "Old Adam within."

"*My* Old Adam is a crocodile, a thing that lies most of the time deep in mud, only snout and eyes protruding . . . a creature with a tough hide and terrible endurance." I told her how I used to visit the crocodile ponds in every zoo I could get to, staring down at the hideous somnolent beast and taking new resolves each time not to let such a monster run my life *its* way, but to tame it and use it for *my* way. I succeeded in confusing my companion to the point of begging to be let off from the proposed meeting. She reminded me that except for the people she worked with daily, like our UNRRA comrades back in Germany, she was still shy in the presence of strangers; moreover, after her long discipline in verbal silence, she had no small talk.

"One doesn't small-talk with Gurdjieff . . . one *listens!*" I said. "Don't disquiet yourself in advance. He'll not be anything like what you may imagine . . . but you'll know, I believe, that you are in the presence of a truly remarkable man. At least, I hope so . . ."

I hoped so because I had the feeling that a long rough road lay ahead of us in Germany. It would be easier to travel it with a comrade to whom I could speak openly of the inner things that mattered most to me. Gurdjieff was the reference point, the source of the only Reality I knew. As Chouka had shared with me her religious past, so I wished to share with her the formative factor of my private secular life. I watched her yield because she could never say No.

"But you would not tell him," she asked, "that I was once a nun?" She still felt the same old anxiety, the same old shame for imagined failure.

"I need only say when I telephone to him, May I bring one friend, Mr. Gurdjieff? That is the formula. Friend is enough. Trust me . . ." I smiled and suppressed the rest of my thought. Gurdjieff would know her past with his first penetrating glance at her inner world.

I had never in all the years of association with Gurdjieff brought any new people to him. Wendy was no exception. She and I had chanced upon him together and together had always been received, almost like a single person with two contrasting natures and potentialities. In the active time of the Rope, Solita and Miss Gordon had occasionally introduced newcomers to his table, friends of the kind I did not possess, people dissatisfied with the lives they were leading.

Having no data on bringing a stranger to Gurdjieff, the emotions I experienced after telephoning to him took me completely by surprise. I telephoned to him from our hotel on the evening of our arrival in Paris, was given an appointment for two o'clock the next afternoon in the flat. My inner commotion was different from the usual excitement at the thought of seeing Gurdjieff once again. A faint edge of anxiety seemed to be part of it. Only after I was in bed and making ready to do my exercises quietly in the dark did the preposterous cause of my excited-anxious state become apparent.

Some old *hausfrau* self seemed to have put on a mob cap and taken possession of me. It ran ahead to the flat to polish up the handle of the big front door, to dust around a bit in the cluttered interior and get a crack of window open to air the muttony odors out of the salon. It wanted to make that hard-lived-in flat, that anachronism of Oriental-Victorian, as attractive as possible for my friend's eyes so that she would understand why, to me, it always seemed a sort of shrine! I laughed quietly to myself as I banished the *hausfrau* idiocy. It was on a par with exhibiting domestic concern for the setting around the Sphinx when taking someone to see it for the first time . . . all that untidy sand, those scabby beggars and mangy camels . . . !

Nevertheless, as I climbed the apartment stairs the next afternoon, clutching the bottle of Polish vodka in one hand and leading the reluctant Chouka behind me with the other, I saw all the threadbare spots in the stairway carpeting and counted the missing tread rods. How I wished that I was a millionaire who could have produced for the master a more "corresponding" establishment, that "more solid place" he had once talked of in the old days when I had thought Wendy might be the one to supply it.

Chouka watched me ring the bell. The external signs of quickening heartbeat she studied perhaps looked like anxiety to her, but they were only the usual manifestations of the Crocodile coming "home." The master was smiling when he

opened the door. I introduced Chouka —"Friend, Mr. Gurdjieff, one who works with me in Germany, a nurse," and
watched her put forth her hand to give him a firm Belgian
handshake which broadened his welcoming smile.

He led us directly to his spice pantry which I had not yet
described to Chouka; nor had I thought to explain that this
depot of comestibles represented in large measure gifts from
"his people" all over the world who, when some rare new
product came on the market, always remembered him, his
vast disciple dinners and the strange unheard-of-delicacies he
often served, always boasting, straight-faced, that they had
been sent to him from "the Planet Karatas."

The spice pantry was now a Lucullan treasure room, its
tiers of shelves stacked with boxed, bagged and tinned
goods, while overhead hung from the ceiling were garlands
of spice bouquets, strung red peppers and imported sausages
of every size and color. Gurdjieff smiled when he saw the
expression on my friend's face. Her nunlike aversion to
ostentation of any sort, particularly to such a gourmet display
as this, was plain to my eyes before she collected herself.
Gurdjieff winked at me, a hint of mischief in his face, as if
he saw what I saw underlying Chouka's astonishment.

We sat opposite him at the little coffee table. He now had a
Turkish coffee in his Thermos and, as he poured, he advised
Chouka to wait for the grounds to settle before drinking, else
they would make "a big scandal" in her throat. The un-
shaded light bulb over the table cast shadows down from his
jutting brows to his great silver moustache. I hoped Chouka
saw the beauty and the power in that musing face, smiling
benevolently as he studied her inwardly for a moment, just
long enough to pass her her cup, long enough for him. Then
he turned his attention to me.

"And so . . . Kroko-deel! How *is* . . . in Gair-*man*ia?"

I told him "how is" in his own idiom. I described my trip into Poland — "like hopeless idiot, Mr. Gurdjieff" — imagining I could encourage home-going among Poles who already knew that Communism had crept into their country, a fact I had missed altogether. "Poland has *auspicious* exterior," I said and he nodded for the unspoken "and *suspicious* interior" which his familiar aphorism implied. I spoke as if alone with him, telling how, in the climate of negative emotions in which I labored, I'd had to begin from the beginning in the Work, to train my nature to stand apart and not identify with every crying Pole around me. I confessed that I was not very successful, a redundant remark under his all-seeing eyes. "But you *try*," he said after a long pause, "you go on trying?"

"Like *red-faced donkey*, Mr. Gurdjieff!" I said fervently and made him laugh for that comical picture he had once made of the *way* I worked on myself . . . the wrong way!

It was all Greek to Chouka but now I felt no concern. I had got her this far, within sight of the master — "a very wise old man sitting in his rich pantry of foods and thoughts," as Janet Flanner had described him in her first letter to the Rope after her return to France. I glanced at my companion sitting very straight on the small chair beside me gazing at Gurdjieff with a puzzled expression. In my gladness for my present situation and its future prospects, I suddenly brought up from the floor the bottle of Polish vodka and set it on the table with a flourish. "The only *good* thing I brought out of Poland, Mr. Gurdjieff!"

He looked from the bottle to me as if surprised; then a mocking expression came over his face. The ageless eyes glinted in readiness for "play," his kind of play that never hurt but always taught. I knew the look; he was going to show me up before my friend and also show himself as the opposite of all I had claimed him to be.

He stood up and took the bottle of vodka from the table. He winked at Chouka, nodded toward me and said, *"Look* what crocodile she is, Miss! She makes *big* ceremony for bringing one speciality she thinks does not exist in Mr. Gurdjieff's pantry!" He went to the shelf behind his chair, pushed away a large carton and exhibited at least a half dozen liters of vodka standing in rows with a dozen other bottles of the "esteemed liquors" for his toasts — Marc, Armagnac, Calvados. He gestured from them to me with a pitying expression and sighed heavily as he thrust my single bottle onto the crowded shelf. The cartons of cigarettes I had also brought, hoarded through months of self-denial of my PX ration, he tossed on another shelf that had American cigarettes stacked like cordwood. "She *also* thinks, Miss," he grinned at Chouka, "that I do not already have very *very* good relations with the American Army!"

His humorous act made the day for me and all but wrecked it for Chouka. Indignation flashed in her eyes as she looked at me, the victim of the most dreadful display of ingratitude she had ever witnessed. How could I accept such treatment? How could I ever have seen Godliness in this mocking man? Her face reflected sorrowing sympathy for me, for my benighted belief in him as a teacher.

That I was laughing appreciatively for the lesson he had given me, cutting my obvious pride down to size with his famous ridicule, was completely incomprehensible to her. Later, I could tell her that I had it coming to me. I could admit that I *had* had a secret pride about that bottle of vodka hauled half across Europe for him. I could explain that what she had witnessed was not a "humiliation" but only a prod at the same old weak spot the master had been poking at for years, but seldom quite as amusingly as this time. This is one of the ways he teaches, *mon amie* . . .

Gurdjieff returned to the table amused for having so easily "put me in galoshes" — his term for showing up the boastful. He carried two boxes of sweetmeats, one of *loucoum* and one of chocolate creams, which he proceeded to divide with exactness. He continued smiling as he patted the candies into place, flakes of cigarette ash now and again dropping down over the boxes. Occasionally he gave Chouka a sly smile, as if only he and she were capable of understanding the anomaly I represented. I saw Chouka relax under the magic of his "language of the smile." He was the grandfather image now, a bit untidy with his cigarette. I heard a kind of phlegmy rattle in his respiratory passages, not a very healthy sound I thought with a pang. He appeared wearier than when we had come in, but it was, I remembered, the hour for his customary after-lunch siesta. His hands moved ever more slowly from box to box, transferring, patting down, making each piece fit precisely. The silence in the pantry hummed with his heavy breathing. Presently his great head sunk slowly forward until his chin came to rest on his chest. He appeared to have fallen asleep.

I signaled my startled friend to sit quietly. I had seen these brief naps before. He came back from them like Antaeus, stronger for having touched the ground. As I contemplated that shaven dome of wisdom tipped toward us, I tried to imagine its inner treasures not meant for our ignorant eyes. So I had always looked at Gurdjieff, I reflected — *from the outside,* the knowledge stored away in that monumental skull, inaccessible to a limited understanding. I must remember to tell Chouka that his kind of knowledge had been built with conscious purpose by conscious artisans into many of the world's great edifices, such as Constantinople's mosque of Santa Sophia. Beneath its golden dome, he had said, there was such a high vibration that even a donkey, led into its interior, could feel "something holy."

Chouka was looking at the master with unconcealed compassion for his seemingly exhausted state. She was the nurse now, listening to that labored breathing. She whispered to me, *"On doit partir, . . . il est très fatigué . . ."* and at that moment Gurdjieff opened one eye, looked sideways at her. His face came alive with a slow spreading smile that lifted up all its tired lines. He nodded at Chouka and said hoarsely in French: *"Petite Soeur de ——,"* naming her former religious Order exactly.

He was dozing again when we tiptoed out of the pantry clutching the candy boxes he had thrust wordlessly toward us across the table. Traces of the cunning smile he had given me after indentifying my friend were still visible on his sleeping face.

Down in the street, I said what I thought Chouka wanted to hear, to put her at ease. "That, of course, could have been pure coincidence. Little Sister of the Poor, of the Sacred Heart, of Charity, of Mercy . . . any one of those could have fitted your compassionate aside to me. He just happened to light on the one that was yours . . ." But I believed otherwise. Nothing ever "just happened" with Gurdjieff. He always knew. Though I had anticipated that he would know Chouka's religious past, he had taken me by complete surprise when, out of a possible fifty female Orders dedicated to good works and charitable thoughts, he had named point-blank her precise Order. It was as if, looking at her, he had seen framing that pointed face the distinctive white coif starched stiff to make the veil fall in its distinctive identifiable way . . .

"Coincidence . . . oui," Chouka was still a bit shaken by the encounter. *"Oui, peut-être . . ."* she said as if talking to herself. *"Quand-même . . . c'est curieux . . ."*

We walked in silence toward the Etoile, each with her private thoughts. I laughed inwardly, remembering Gurdjieff's tired smile of cunning that plainly told of his pleasure at having put me "in galoshes" twice in one hour — once for my coals-to-Newcastle presents, once for my friend whose qualifications I had so discreetly withheld from him!

CHAPTER FIFTEEN

THAT first sortie outside Germany made everything on the inside seem sadder, yet in one sense more bearable. The discovery that life beyond our battered frontiers had begun to resume its normal pace made our upside-down world of the Displaced seem more a passing phenomenon than a permanent distortion of hundreds of thousands of human lives for which (as despair had often tempted us to believe) no solution or amelioration would ever be found.

My visits with Gurdjieff (I had gone back to him twice while on furlough) had sharpened my thoughts about the "humanity-ness" he exemplified. With fresh eyes I saw our United Nations workers as practitioners of the lost cause of brotherhood in their daily lives — *engagés,* as artists use that nearly untranslatable word, in pawn, committed. We were (though such a continuity was then quite unimaginable) the precursors of the worldwide movement in humanitarianism which would appear fifteen years later as the Peace Corps.

The volume of our labor and the depth of our commitment to it was expressed in one of the round-robin letters I regularly produced for family and friends, notes for the DP book I hoped one day to write:

As we approach our one-year anniversary of arrival in Wildflecken (August 4th, 1946) we begin to see something of the long view of events that have happened here. I noted the other day that since we have been here 79,000 DP's have been admitted to or evacuated from this camp. I stared a long time at that unexpected total. In it I saw all the reasons for our deep fatigue. We have had to pay out the milk of human kindness to 79,000 transients in the past twelve months, while simultaneously caring for the 12,000 "unrepatriables" who live here all the time. It's a fair job, as the English say, quite a little show in itself. Most of the workers left in the field are like me. They care about people as persons and they give a lot to each. There wasn't one of the 35,000 Poles who left Wildflecken in the past year who did not have special clothes for departure, goodies for the children, some of our PX chocolate bars in his luggage and, at last — whether he went by truck or boxcar — a great goodbye from us all . . . *Dobre zehn* . . . until we meet again. How many promises did I make to visit them in Poland when all this is over? How many tears, not crocodile, have I shed seeing trusting faces calling farewells from cattle-car doors? There wasn't one of the 44,000 DP's transferred into Wildflecken in these past twelve months who lacked care and attention. I speak about the *little things* — his food, billeting and medical needs were taken care of automatically. I speak of writing letters to other camps, inquiring for a missing mother, sister, brother of a new arrival. I speak of writing to GI's demobilized in the States for help for the DP girls left behind who are carrying their babies. There were thousands upon thousands of *little* things to do always, for 79,000 displaced persons . . .

Everybody had acquired some kind of domestic pet before the end of that first year in the field. The cats and dogs which my frazzled team comrades began to collect gave them at the end of their momentous days the most superb "idiot relief" of all. The men on the team preferred the larger breeds — German shepherds, Dobermans, boxers; the women the smaller — dachshunds, miniature schnauzers, and cats of all stripes.

Chouka came down from camp one night carrying a small white kitten — a gift from one of her Polish nurses. She was transformed with the joy of the born animal lover who at last had a pet of her own. We named the kitten Framboise, because of her raspberry nose and paw pads, and soon that small pink-and-white ball became our center of gravity in all off-duty hours. Shortly after the advent of Framboise, I gave her the pet I knew she yearned for — a pedigreed German shepherd dog such as her father loved, the only breed he considered truly noble, the dog of her childhood. I found a proper puppy in the bombed-out city of Schweinfurt, in a German kennel which despite all the wreckage and starvation of war had managed to keep its shepherd bloodlines pure. I bought him for two cartons of cigarettes, *"mitt papieren."* These pedigree papers named him Lummel von der Wanderschaefferei — Lummel signifying "lummox" in German, a homely endearing name that fitted him perfectly. He was fawn-colored with a coal black mask, just seven weeks old. I brought him home after one of my day-long trips down to Wurzburg to fetch the team's PX ration. Chouka and Framboise were waiting for me on the balcony that overlooked the UNRRA billet street. I heard her startled cry as I got out of the truck carrying the puppy. She rushed down into the street to meet me and when I laid Lummel in her arms, it was as if I had given to her every worldly joy she had done without during her seventeen years vowed to poverty, chastity and obedience.

So began for us what I call "the time of the pets," a time that was not to end for the five years we remained in Germany.

Early in 1947 UNRRA began to reduce its staff of 25,000 officers in preparation for the closeout of the organization on June thirtieth. A "temporary specialized agency of UN" called IRO (International Refugee Organization) was to take over the unfinished DP business. Terminations started to filter down to the field by February. Each time a team comrade went home (with cat or dog or both) the rest of us took over his or her job since there was no appreciable diminution of the DP population.

After Pierre left, I was sure I would be the next on the list; deputy directors were not featured in IRO's job categories. I told Chouka that I would go promptly to work on the long overdue book which would tell the truth about the gallant field teams, the backbone of the UNRRA ideal. I had a sense of mission about this, especially after *Life* magazine published an editorial celebrating the coming end of UNRRA. The piece was captioned "GET A HORSE" and although it called UNRRA "the most ambitious humanitarian effort ever undertaken by mankind," it went on to explain how it had been "cursed with inefficiency" and was "licked before it got fairly started." It cited the shiploads of UNRRA supplies to Italy, Greece, China, Yugoslavia and Poland, much of which had either gone down the drain into black markets or had disappeared behind the Iron Curtain. No reference was made to the human side of that relief picture; the small vital segment of the huge UNRRA operation known as "Displaced Persons Mission in Germany" was not even mentioned. I seethed for days after reading it and lay awake nights writing the book I had lived in sweat and tears, unaware that I had lived only the first easy chapters of it.

In early March, instead of being terminated, I was promoted to the post of director of the Aschaffenburg camps, replacing two male directors who had been moved into other areas. The Aschaffenburg camps were "static camps," populated mainly by Ukrainians, Estonians and Belo- or White Russians, all unrepatriables whose homelands were now in Stalin's pocket. The day before my transfer became effective, I drove over to Aschaffenburg to receive from one of the departing directors a casual briefing on the setup of my new territory. Though only two and a half hours by motor from Wildflecken, Aschaffenburg was like another planet in the refugee system, far from the wildness and unpredictability of my vast Polish camp. It had an old established look; its mood was sit-down, wait-and-see. The total population of its seven scattered camps was only nine thousand but it comprised five distinct national groups, all organized like little Tammany Halls, all bristling with national antagonisms.

I drove back to Wildflecken for the last time, with a stone in my heart. It was two years too late to be able to say *We will not identify.* I was identified with every pine tree in my mountain camp, with every blue-eyed Pole who sneaked out to commit mayhem in the cow towns roundabout, with every newborn Polish baby to whom I was godmother. And above all, closest to my heart, was my strange little family — a Belgian nurse, a German shepherd dog and a royal alley cat.

Framboise came halfway down the billet stairs to meet me, purring all the way. Chouka was waiting in the room, her bird face sharp and white, with Lummel leaning hard against her knees. He had known for days that something dreadful was happening.

"I'll get you all over there," I said to them. "By God I will . . . it's the pound of flesh I'll demand from this dying old UNRRA in return for what it asks *me* to do . . . *to begin again* at this late date . . ." I choked, unable to go on. Chouka sent Lummel to comfort me and went to prepare our last nightly drink together.

Through my tears I watched her set out a tin of PX grapefruit juice, the bottle of London Dry Gin from our last liquor ration, a tray of fresh eggs which her Polish driver regularly brought her. "Two *coups de gin* this time," she said; "*on les mérite.*" She poured two ounces for each with her nurse's measuring eye, went out on the balcony and scooped snow into the shaker with the beaten eggs, fruit juice and gin, shook, then poured the golden froth into two glasses already chilled. I thought what a long way "in the world" she had come since that day so long ago when she had sobbed for her "failure." She no longer needed protection of any sort from me; she had completely caught up on the ways of the world, even to the point of playing bartender. "We've come a long way together, *mon amie,*" I said as we touched glasses. Her eyes were clouded with domestic worries — Would I remember my trenchcoat when riding in open jeeps? . . . Who would find the reading glasses I was always misplacing? . . . Who would see that I ate properly? — but she did not speak of these things.

"I'll pray for you each night, Kate-cha," she said softly. "I'll ask the Blessed Virgin to watch over you." She gave me a nunlike smile secure in the assurance that her petition would be granted, as if that request would be going forth to a very personal friend who could deny her nothing. We drank the fizzes slowly while Lummel and Framboise entertained us with a hissing yelping wrestling match on the floor.

I looked around at all I would be leaving early next morning — the dear familiar room, a trusted friend, my two pets, and I began to talk like a martyr.

Chouka put a fresh glass in my hand. "Here, drink this," she said sternly. "Weren't *you* the one who called self-pity the most depleting of all the negative emotions? All your cherished Gurdjieff teachings . . . is *this* how you practice what he preached?" She had flecks of fizz foam on her lips as she scolded me out of my low mood. As once, long ago, I had helped her, so now, "as hand washes hand," she uplifted me. She spoke proudly of my promotion and of the challenge of the new job which I would pick up with ease. "After all we've gone through here, Aschaffenburg will seem like a tea party," she said.

I drove away before sunrise the next morning so I would not have to say goodbye to the team. Chouka stood on the balcony with Framboise in her arms and Lummel, forepaws on the railing, close beside her, was nearly as tall as she. I did not look back after the barricade of the main gate dropped behind me.

In the pocket of my battle jacket I had the schedule of my day's activities in Aschaffenburg which I had blocked out very simply the night before:

1. See the Ukrainian Police, make friends.
2. See the Orthodox priests,   "   "
3. See the National Group Leaders, make friends *if* you can.
4. Speak with the office staff without whose help you will sink.

I made up the speeches I would give to each group as I drove through the waking countryside. Police Chiefs first. The DP police of Aschaffenburg, organized like a para-military outfit, had been the special "baby" of the preceding male directors. To win them over to a woman boss, I would have to talk and act like a man. Not too difficult for me, I reflected, after that year and a half of man's work in the shipyards . . .

I might not have remembered the momentum of my first week in Aschaffenburg had I not preserved in a hasty round-robin some of its highlights:

My week started off with three of the most astonishing days. On the first day, the CIC (Counter Intelligence Corps) came to visit me, to warn me specifically about several of my office staff on whom I had already begun to depend. On the second day the French nurse on the team (a magnificent workhorse whom Chouka knew and for whom she had said prayers of thanksgiving that I had a stalwart aid beside me) came to my room, told me she had been secretly married to a DP, had known herself to be pregnant since January and now was about to have a miscarriage! I called for an Army ambulance and escorted her myself to Frankfurt. The third day, the Army detachment in Wurzburg telephoned to ask me to billet in our UNRRA house three enlisted men and one sergeant for the night, which I agreed to do, until I heard further that those GI's were coming up here with 5000 pounds of TNT (for a demolition squad working in the region) which I was expected to keep in an UNRRA warehouse with a detachment of my DP police to stand guard. That was the first time in those first days that I really sounded female. I shrieked like a harpy into the field phone, refusing to take responsibility for security in my area with 5000 pounds of TNT under the surveillance of a DP police that was looking at a new woman commander with crafty measuring eyes, not yet convinced she meant business. My high-pitched cries of dismay got me off that TNT hook and fast!

The thorny experience of the ambulance ride to Frankfurt with a team sister having a hemorrhage resulted in the eventual transfer of Chouka to Aschaffenburg to replace the French nurse now invalided home. Since Chouka was attached to my team without any request or intervention on my part, I took her coming as a sign that I really had one of those guardian angels, which Catholics always spoke of with such confidence, watching over my personal affairs — even over my professional affairs. Chouka arrived just before the camps' Orthodox Easter celebrations, in time to school me on how to behave in the presence of the bearded archbishops in magenta robes and gold miters. With the total camp population watching every gesture of their new director, I could not afford a false move in any direction, including the ecclesiastical.

Now that my trusted confidante was at my side (and Lummel and Framboise to complete the picture) I felt able to face the upheaval of UNRRA's phase-out in the summer and the uncertainties of continuance with the shadowy new IRO that would have to operate the same mass-relief program on a beggar's budget. The shrinkage of the Aschaffenburg team was an index of what was going on all over the U.S. Zone. Instead of the score of UNRRA officers who had previously supervised the seven camps (spread out through the town and into the valleys on the other side of the River Main), I had exactly two females, Chouka and a Norwegian welfare girl, and one Belgian supply man to do the job. Fortunately we were all seasoned, having been with the program since its inception. In my prejudiced eyes, my small band was the cream that remained after many waves of "reduction in force" had passed over us.

Long before my appointment to the International Refugee Organization came through (May of '47) I felt that, if asked, I might have no choice but to remain in the sorry "DP business" to the bitter end. All personal ambitions, even my driving desire to get back to writing and the Gurdjieff work, were as nothing before the needs of the refugees we served. My own individuality was submerged in the human mass about me. The slow smiles I knew how to bring to the desolate faces of my refugees were the me that was in them, by them and for them.

Especially I saw their dependence when I addressed them in assembly, group after group, camp after camp, time after time — myself so deeply involved in their homeless situation that I never needed to make a conscious effort to "enter into it" as Gurdjieff had taught, but only to bring forth the right words "to correspond" with what I saw — words of reckless optimism about those Golden Doors of America that would one day open to them.

I looked down on those doors as I flew over the Statue of Liberty in July of '47, coming into the New York airport, on my first home leave in over two years. The famous symbol looked quite stunted from the air and was gazing in the wrong direction; she should have been looking toward Washington where Congress was endlessly debating and shelving a Displaced Persons Act, hanging restrictive clauses to it that would never give her "the wretched refuse" she cried for, but only the able and healthy, only the "suitably employable." I cringed as we passed over her, remembering the buildup I had given her in the assembly halls of my DP camps.

I returned to my team twenty days after leaving it, so glad to be back among people who spoke my DP language that I swore to Chouka I would never again take a home leave until IRO folded and wrote finis to our task. Outside of my mother's quiet apartment in San Francisco, nobody had seemed the least bit interested in Europe's million homeless whose cause I tried to plead, privately and unofficially (IRO's muzzling restrictions on public utterances by employees were the same as UNRRA's). Nobody could talk of anything but the Marshall Plan and what its proposed twelve billion dollars might do to revive the European economy. When, among friends, I managed to get a word in about the DP's, I was treated, so to speak, therapeutically — advised to "forget them" while on vacation, have fun and "be your old gay self for a change." The old gay self they remembered had been so long dead I'd forgotten even where its bones were buried.

Nowadays, when refugees (Tibetan, Arab, Congolese, Cuban, Chinese, Indian, Vietnamese) have become a common phenomenon, our total involvement with those first Displaced of twenty years ago must appear quixotic. Our passionate belief that we were witness-participants of the last great human uprooting that would be seen on earth seems naïve in retrospect. Civilization would not permit a repetition of such an outrage to the dignity of mankind, we said . . . like innocents, like the DP's themselves.

All through '47 and most of '48 we waited for the world to remember its promises to our homeless, to open up a door for them somewhere, anywhere outside Germany. A few trickled out — coal miners to Belgium, domestic workers to Canada, sheepherders to Australia. We worked madly for each emigration mission that came in to the Zone to inspect the human goods we had on display. Analogies with the old slave trade were difficult to suppress. "Bodies for sale — strong-backed, well-muscled, not a cough in a carload," I wrote to my mother in bitterness; "There's a black market started up for chest x-ray pictures of good clean lungs — no TB's accepted by any mission."

Our domestic pets provided the only balm for our heavy spirits, laughter, and sometimes tears, at the end of difficult days. Framboise had an affair with a tortoise-shell tomcat and produced kittens, which Lummel guarded like a father before he had a fatal encounter with one of the wild boars in the forest of that boar-hunting region so favored by Goerring. We replaced him with two pedigreed shepherd puppies — Helga and Lady — champion females who eventually sailed with us to America.

In the fall of '48 our team was transferred to Wurzburg to take over a newly consolidated area that stretched all the way to the Russian Zone in the East and to the Tyrol in the South, with some 65,000 DP's living in seventy-three widely scattered installations. Chouka was promoted to Area Chief Nurse and I to Chief of Care and Maintenance which included in its duties the setting up of vocational-training schools to prepare our DP's for jobs that might make them acceptable for emigration to the States under a Displaced Persons Act which the Eightieth Congress finally passed on June 25, 1948. That DP Act was barbed with restrictions, quotas and preferences, but we were mercifully unaware of this for some months as we prepared our refugee flocks for the Great Exodus.

All of us caretakers were more than ready for that exodus. After the months of living in Aschaffenburg under the Berlin Airlift, listening to the planes flying through the pea-soup fogs that covered the Main River valleys with more than two million tons of food and coal for West Berlin, knowing Czechoslovakia had fallen to the Communists and Finland was about to go into Stalin's pocket under a "pact" that spelled pocket to us — now we saw ourselves ringed in with our DP's like the hole in the doughnut.

To give ourselves strength to face a fourth Christmas with the DP's, I guided three of my team (who had never been to Italy) to Florence over the long Thanksgiving weekend of

'48 — Chouka and two Americans, a young woman welfare worker and a male resettlement officer. The impact of that three-day holiday in Florence after nearly four years in DP-land made us all mad with joy. Since my prewar visits, Florence had added to the splendors of the Duomo, the Baptistry and Giotto's campanile — now spotlights lifted those wonders of green, white and red marbles straight up into the night sky. The Cellini Perseus in Loggia dei Lanzi . . . the Signoria . . . the Church of San Lorenzo where Michelangelo figures reclined on the Medici tombs . . . We walked and I talked. Like a proper guide, I allowed time out for shopping — gloves and scarves, leathers and art goods — and for long teas in the pastry shops of the Via Tornabuoni, to gather strength for the Pitti and Uffizi galleries.

Only once in those three days of a happier life did I remember the DP's. On our last morning I told my footsore company that they could not leave Florence without seeing the Della Robbia *bambini* in a fifteenth-century convent established to care for foundlings. An old caretaker in frayed overcoat followed us through the arcades and led us inside the convent to see two Della Robbias in the nuns' art gallery — a madonna and babe statue in pure white porcelain, no blue, and a Holy Trinity in white on a blue ground. Chouka's face took them to her heart. She seemed unaware that we were inside a cloister with black-robed nuns gliding in the background. Our frayed old guide now offered to show us the treasure of the convent and led us into a chapel that was chilly and dark. He turned on the electric lights, and there flared before our eyes, above the altar, a magnificent scarlet Ghirlandaio — the Adoration of the Magi in a great triangular composition, the Wise Men gleaming in crimson and gold and an adorable Virgin enthroned amid crowds of Florentine nobility robed in satins and jewels.

In prewar travels I had missed that great altar painting. As my eyes moved from the high Virgin down to the foreground, I saw the only two figures in it not dressed in scarlet — two little foundling children kneeling in ragged white dresses, with tiny gold halos above their heads. *"Due innocenti . . ."* the old man whispered. Two little innocents. I stared at them, seeing my DP kids, the foundlings born in the camps, already grown to three or four years without ever knowing that there was any other kind of life than that of their refugee world. At once I recognized the "reminding factor" that told me with dreadful finality why I could never give up and go home until the last baby innocent was safely taken out of Germany.

CHAPTER SIXTEEN

IT is said that every seven years the pattern of one's life changes. Always I had interpreted that engaging Old Wives' saying, in terms of the musical octave — seven notes struck, then on to the new octave. I had traced in my personal chronology the new turns my life had taken after seven, fourteen, twenty-one years — though sometimes I had to twist developments slightly to fit the dates. But now, looking back on 1949 (one of the multiples of seven in my own mortal span) I see a kind of arcane confirmation. Nineteen forty-nine was my year of twofold loss and spiritual desolation; my mother died during that summer and Gurdjieff in that autumn. It was certainly a year of tragic changes and at the end of it, I felt that I walked alone on the planet.

The only omen I had that 1949 might be a tragic year was the fact, observable in occasional wandering letters, that my mother was growing old while waiting for me to come home "for good," as she always expressed it, with treble clefs and grace notes penned above the two words. I decided to take advantage of an unused annual leave with IRO to fly to San Francisco and see with my own eyes how things were with her. I left the arrangements to IRO, specifying only that the leave be in January — when I knew Gurdjieff would be in

New York visiting his American groups. When the double aim was assured, seeing my precious mother and teacher, in a full month of leave, I told Chouka happily that with such an auspicious start, 1949 was sure to be my year of roses, roses. It was not until I was riding up the autobahn to Frankfurt, reading through the sheaves of furlough papers and plane tickets, that I realized IRO had inadvertently sent me off on Gurdjieff's birthday — a coincidence which scattered a few more roses through my thoughts as I flew west over the Atlantic. The "thorns" I had forgotten about were awaiting me in New York.

At my hotel I found a letter from my sister, who wrote to "prepare me" for what I would find at home: my mother might not recognize me, might confuse me with a niece named after me. Her wonderful mind had "given way," leaving her at times like a child. My task would be to coax her into a rest home where she could have the reliable care she needed now.

The news crushed me. My mind refused to believe that an intellect like my mother's could suddenly "give way"; the kind of brain matter she had could not dissolve into nothingness in the short time since her last perfectly coherent letters to me — always about my DP's, always urging that I stay with them to the end, always promising that she would "wait for me." I wept as I talked to myself in the hotel room. Then suddenly a thought stopped the tears . . .

Gurdjieff might "make something" for my mother. This was why I had pressed so hard on IRO for a January leave to coincide with his New York sojourn. This was an example of the "conjury" he had once declared operated in individual lives, operating *not* as magic, but as something *you* do which

will be good for you (but for no one else) because *you* do it.
I looked in the notebook that always traveled with me. It was
on the Riviera trip in February of '37 when he had spoken so
cryptically about "conjury." "Wish or not wish, conjury you
must believe because all life consists of conjury." We had
had one of the etymological discussions so dear to the
master's heart. Conjury — *con,* with; *jure,* to swear — "with
swearing" the Canary had suggested hopefully but Gurdjieff
said no, *that* was not the conjury he meant. (Later, pursuing
the old Latin root of *jure* or *iūs,* we discovered for ourselves
that one of its original meanings was "a religious formula
having the force of law.")

I telephoned then to Solita, listened to her Canary voice
singing for my safe arrival in abominable flying weather
"which only a Crocodile would venture into." I told her that
conjury had brought me back at the right time and read her
my sister's letter. And Gurdjieff? I asked. Back in the Hotel
Wellington, she said, and *of course* I must tell him about my
mother; she was sure he would give help. She would meet
me next day.

The next day was January 13, 1949. I write the date out in
full because it also was "conjury" that I happened to be there
on that particular day when Gurdjieff was to make an an-
nouncement of tremendous importance. I could never have
planned such perfect timing. Conjury, I say it was, and so
shall always believe. I was, however, separated from close
contact with the Work, still somehow within reach of whatever strange force brought "his people" near to him when
something important was about to take place.

Crowds of people I had never seen before; rooms jammed
wall to wall with his followers; the piles of overcoats in the

foyer four feet deep the length of it; early arrivals seated on the floor around his sofa, cross-legged; everyone present awaited the voice of the master. I found a place with the standees around the walls and looked at him, seeing only him, brown and benign of countenance.

No one moved when Gurdjieff took a letter from his pocket and handed it to a tall Englishman sitting near him. "Read, read — is for everybody," he said and listened as if weighing each word: "This circular is addressed to all my present and former adepts and to all who have been directly or indirectly influenced by my ideas and have sensed and understood that they contain something which is necessary for the good of humanity. After fifty years of preparation and having overcome the greatest difficulties and obstacles, I have decided to publish the first series of my writings in three books under the title of *An Objectively Impartial Criticism of the Life of Man,* or, *Beelzebub's Tales to His Grandson* . . ." A description of the first edition followed, a volume of nearly one thousand pages to be printed in four languages; then ". . . in order to make it possible I ask you and all my other pupils to buy one copy of the first printing for a sum of one hundred pounds (or $400 for Americans) . . . By means of this action it will be possible for all those who have gained personal help from contact with my ideas to do something to repay and to help reap the harvest which I have sown. Signed G. Gurdjieff."

The room buzzed with excited comments. I stepped forward to the group around Lord Pentland whom Gurdjieff had named as his representative in America, and put my name fourth on the subscription list, writing out my check for four hundred dollars on the spot. Gurdjieff saw me then.

He expressed no surprise that I was there, only that I was paying up so promptly. I told him that I would not be staying, that I had to fly to California. "Mother business, Mr. Gurdjieff," I said keeping my voice calm. He read the desire I naïvely thought to conceal. "You wish to speak aside, Krokodeel?" he asked, despite my intention not to steal an instant of his "dear Time" on this day of days.

During the prolonged and somewhat boisterous lunch served on paper plates, I looked over the largest crowd I had ever seen gathered about him. Some of the old American group I now recognized, but all in the large English group were strangers — those Ouspensky disciples who had come to Gurdjieff after Ouspensky's death two years before, said Solita. The Londoners had a double interest in Gurdjieff's publication, since it meant that Ouspensky's long withheld book about his early years with Gurdjieff would also be published soon after.

Everything I heard that day was fresh news to me. During my years in Germany, cut off from all information on the spread of the "Gurdjieff movement," the master whom I knew mainly from the intimate days of the Rope ten years before had apparently become a towering figure in the Western world and groups had been established in Holland, Sweden, Germany, South America . . .

Now and again I gazed across the smoke-filled apartment at Gurdjieff, installed on his sofa with one leg as always tucked under him. He looked the same as I had always known him. Take away the crowd trying to speak with him, put a mustard and rose striped wallpaper behind him, and he could have been sitting in that Left Bank hotel room of fourteen years ago, on the sofa that sprouted its springs from the underside . . . Thus my Crocodile comforted me as I wondered how I had ventured to bring my small subjective problem to the attention of a master who now belonged to the world.

After lunch, he beckoned me to follow him to his bedroom. "Now tell . . ." he said. And looking straight into his serious black eyes I told how I had to go home — "to put my mother away, as we say, Mr. Gurdjieff" — because apparently her mind was failing and she could no longer live alone. I told him how my conscience tormented me because I could not stay with her, having recently signed a contract for another year in Germany — necessary for her sake, since I was her sole support. His eyes compelled me to speak fast and accurately, without emotion. When I finished, he went to a cabinet and took out a bottle of colorless liquid. "You do exact what I now tell, Krokodeel . . ." I was to massage all this liquid over the solar plexus region of my mother, then take a photograph of her and bring it back to him . . . wrapped tightly, in black paper, no light, understand? His stern face softened but he did not smile. "You do *exact* . . . then, *if not too late,* perhaps I can make something . . ." He smiled then said, "Now go . . ." before I could get the knot out of my throat to thank him.

In the plane flying West I was nearer to a dragon than a crocodile. I was flying help to my mother, a strange and magical aid to be sure, but believed in utterly by me. My spirits soared, the powerful stratoliner was like an extension of my dragon driving through the night. The beacons ten thousand feet below stretched across the continent, no light out of sight of the succeeding one. I said no prayers as we flew over them. I felt no need to. My whole being was wrapped in a state of thanksgiving . . . *"If not too late, perhaps I can make something,"* he had said.

Once I took the bottle from my briefcase, uncorked it and sniffed the scent — a hint of attar of roses. I recalled how, long ago in Paris in the early days of the Rope, Gurdjieff used to compose certain scents and put us all to work shaking the bottles to make a good mixing. Once he had given to each of us a bottle of an "objective scent" he had specially composed "to make light all the sorrows of the Inner World." The bottle I now carried smelled like something in that category, but it must be quite different. I was only to do with it exactly as told and leave the rest to him . . . Like the water of Lourdes? Chouka had told me about that, how the pilgrims used it and left the rest to the Virgin of the Grotto with faith. I saw nothing strange in my own faith in a master whose "cures" I had witnessed more than once.

It would have been a heartbreaking mission to my mother had I not been given an exact task to do with a small bottle of unguent and a camera. I wanted her to remember me before I performed that task. At first she thought me a stranger who had come from afar — "All the way from Germany, you say?" — to visit her. Then, as she grew accustomed to my presence, memory returned and one day out of a blue sky she asked me who was taking care of my dog Lady, while I was home on leave. We began talking together again like the two cronies we had always been.

That evening after helping her to bed, I shook up the bottle of scented fluid and rubbed it gently all over her while telling her about "a wonderful Russian man" I knew who had sent it to her and had promised that he would "hold the thought" for her after I returned to my refugees. That a man she did not know, had never met or heard of, would be "holding the thought" for her struck her as utterly generous and delightful. She laughed softly as I anointed her satiny skin — the skin of a schoolgirl, I thought, with anguish as I remembered that her age was now seventy-seven.

I photographed her sitting out in the patio of my sister's home, spent a roll of film that caught her in every mood from serious to gay, with her beautiful pompadour shining in the morning light.

In the fortnight that followed, I found a suitable rest home on the outskirts of Palo Alto, in a grove of California live oaks. I lured her to it, first by a description, then by a short walking tour under its ancient oaks. As in my childhood, we explored the oak tree holes for elfin faces and laughed happily together each time we discovered one looking down upon us. Until I was flying back to New York, I had not realized that I had gone into her second childhood with her before saying my last goodbye.

Nor did I realize, until I saw Gurdjieff's face when I handed him the prints I had developed in California, that in my joy for having brought my mother's memory back for a little while, I had forgotten the part of his instruction about bringing the film covered tightly, no light, wrapped in dark paper. He did not rant as in the old days. He simply looked at me, sighed heavily and put one glossy print into his wallet, shaking his head as if to say, You have redoubled now for me the work I do . . .

He went to his trunk, took from it a postcard-sized photograph of a strong-faced old lady in a black head shawl and cape, sitting on a wicker chair near a large tree, her feet planted firmly on the ground and one of those chaplets of black beads in her hand. "My mother," he said. He then gave me an exercise, totally different from any previous instruction yet including steps from many of the earlier "spiritual" disciplines. I must always be alone in a room when I performed it, alone with two empty chairs before me, on which I was to see "with inner eye" his mother and my mother sitting side by side. Step by step he went through the instruction which, I gathered, might enable me to draw into myself a force to send to them — a kind of "help" for his mother and mine. Then he called Madame S., his oldest and most trusted Russian assistant, told her to go over it once again, step by step with me, and abruptly left the room.

It was the last exercise he was ever to give to me. I stood alone in the bedroom staring at the two empty chairs Gurdjieff had drawn hastily together. They were bogus-gothic hotel chairs with red velvet seats, tasseled at the corners. Nobody was sitting in them. Not yet, not yet . . . I put the picture of his mother in my purse and went out into the living room.

The English disciples were crowded about Gurdjieff's sofa talking of the book with him, advising on the size it should be, something to fit in a man's pocket, they suggested, easy to carry everywhere, like the chaplet of black beads I was carrying. I fingered them unobtrusively and did the "sensing exercise" with them while listening to the book talk. The wish to show my chaplet to the master, to let him know that however else I failed him I still carried those precious beads and worked with them, propelled me toward his sofa. I waited until the editorial discussion tapered off, then took the chaplet from my pocket and showed it to him.

He looked at the chaplet and then at me, with quite the most lovely smile I had ever seen. He put forth his hand without a word and I gave him my chaplet to hold. As if caressing them, he passed a few beads through his fingers, then held up the chaplet for all in the room to see. *"Is moth-er thing . . ."* he said, drawing out "mother" in tones of love. Then with a nod of satisfaction he dropped my chaplet into his own pocket and that was the last I saw of those black beads that had been my talisman and "Inanimate Helper" for thirteen years. Did he take them back because I looked boastful in displaying them? Or because someone else now needed them more than I? I would never know, I could never ask. Gurdjieff's hoarse husky voice saying "Is moth-er thing," was to echo often in my ears when, later in life as a practicing Catholic, I passed another kind of rosary through my fingers, a longer one spaced out in decades of beads. The Catholic rosary never seemed strange to me, never an object of "Romish mumbo-jumbo" as some Protestant friends termed it. *"Is mother thing . . ."* was my silent answer from my inner world.

I saw Gurdjieff daily for a week before flying back to Germany. One of the last sessions in his always crowded hotel rooms is mainly a memory of laughter — his laughter, deep and infectious, unintentionally provoked by me. Its origin was the story of a four-year-old girl who sat by me on the plane that had brought me back from California. She was flying alone across the continent, and although she had never before been on a plane she acted with such consummate mastery of her tiny self that she stole my heart. All her natural terrors on a first flight she attributed to her doll, talking to it in a fluty voice, telling it not to be afraid, rocking it in her arms and singing to it whenever we ran into rough weather.

I told the story of that child to a group of disciples'

children who came to the hotel one day after lunch to see with their own eyes the "great man" whom their parents called Teacher. Possibly the Armagnac I had drunk during the lunch loosened my tongue unduly; possibly the sight of Gurdjieff chuckling with pleasure as he looked down into those innocent upturned faces, a second generation of followers, prompted my urge to contribute to the happiness of the occasion. In any event, I found myself asking Gurdjieff for permission to "tell a little story" to those assembled children. I was sitting on the floor with Solita, near his sofa, and he looked down on me a bit dubiously, as if measuring motive against capability, then nodded consent.

I did not know that one of the men had concealed a recorder beneath the sofa to register Gurdjieff's words. I did not dream that my impassioned Crocodile account of a small girl flying alone across the continent, all alone through the night, talking courage into herself by talking to her doll, was going to be played back to me in every session of the remaining days in life with the master . . . played back on the rolling waves of his laughter as Solita chirped her editorial comments on my heartrending report of one small girl's inner bravery "flying all alone . . . *all alone* . . . ("We've had that, Katie, *get on* with the story!") . . . my voice thickening with emotion, caught like a phonograph needle in the groove mourning "all alone . . . all alone" while Gurdjieff's great laughter mixed with the children's high hilarity all but drowned me out. Afterwards, in a voice worn hoarse from laughing, Gurdjieff told the children they had been listening to a Crocodile, this was what it meant to *be* a Crocodile . . . "Crocodile tears, you *know* what means crocodile tears?" And he laughed again with them as he looked at me wiping tears of fury from my eyes for having made a spectacle of myself.

He laughed anew over that dreadful recording every other time I saw him on that last visit, always ordering it to be played back while I was there, adding new laughter to his own recorded laughter when I beseeched him to have mercy and not make me hear once again how I sounded when I let the emotions lead me into self-forgetting. On my last day in New York, I wept genuine tears when I heard it because then, after so many repetitions, I was hearing only my own lugubrious voice carrying on like a wound-up talking machine beneath the sounds of the master's mirth, and nothing the other disciples said to me afterwards — "You should be *glad* you were able to make him laugh like that!" — could change my inner fury and self-disgust.

Gurdjieff still had a glint of amusement in his eyes when I approached him to say goodbye. With so many people waiting to speak with him, I made the leave-taking brief. I thanked him for his help with my mother, for the new exercise, for everything, in short, including the merciless last lessons he had given me which showed me to myself as I had never seen myself before.

Last inner-world exercise, last in-life lessons, last look at him alive. The next time I was to see him, he would be a fallen Colossus with his glowing eyes closed forever. Then, and only then, would I remember with gladness, that last great laugh I had drawn from him . . .

Back in Germany, the exigencies of my job seemed to have tripled in my absence. The U.S. Emigration program was now going full tilt, going nowhere. Every refugee I had ever known and loved was caught somewhere in the papermill of the Resettlement Center, somewhere between Medical, Security and Immigration Service checks and rechecks. My daily life became a kind of manhunt tracing case files of the humans hung up along the processing line which had to, by law, culminate in consular visa four months after the "case numbers" were given, else they became invalid. I was like a furious huntress following that processing trapline, trying to free the caught ones whose names were Ignatz, Sofia, Vladimir, Vitalij, names so familiar to me. I was back, in short, in the only kind of life for which I had true "fingering" — *doigté,* as Chouka expressed it, a fingering for humanity.

I had a wall-wide chart in my office, marked off in columns under headings that described the steps of emigration processing. Between the first column — *Case-Numbers Received* — and the last — *Total DP's Visaed & Shipped Out* — lay the battleground my team and I fought each day. I had four phones on my desk which rang constantly. Frankfurt Control to dictate new case numbers received for DP's in my area, Bremen Embarkation Center to give names of families being sent back because of some last-minute discovery of "irregularities" in their documents, the International Tracing Bureau, the CIC, the DP Commission . . . I talked myself blue in the face with begging. "Don't take action till I call you back, there *must* be some mistake . . . I'll put my nurse on the case right away . . . My welfare worker knows that family personally . . ."

On and on it went, day after day, all through the beautiful springtime of '49 when the Main River valley around Wurzburg burst into sudden wild colors of fruit trees and vineyard slopes, giving me something more than our doleful human scene to write home about. On a day in mid-June I took the usual number of morning calls, first from Frankfurt, then on around the DP circuit from Bremen to Munich, jotting down the good news with the bad and winding up with the worst of all — a call from Chouka in the area hospital to say that I'd better remove Ignatz, my Polish driver, from the processing rolls; the lung x-ray of his eldest child had just come through from Medical; it showed active TB. She had talked to the boy we both loved, and failed to convince him that he should go on ahead to the States and trust us to get his child to him as soon as her lungs were clean — in a year at most, quite possibly less. "He refuses categorically, says he will stay in Germany until they can all emigrate together. You know him . . ." I had known him since Wildflecken days. Like a brother, I thought, as I stared at my chart, mentally subtracting one number from the Medical column and adding it to the column captioned Deferred Indefinitely.

When the phone rang again I let it ring. It rang perhaps half a dozen times before I could summon courage to answer. It was Military Switch from Frankfurt with a long-distance call from my sister in California. I knew what the news had to be. "Our mother . . . died in her sleep last night . . . No special cause . . . just a wearing away, they say."

Just a wearing away, they say . . . worn out waiting for me to come home for good. I stared at the columned chart that had trapped me, along with all those thousands of processing refugees, for at least another year until all those columns except the last one added up to zero. The relentless phone rang again — Resettlement Center to ask if I would come out to the plaza and give the official send-off to a transport of visaed DP's starting out for Bremen Embarkation. Always a joyful scene, those final transports, always the basis for a letter to my mother. I went out to watch it for her, still unable to take in the fact that she was no longer there to be written to. I found myself automatically gathering up the little "human interest vignettes" she loved.

Four months later, there was a second great loss and refusal of the mind to believe that here was the body of Gurdjieff before me, eyes closed, his great shaved head sunk into a silk pillow, denting it deep with its weight.

He had been still alive when I arrived in Paris on October twenty-eighth, but was already in the hospital. I joined Solita in the lobby to await news from the room above where he lay in great pain, it was said. We remained until closing time and returned the next morning. More people had joined the vigil and there was again that curious awareness of some strange force drawing his disciples close in a crucial time . . . as it had drawn me out of Germany on a sudden three-day leave.

He died on Sunday morning, October 29.

The hospital chapel had space for just one row of mourners between the low mortuary table and the walls. From where I was crouched on the floor with my back to a wall, Gurdjieff's body beneath a satin coverlet scattered with red roses was nearly level with my eyes, and he seemed to be breathing as I stared at his profile, his respiration slow and steady matching my own even breathing — a common phenomenon, Chouka was to tell me later, but startling to me on first experiencing. There was not a sound in the crowded chapel until a bearded Russian priest arrived and began to chant prayers from the foot of the bier in a golden voice.

"Never to hear my name called again by you . . . Krokodeel, Kroko-*deel!* . . . and now what? Now where? Now *who?* . . ." My questions flowed in an interior monologue, urgent and agonized. They united with the other silent supplications around the bier, a vibration of common grief so sharp as to seem audible; but the only sound was the priest chanting a Russian hymn.

I sat all through that night until four the next morning, while a continuous changing of the vigilants went on around the bier. The French disciples, summoned by telephone or telegram, arrived early in the evening; later the British from across the Channel came into the chapel direct from the station, with traveling bags and steamer rugs still in their hands. When at last I stumbled out into the Monday morning dark, I saw rows of pilgrim disciples sitting like Mexican Indians along the icy paths, wrapped in overcoats and rugs, with arms clasped around their knees and heads bent down, awaiting their turn in the chapel.

On Monday afternoon, I went back to Germany. The advance guard of the American group had flown in during the night from New York. The path from the hospital lobby to the chapel was a processional of "his people" come to say their farewells to the master who had taught them how to say *I AM.* Inside the chapel, another Russian priest chanted the prayers of the Orthodox ritual. The flowers had been changed from roses to carnations and two small bouquets of tuberoses and violets lay on the pillow on either side of Gurdjieff's face, now gone a little gray, like stone. I stared at the body that no longer seemed to breathe, at the closed eyes that had read me like a book. I knelt before a little ikon of St. George at the foot of the bier — his saint, the one he had called "a very expensive saint," whose help was not procured with money or candles, but only with suffering. "He, your namesake, told us," I reminded St. George, "that you are interested only when he *made something* for his inner world, and that you *always* knew . . . Now you know all that he made, and you must be helping him, *as he helped us* . . ."

In a slow-paced line of mourners unknown to me, I moved around the body toward the head of the bier. As I lingered for my look down at the beloved countenance, the Crocodile that I thought had died suddenly spoke up: "Kiss him goodbye . . . *don't be afraid!*" I bent and touched my lips to the monumental skull.

In the train for Frankfurt that night, I reviewed my "Gurdjieff years" like a drowning person seeing his whole life pass before him. Only seventeen years since I had first advanced haltingly to his table in the Café de la Paix . . . yet, a *whole* life, I thought. Where now, with the master gone, could any equivalent ever again be found? Where now, on *this* side of the great separation?

The train rumbled like his voice. "As long as *with inside* we have same ideas, Kroko-deel, *we will not be separated* . . ."

CHAPTER SEVENTEEN

NOTHING of my chaotic inner state even faintly reflected in my work after the return from Paris. The efficient UN executive functioned like a unit of highly calibrated machinery designed to produce candidates eligible for the States. I observed myself smiling and sweet-talking my way through our Area 3 emigration mill, inching up toward consular visas the case files of our DP's, never blowing up with inner rage for bureaucratic blundering, but only acting in pretended anger when it seemed useful to do so to get the job done. Had I finally learned to keep my inner world inviolable and apart from the in-life activities that claimed all of my waking hours? Had the shock of my double loss enabled me at last to live in one place within myself and to labor in another?

This felt nevertheless like an exceptionally productive way of being. IRO seemed to think so too. I was promoted to chief of the U.S. Desk, responsible for overall supervision of operation of the U.S. emigration program in the entire U.S. Zone, reporting directly to my counterpart at Geneva HQ level. The demands of the new position did not intimidate. I had the dauntless Crocodile working for me now, its nature tamed, its strength mine to use at will. Thus it was to remain for the duration of my overseas service, a powerful silent partner in the windup of the immense humanitarian job which was to end for me when the last eligible DP in the Zone had been covered by a case number for the States — in the spring of '51.

Roses in one's outer world, thorns in one's inner . . . and a spiritual loneliness. My thoughts were endlessly asking *where? what now?* Solita had written that there were to be Work groups with Gurdjieff's trained assistants, but how could one attach oneself to one of those, once having fed at the Source? Moreover, except for the close days of the Rope, I had always been a sort of maverick among the master's disciples, appearing in his various groups, briefly reporting only to him down the years, a prodigal he had put up with, and in that forbearance, I realized, he had put into me what he called "an unquenchable impulse of desire" for *his* things.

Where next? How to continue? This was my dilemma. With Chouka gone off as escort nurse on a ship bound for Mombasa (to pick up a small colony of DP's from British East Africa and escort them to England) I had no one with whom I could talk, except the two dogs Helga and Lady. They made beautiful listeners. Their ears pointed like radar cones to catch my every sigh. They knew of my emotion when I received a copy of Ouspensky's *In Search of the Miraculous.* They lay on my feet, as if to hold me down, as I read.

In the opening chapters when Ouspensky described his initial encounters and conversations with the master, it seemed as if I were hearing Gurdjieff talk again, minus his accent and abbreviated locutions, and in much greater detail than he had ever revealed to the Rope. There were brilliant clarifications of things that had always puzzled me. I saw, for the first time, the scope of Gurdjieff's concept, mathematically formulated and diagrammed, a picture of the universe from Godhead to Man, every part of the chain ordered and connected. "As above, so below . . ." *Below* — all the way down from God's omnipotence through suns and planets to earth and to the sentient atom of humanity that was I, a part of the immense design. A *working* part it must continue to be. Ouspensky's recapitulation of the master's "three ways" of striving amplified what I knew in outline about the Way of the Fakir (struggle with the physical body), the Way of the Monk (striving through religious feelings, emotions) and the Way of the Yogi (through the mind, for which a man must have a teacher). I read and reread the paragraphs on the "monk's" way, the way of subjecting all his other emotions to the single one of faith, to develop unity within himself. I began to get answers about how to continue without the master.

The "monk's" way was a slower way than his own "short-cut" method but it led in the same direction. "On the way of the monk," Ouspensky had quoted the master, "a man has a teacher, and a part of his duty, a part of his work, consists in having absolute faith in the teacher, in submitting to him absolutely, *in obedience.* But the chief thing on the way of the monk is faith in God, in the love of God, in constant efforts to obey and serve God, although, in his understanding of the idea of God and of serving God, there may be much that is subjective and contradictory."

I studied those lines like a road map depicting a journey I had already begun, trudging out its first miles under the guidance of a teacher in whom I had had "absolute faith." Now the guide was gone but the road was still there. With the help of God now, I would go it alone, wherever it might lead. All I knew about it with "sure-ing" was that it led in the right direction.

In my outer-world life I knew exactly where I was going. I would first finish my refugee job as honorably as the law allowed, then sail for the States with Chouka and the dogs and try again to be a writer. Since Chouka did not wish to return to Belgium after IRO ended, I had suggested that she go with me and make her own try for a new life abroad. For the first time in all my working years I now had a bank account (UNRRA and IRO savings) sufficient not only to guarantee myself a year of uninterrupted writing, but also to guarantee sponsorship for her as an immigrant under the Belgian quota. Chouka had filed her application with the American Consulate in Antwerp for a visa number. She was warned that she would probably receive her number in the next month or so and must be en route to the States within one year from its date of issue, else it became invalid.

I remember the drive back from Antwerp to Germany as the first completely lighthearted time I had experienced since my mother's and Gurdjieff's deaths. It was as if I were already embarked on my new life after IRO. I described for my companion the U.S. Route 66, the big southern swing from East to West coasts which we would follow in our search for a new home, a place where she could "get her feet wet" in American nursing while I tackled the long postponed DP book. "California, Arizona, anywhere that feels right for a new beginning — nursing, writing. We'll simply keep driv-

ing till we find it!" I was already halfway there in spirit
before we crossed the frontier into Germany.

My last months as Zone chief of the U.S. Desk were a
race against time and events. Chouka received her visa number one month after filing her application, and I was determined to sail with her as sponsor, to make sure she got past
the gorgon Immigration Service (whose devious ways I knew
only too well). February of '51 had to be our departure date. I
became a sort of traveling salesman riding the autobahns
between Frankfurt, Bremen and Munich, selling pieces of
myself for goodwill in every meeting with the Big Brass of
the higher echelons. If I sound now as if I carried the whole
of the U.S. program on my back during its final period, that
was the way I felt, the way I worked.

On June 16, 1950, Congress voted an extension of the DP
Act with its Section 13 (the "security section") so greatly
expanded that it seemed next to impossible that any U.S.-
bound DP could complete his processing toward the final
visa. Nine days later, North Korea crossed the thirty-eighth
parallel into South Korea and our employer, the United
Nations, was asked to intervene in what President Truman
termed "a police action." But we knew better. We knew the
look and smell of war.

Now the DP's of military age who managed to get
through the mystic maze of the security check and up to
Consul had to consent to fight, if drafted, in the United
States Army before their visas were granted!

It was a world going mad again, making ready to repeat its
pattern of errors. I foresaw the bundle-toting new refugees
the Korean War would spew forth to add to earth's homeless

and said, *It will never end!* Nor would it, as long as there were refugees on the face of the earth. Some of my UN comrades were already applying for a transfer to Korea. Not I, I told myself fiercely as I felt the old battle-loving Crocodile stir within me. Not I. I had done my share and all but done myself in, doing it. Not even the shipyards had so exhausted me as those final months in IRO. I wrote my letter of resignation to become effective in February of '51 when, by my calculation, just about all the case numbers for emigration under the extended DP Act would be assigned.

I was billeted in Munich for my final months in IRO, rooming with an idealistic Canadian woman attached to the Zone Resettlement and Repatriation Division. We had an apartment in a reconstructed Wehrmacht *Kaserne* spacious enough to include the two dogs, my Lady and Chouka's Helga, whom I was boarding while she made her final trip as escort nurse — to Australia with two thousand resettled DP's. I had a twinge of envy for the way Chouka was ending her UN service — *with* the DP's in their dramatic moment of delivery to a new life in a new land.

I fitted into the higher level like a square peg in a round hole. I disliked the atmosphere of the Zone HQ. Division chiefs behaved often like little tin gods and referred to the DP's as "bodies." There were hints of "empire-building" in a few of those toplofty chiefs who seemed to want their divisions to go on indefinitely, whether essential to the program or not, in order to stay in their cushioned jobs with luxurious fringe benefits. I called this "living off the backs of the DP's" and ceased to care who heard me. I supposed that "empire-building" would go on as long as there was a refugee left in the field to squabble over, a "body" to be snatched from one division to pad out the statistical reports of another. The humanitarianism that had characterized the early days of UNRRA appeared to have come full circle; it was a cloak-and-dagger business now. I counted the days until my walking papers would deliver me. It was nip-and-tuck, I said to my roommate, whether I would get out with a shred of faith in my fellow beings left. In short, I was fighting mad.

Chouka returned soon after Christmas with stories of the voyage that made me laugh and cry. I finally ended up being proud of our great bumbling international organization and what it had accomplished. I clutched my crested IRO testimonial as if it were a parchment conferring nobility. Between its finely engraved lines were six years of my life, the most momentous years I would ever have in my outer-world affairs, the most transforming for international thinking and feeling. I could never again fit into the narrow cast of chauvinistic nationalism.

In Belgium we rested for a fortnight in the summer chalet Chouka's father had built near the Dutch border in a lovely region of sand dunes and pine woods. Relatives came to visit Chouka, listening with admiration to her tales of Mombasa, Australia, her flight back in a Flying Tiger, alone with its genial American crew; Melbourne, Capetown, Colombo, Aden, Athens and Port Said came into her odyssey, places they knew only as stamp collectors. "And now to America . . ." Chouka ended, all diffidence with her family wiped away by their new respect for her. All the hatchets, I thought, real or imaginary, are buried for good — that's the way it should be.

We sailed from Rotterdam on the S.S. *Noordam,* a slow one-cabin ship chosen because it had kennels for our dogs and an open afterdeck where we could exercise them. As they influenced our choice of ship so were they to affect all subsequent choices of living places — always on the outskirts of cities, always in surroundings where there would be trees, unpaved roads and uncontaminated skies. Their canine needs corresponded ideally with those of their mistresses.

In one sense, I was as much of a DP on my return to the States as any of my refugees. In my six years away from America (nearly eight if I counted the shipyard time) I had lost not only every familiar contact but even the feeling that I had ever belonged to my country. Like any immigrant, I examined in New York's show windows the new parapher-nalia of American life — television sets, "do-it-yourself" kits (for the construction of anything from a house to a bird cage), long-playing records, best-selling books by authors I had never heard of. I postponed calling on my literary agent until my astonishment subsided; and I concealed from Chouka the uneasiness I felt that my name might not even be remembered by the agency that had sold my last book exactly twelve years before. Happily, it was remembered and I was received, encouraged and returned to my interrupted past — no longer a DP wondering where and how to make a fresh start. The title for my new book came to my mind even before the elevator brought me down to the lobby where Chouka was waiting. I gave her the victory sign. "I thought of the title in the elevator," I said. "It's *The Wild Place.*"

The next morning we started out on the long drive to California. Even if I had not resolved to make that trip a scenic and leisurely one, the needs of the dogs determined our innumerable detours, looking for motels which would accept pets. I learned to relate advertisements of "wall-to-wall carpeting" with the NO PETS signs invariably on view in the motel managers' offices; and finally found the simpler cabins frequented by transcontinental truck drivers. Their parked ten-ton trailers also showed me the way to the best eating places along the highways where all "Hamburger & Pie" signs otherwise looked alike. That was how we discovered the unspoiled America — by following the lead of its brave and knowledgeable truck drivers.

Arizona looked and felt like the place for us. It had that "feeling of wide" I was ardently seeking; it also had tract houses, five to an acre of land, built on the outskirts of its cities, with empty desert for backyards. "Two-bedroom homes for rent, completely furnished, seventy-five dollars a month" — exactly right for our purses. Nevertheless, we drove first to California to make sure we were not missing perhaps some ideal little hideaway to be had for a song somewhere in the Bay region near San Francisco.

It was a turn-around trip to the coast and back to Arizona. Only millionaires in the Golden Gate State could afford a bit of wilderness for backyard! Every aspect of Arizona living provided new experiences for all four of us, a stimulating way to start our various new lives. The dogs shed their heavy Bavarian undercoats and learned that the irrigation canals were made for swimming. Chouka, working in a local hospital, discovered in her Navajo patients a stoicism beyond any fortitude she had ever before encountered, even among tribal chiefs of the Congo. As for me, with long vistas of sagebrush and sand to stare at from my window, I found that words would rush to my rusty writer's mind as I began my first chapters of *The Wild Place*. For the first time in my life I could produce more than five hundred *keep-able* words in my daily work stint while my discarded pages lay about my feet, startling Chouka because she had never seen a writer at work. Each evening I read her my daily production and always knew from her face when I had gone overboard into what she tactfully termed *"les fleurs de rhétorique."*

Yet, for all the satisfaction of seeing my manuscript growing thicker day by day, I had a hidden hunger that my book could not appease. I knew its cause, had lived with it since Gurdjieff's death. My inner-life activity had come to a standstill . . . I began going to Sunday Mass with Chouka, at first observing with uncomprehending eyes the solemnity of Christ's Last Supper, the essence of the Mass . . . a continuous remembering. I recalled Gurdjieff's admonition: *Accustom yourself to forget nothing*. Gradually I saw the Mass as an "accustoming" that went back to man's beginnings as a Christian, an extension of "remembering" which antedated one's individual experiencings. "As often as ye shall do these things, ye shall do them in remembrance of Me." In the silence of the Consecration there was a fulfillment and a benediction for me.

I became a convert to the Catholic Church while finishing my DP book, after a month of instruction by a Jesuit Father who told me at the outset that it would do me "no harm" to learn something about the Church since I was a writer for whom everything could be grist to the mill, whether I eventually entered the Church or not. My Protestant heritage had instilled in me the usual notion that once the Church got its hands on you it never let go. The Father's easy words erased that ancient suspicion, even to the point of making it sound as if the Church could quite comfortably get along without me. He appeared to be much more interested in educating me on its long combative history. To this end he introduced me to the Scholastics — St. Augustine, St. Thomas Aquinas, Roger Bacon, Duns Scotus — and discussed them with me after reading, as if my illogical untrained mind equaled his Jesuit formation. He even read Ouspensky at my request, after I told him that if anything in the Church forbade "this kind of thinking about man and aim of life" then I could not with clear conscience accept baptism. I forget his exact words when he returned the book to me with a gentle smile, saying that he saw "no hindrance."

Years later, in one of those terrifying "meet the author" luncheons for which writers are called upon to speak, I talked about my conversion to an audience predominantly Catholic. In the question period following my address, a birdlike little woman stood up and said, "I would like you to tell me just when does a convert *cease* being a convert and settle down to being just a plain Catholic?" Her rudeness left me silent then, but I can answer her now. The answer, as I know it, is *never!*

When my book was finished and sent to my agent at the end of our Arizona year, we went back to California. In Eagle Rock on the outskirts of Pasadena we found a small redwood house, delightfully perched on a hilltop. It seemed to have been built with us in mind, although it must have been forty years old when we made our down payment on it, an advanced age by Southland standards. The steep switchback path was bordered with white azaleas and shaded by oak

trees. My restlessness as a writer between books was forgotten in the excitement of owning a first home, painting it
(a coat of redwood-log oil over its entire exterior) and
furnishing it. I used to look up at it sometimes from the
winding street below and wonder what kind of book I would
write in that adorable eyrie.

One day I knew. A telegram came from my agent saying
that *The Wild Place* had won a literary prize and I must fly to
Boston to receive it. All day I saw Chouka wearing a
thoughtful face. That night she asked me what I would say
to my editor when he brought up the subject of my next
book. "Oh, I'll think of something," I said with small
assurance. Then she said with a shy look: "Why don't you
suggest *my* story, a bit — how do you say — fictionized, of
course?"

I remember how I stared at her trusting face, unable to
believe my ears. This story was what I had dreamed of
writing during all the Wildflecken years when we had talked
of her strange veiled past, those long seven years when I had
shared every step of her struggle for an inner perfection.
When at last I could speak, I asked her, *"Why now? Why?*
After nearly ten years of guarding your secret?"

She met my demand eye to eye. "Because . . ." she said
steadily, "I think it might *do some good.*"

Because it might do some good! Because she had seen in
her new country the fragmented state of the Christian faith,
because she had read in newspapers the pages of church
advertisements, each with their separate calls and claims,
dividing faith in God into sects, bits of Him seeming to
belong not to all but to each, a confusion to confuse all

believers; because she had seen at the bedside of her dying patients the longing look of the nonbelievers and had heard their final cries to a God, no longer denied.

Because it might do some good . . . these were the words of a nun, words of faith and hope, illumined with the sweet charity of wishing to share her hard-earned treasure of impregnable belief with all those who — in the words of Gurdjieff — were *"hungry for something more."*